INJUSTICE
FOR ALL

INJUSTICE FOR ALL

Anne Strick

BARRICADE BOOKS
New York

Published by Barricade Books Inc.
150 Fifth Avenue
New York, NY 10011

Printed in the United States of America.

Library of Congress Cataloging-in-Publication Data

Stick, Anne.
        Injustice for all: how our adversary system of law vicitimizes us and subverts true justice / Anne Strick
                p.   cm.
        ISBN 1-56980-065-0
        1. Adversary system (Law)—United States. 2. Justice, Administration of—United States. I. Title.
KF384.S77 1996
347.73—dc20   95-51180
(347.307)   CIP

"For the memories
of my mother and my father
and of Harry Laskin too.

For Amanda, Adam, and Gabriel,
And for myself."

Acknowledgments

Over the years of researching and writing this book, help has come from sources both likely and unlikely.

Viewpoints Institute, where I studied under Dr. J. Samuel Bois and Ethel Longstreet, gave me a great part of the conceptual framework upon which I structured the particular vision which informs this book. Richard Renneker, MD, spent many long hours patiently reading and critically reacting to the groping beginnings of my theme. His encouragement, throughout those early days, was invaluable. Without Bois, Longstreet, and Renneker, this would be a different book, and I believe a lesser one—though I alone am responsible for what I have made of their diverse offerings.

The critical comments, interest, and loving energies of my mother, Rhea Wachsman, and my uncle, Edward Biberman, were of inestimable emotional support and practical help throughout. The late Judge Robert W. Kenny was the first member of the legal profession to read the manuscript, and his unqualifiedly positive response was an amazement and a joy. Judge Armond Jewell's similarly positive response helped me believe that Judge Kenny *had* actually read the book. Judge Harold Rothwax's dislike of the book was almost equally satisfying in its length and intensity. William Kay Kirby, then Judge Jewell's law clerk, presented me a critique combining approval and caustic disagreement in fruitful measure.

Lawyers Daniella Sapriel, Marge Buckley, and especially editor Ned Chase, raised important questions and indicated areas needing expansion, modification, and clarification. Dorothy W. Nelson, Dean of USC Law Center, found time in her extraordinarily busy schedule to read, consider seriously, praise, differ, and make suggestions in great and productive detail.

John Collier's reflections upon the manuscripts's original version, Sylvia Jarrico's editorial eye upon the first two chapters, and Catherine Turney's and Joseph Morganstern's notes upon the whole, were most useful. Daniella Sapriel's diligent blue pencil was indispensable. My daughter Betsy Strick, and my sons David and Jeremy, each read thoroughly and thoughtfully, and each made different and extremely constructive contributions. I appreciated Philip Dunne's stylistic comments, and his consistent, generous proffering of personal introductions opened important new channels of assistance. Renée Gould's introductions, also, as well as Ruth Lipton's, were of great value, and the enthusiasm of both urged me on. The courtesy and effort extended, in my behalf, by Leonard Boudin, William vanden Heuvel, and Arthur Schlesinger, Jr., have been truly remarkable.

Shirley Burke has been agent, critic, and—from the first—friend without peer. I am deeply grateful to her, as I am to my editor, Edward Chase, for his original belief in the book, and for the continuing care he and his assistant, Gail Hochman, have devoted to it. The rich facilities of the UCLA Law Library, and the expertise of its personnel, in particular Booker T. Davis and Sylvia Merritt, expedited my labors. Isobel Estorick and Muriel Slatkin volunteered—and spent—long, grueling hours proofing the galleys with me; Maggie O'Rourke, too, donated precious free time in pagework.

To all the foregoing, and to all those literally too numerous to mention in the space allotted here, yet who gave time, cheer, and aid of all kinds, my most profound thanks forevermore.

ANNE STRICK
1977

CONTENTS

PREFACE

"Are we fools?" cried Fred Goldman, father of the slain Ronald Lyle Goldman, decrying to the press—in the midst of the trial of Orenthal James Simpson for double murder—the defense's divert-and-distract tactics. "Are we all fools?"

Goldman was not alone in his dismay. The Simpson trial has been called variously a fiasco, a travesty, an embarrassment to the legal system. Christopher Darden, one of its prosecutors, publicly declared that all involved in the case have been tarnished by it.

But Erwin Chemerinsky, Legion Lex Professor of Law at the University of Southern California Law Center, finds those assessments "baffling." In an article in the *Los Angeles Times* on August 18, 1995, he called the trial something else: It was instead "...the legal system at its very best.. Excellent prosecutors carefully presented a vast array of often sophisticated evidence and excellent defense attorneys subjected it to rigorous cross-examination. An always conscientious, highly intelligent judge...presided...."

Conflicting opinions? Yes. Essential contradiction? No. Both opinions—polar though they be—join in one overarching fact: the best that our adversary trial system offers is nonetheless a travesty of all we mean it to be. It can give us no better. And that, in fact, is the point of this book—the first point.

The Simpson trial—fiasco, travesty, embarrassment, tarnishing all involved—does indeed at the same time represent the American

1

adversary or "fight" approach to trial justice at its best. That "best" is a take-no-prisoners battle which—because adversary theory ordains that whoever wins is "right"—inevitably justifies "anything goes in order to win."

Centuries ago, the adversary approach to dispute settlement—derived in significant degree from such ordeals as trial by battle—represented an historic advance. Today it is an anachronism; increasingly inappropriate to the issues that come before it, increasingly diminishing public trust in our courts, increasingly destructive, finally, of our judicial system's moral authority. And therein lies loss—incalculable loss—for us all. I believe that better ways can be found.

Consider: The Simpson defense mustered a team comprising some of the foremost legal talent in the entire country. The County of Los Angeles spent some nine million dollars of taxpayer money in prosecution. Simpson spent an estimated six million. There were 126 witnesses, 133 days of testimony, 857 exhibits, more than 50,000 pages of trial transcript, and twenty courtroom attorneys (prosecution nine, defense eleven). The trial took nine months. The jury took less than four hours. And a country was left the worse. The truth, the whole truth, and nothing but the truth is always hard to find. It cannot be found in adversary trial.

Professor Chemerinsky, however—urging against any effort to change our trial system—calls the Simpson case "truly unique." Most pundits share that view.

No.

In its essential elements, it was not unique at all. The Simpson case was unique only in its magnified theatricality: magnified beyond any prior experience, on television screens nationwide; worldwide. (Magnified, also, by its symbolisms that, postverdict, quickly became clear. Rorschach-style, the case represented a spectrum of attitudes, assumptions, and beliefs both inside the black and the nonblack communities, and between them.) Within the courtroom, however, were contained exactly the same behaviors manifest in adversary trial anywhere in America: bombast and snake oil, reason and hyperbole, genuine passion and simulated passion, skill and ineptitude, effort honest and dishonest, significant information obfuscated and withheld, practiced memories, facts misrepresented and falsely implied; and the bullying, humiliating and treating with contempt—by both sides—of almost every witness unfortunate enough to appear. Missing only—and as always from the adversary courtroom—was any "search for truth" at all.

For contrary to myth, contrary to general belief and hope, no one within that courtroom is either directed or empowered to make such a search. No one: not judge, not jury, not lawyer on either side. (Famed trial attorney Gerry Spence, writes a colleague in the book *Reconstructing Justice,* advocates in his lectures and articles "putting as much improper evidence as possible before the jury by asking improper questions. He reasons that this will sufficiently prejudice the jury to decide favorably despite the facts and the law.")[1]

Conflict, in human interaction, is inevitable. It is the method of resolution that is critical.

A fight system, by definition—whether featuring in closeup, from the film capital of the world, glamorous O.J. Simpson or weeping Menendez brothers, or in some obscure courtroom in middle America, plain John Doe—seeks only a victor. It seeks neither truth, nor equity, nor even all information that might help explain "what actually happened," but fails to support the story each party has determined to sell. That victory—as in any war—goes to greater power, wealth, skill, chicanery; or, often enough, simply luck. ("There has been," explained Harvard Law Professor and attorney Alan Dershowitz, in his book *The Best Defense,* "almost no correlation between the guilt or innocence of my clients and whether they served time or got off.")[2]

Theater, in adversary trial, is one of the essential tools of battle; the effective trial attorney is a first-rate actor who (like all effective performers) believes, at least while he/she is on stage, in his lines. The Simpson trial offered a big-screen amalgam of high-concept theatrical elements: a luminary defendant—handsome, charismatic, wealthy, a sports-celebrity and folk-hero whose ingratiating public persona was imprinted indelibly upon the hearts of so many (an "unconvictable defendant") who was discovered to have been also a many-time wife-batterer; an exotic but troubled interracial marriage to a woman whose sexuality leapt from tabloid pages everywhere; a crime of stunning brutality; and a police department and coroner's office whose dark-side flaws were all too clear. All these elements joined—with a supporting cast of the defendant's theatre-wise, nationally famed "dream team"—to magnify the show. It is only the degree of magnification that was "truly unique."

"Do they take us all for morons?" demanded the anguished Fred Goldman, "...we all know what they want is to inflame the emotions of the jury...with issues that don't relate to this trial."

The answer is Yes. Yes, they take us for morons. Yes, of course their purpose is to inflame the emotions of the jury. Like good hucksters everywhere, lawyers assess and then try to sell to their audience—the jury, the public—what they believe it will buy.

Don't blame the lawyers.

That—within our adversary trial system—is exactly what they are supposed to do. Within that system, such behavior is called only "zealous advocacy"; to which the lawyer has sworn an oath as a condition of admission to the bar. A defense attorney who failed to reach for the most effective weapon at hand—whatever its nature—would be considered remiss in duty. Don't blame the lawyers.

Blame the system within which they are required to operate. There is no other. And blame us. Blame us for buying that system, and its ethic. The adversary ethic, whose highest virtue is "winning" *no matter the means or social cost.* And which, overriding competing codes of personal and social responsibility, of integrity and the Golden Rule, infects our society as fatally as any plague. A legal system cannot escape the society in which it rests. And that is this book's second point.

Blame us for accepting for so long, accepting without question, for centuries—in our law, our society and our lives—an ethic that does not cool fires, personal or societal, but fans them. An ethic that brings neither understanding nor resolution, but only a winner and a loser, both the worse for battle. An ethic that—centered in a primary cultural institution meant to exemplify our "best"—instead mocks our highest judicial intentions; promulgating and then rewarding those very behaviors we mean it to oppose. For no one directly involved can remain for long untarnished by those weapons which even the noblest of legal ends demand and sanction. Thus, inevitably, our adversary trial system creates disrespect for lawyers, judges—and law itself. And, as it represents a kind of moral schizophrenia—claiming a search for truth and at the same time refusing truth wherever victory beckons—ceaselessly recontaminates the society from which it springs. Like war, adversary battle inflicts irretrievable damage—upon not only the participants, but upon the civilian population on both sides.

Small trials contaminate the social fabric anonymously, poisoning in small, quiet but ceaseless drops, over the decades. Large trials contaminate in sudden great waves that now and then threaten to overwhelm the body politic. Menendez (two young men who, having confessed to slaughtering their parents as they sat watching television and eating vanilla ice cream, claimed self-defense) raised denial of responsibility, our growing national illness (the perpetrator-as-victim switch) to new heights of invention. (Nonresponsibility of the self and blame of "the other" is basic to adversary thinking.) Buying that switch, two juries, unable to decide between verdicts of first-degree murder or manslaughter, deadlocked. Simpson both reflected and significantly aggravated pressure along our societal fault lines—between white and black, black and Jew; pressure that an increasingly Balkanized society can ill afford. Both trials—Menendez and Simpson—accelerated a truly dangerous growing contempt for our entire judicial process.

Professor Chemerinsky, however—together with most members of the legal profession—believes we can do no better. "[in the matter of Simpson]...Both the state and the defendant have received as fair a trial as any human system can possibly provide."

Again, No.

I am more optimistic than that. I believe that we can do better, if we will only try. If we will understand that, within an adversary frame, all the patching and tinkering in the world—jury reform, tougher judges, gag orders on attorneys, harsher laws—will ultimately make little difference. If we will only face squarely the central issue—the adversary ethic, keystone and high holy of our current trial system, upon which all else rests, from which all else flows. Altering weapons will not make war intrinsically less murderous, less devastating to a society.

I believe that we must begin a national dialogue directed at designing a new judicial system: a system based on a nonadversary ethic and on the concept of personal responsibility; one which *reconceives* the roles of lawyer, judge, and jury and entirely rethinks such matters as sentencing together with the purposes of imprisonment and uses of restitution. Experimental designs might be established in selected small jurisdictions, and fine-tuned over a period of time. Here and there (and detailed in Chapter 16), initial small steps in that direction are being made.

I believe we must at the same time recognize the inescapable connections between a legal system and other formative aspects of a society: those connections between, for instance, education, family stability, public health, economic opportunity, and the behaviors shaped therefrom—and the problems that that behavior feeds into our courts. Above all, we must acknowledge the ineradicable connection between societal ethic and both individual and institutional behavior. The adversary ethic—the ethic that significantly shapes our society as well as our courts—is both divisive and intrinsically amoral. "I do not apologize for (or feel guilty about)," wrote Alan Dershowitz, "helping to let a murderer go free—even though I realize that someday one of my clients may go out and kill again."[3]

A society that pledges "justice for all" but is fragmented into groups that demonize one another, cannot have a trial system that delivers a commonly perceived justice. A society without a unifying, overarching moral code of integrity, of compassion, of personal responsibility for every single action, a society without transracial justice standards—cannot have a trial system that commands general respect. A society where the strong dismiss the weak and the self-interest of each is not seen as ultimately inseparable from the welfare of all, cannot deliver equity in its courts. A society where the prize supercedes its *means of achievement*, where there is no bitter taste in the prize won dishonestly, nor valuing of honest effort that fails to win the prize— cannot have a trial system that delivers justice for all.

Competitiveness carries enormous energy. Framed within a positive moral code, it can fuel the drive for excellence. Or, framed negatively by the win-at-any-cost ethic, can be equally destructive. Thus competition has been a significant source of American individual and national progress, as well as of many of our darker chapters. But a society in which the "anything goes" adversary ethic continues, at levels both personal and institutional, to shape the drive to succeed, a society in which the interests of "the other" are regularly overriden by too many in sole service of the self—will finally splinter.

Consider these fruits of that ethic:

Consider, for instance, the 40 percent to 90 percent of students recently estimated by the Carnegie Foundation for the Advancement of Teaching to regularly cheat on papers and exams.[4] Consider the rash of cheating at the prestigious Massachusetts Institute of Technology[5] and the 1992 cheating scandal at Annapolis.[6] Consider the findings of a landmark survey of some 6000 students in thirty-one of the country's most eminent colleges and universities, conducted in 1992: nearly 70 percent had cheated—80 percent in nonhonor-code schools; 60 percent in those schools *with* such codes.[7] "Cheating," comments Rutgers student Michael Moore, author of the highly successful book *Cheating 101: The Benefits and Fundamentals of*

Earning the Easy "A," "has become the American way."[8] These students have learned to seek the prize, *no matter the means*. Consider the outcry—from parents, from school administrators, from media, church and political leaders—that we do not hear.

Consider the 1,952 young men of South Carolina's Citadel—a military academy devoted, nominally, to the induction of boys into manhood. Consider the insults and death threats with which the cadets demonstrated that manhood—bravely bullying from their ranks one lone female; their T-shirted chests bearing the proud and literate legend "1,952 Bulldogs and 1 Bitch."[9] Consider the public apology the Citadel's administrators failed to make for the method that yielded that victory. Consider the lesson implicit: winning *no-matter-the-means—no-matter-the-target—is endorsed*.

Consider, finally, former tobacco lobbyist Victor Crawford (a life-long smoker dying now of lung cancer) explaining his selling to Congress and the American public the harmlessness of cigarettes, though he and his companies both knew he was selling death (*Sixty Minutes*, July 23, 1995)."Was I lying?...Yes...My job was to win. Even if you're going out lying about a product that's going to hurt kids. Your job is to win...It's the American way." Consider our tax dollars that support with subsidies that *in-no-matter-the-means-or-social-cost* industry. Consider the outcry against that support that does not swell across the land.

George Regas, rector emeritus, All Saints Church in Pasadena, California, speaks of a disease of the heart: "Suspicion, fear and hatred of the 'other'—the one not like me—is the fundamental disease of the world today. This disease of the heart is the source of every genocide, every holocaust, every ethnic cleansing, every gay bashing, every urban riot, every skinhead outbreak. And today's political climate is playing this card of hate. Our hope is in setting our faces against the tide..."[10]

Adversariness is a condition of the mind, as well: it offers a limited, the other-be-damned, view of the world. That view has always been with us. But to the degree that it is a simplistic vision, it becomes, in our rapidly complexifying lives, more perilous every day. "We are plunging headlong," wrote a former United States secretary of health, education and welfare, in 1972, "into an unknown future, dragging with us the outworn slogans, attitudes and institutional apparatus of a world that is vanishing."[11]

In a secular society, where the judicial system is the highest institutional arbiter of morality, our survival rests upon the moral authority of that institution. And that institution, in turn, reflects every last one of us. If we fail to face the adversary ethic which informs all our institutions, which shapes too many of our unspoken assumptions and daily interactions, and which is a toxin at our societal core, our society—increasingly anarchic, increasingly sociopathic, increasingly paranoid and increasingly armed—will ultimately destroy itself. On the eve of a new century, I believe that better ways can be found; and in fact are (detailed again in Chapter 16) increasingly underway.

This book was first published nineteen years ago. Before John Wayne Bobbitt was charged, before one jury, with marital sexual assault and victimization of his wife—and acquitted as *her* victim. Before Lorena Bobbitt (who had severed her husband's penis with a knife) was charged, three weeks later and before another jury, with malicious assault—and also acquitted; on grounds that long-term victimization by *him* had rendered her temporarily insane. The same prosecutor brought both blame-game cases and lost them both to defenses that successfully shifted the blame-target.

This book was first published before the police who had beaten (viciously, continuously, and on videotape) a prostrate Rodney King were acquitted by an all-white jury in one venue and in a second trial, in a different venue with a different population and jury composition, were instead found guilty. Before a third trial in thirty years finally found Byron de la Beckwith guilty of the murder—a murder charge which had ended in his freeing, by two prior deadlocked all-white juries in 1964—of black Mississippi civil rights leader Medgar Evars. Before Damian Monroe Williams was videotaped braining almost to death Reginald Denny in the midst of the Los Angeles riots and was found guilty only of simple mayhem—rather than attempted murder or aggravated mayhem—on his lawyer's plea that Williams was a victim of mob hysteria (which the defendant described as getting "caught up in the rapture"). Denny has since required repeated brain surgery.

This book was first published before the trial of William Kennedy Smith for rape, before the Menendez brothers and Orenthal James Simpson. Before the spread of radio talk shows, before cable television; and before Court TV. Before public awareness and public cynicism about our trial system had risen to its current level—a level heretofore, I believe, unseen in the United States. In 1977, I wrote that "public confidence in our system of justice is at low ebb." Today the well is almost dry.

In order to bring this material into the present, I have rewritten portions of the final chapter to include new information, and have updated those statistics, in Chapters Two and Fifteen, which were then current.

Otherwise, nineteen years later, the book—and my argument—remain exactly the same.

PART ONE

Agent of Lawlessness

The doctrine of contentious procedure ". . . is peculiar to Anglo-American law . . . [it] disfigures our judicial administration at every point . . . [it] give[s] to
the whole community a false notion of the purpose and
end of law. . . . Thus the courts . . . are made
agents or abettors of lawlessness."

—*Roscoe Pound*[1]

1

THE PATRIOTIC FICTION

Our legal system too often betrays us—from law that is lenient for the mighty but harsh for the weak, to killer freed to kill again, to Watergate, the "lawyer's scandal." That betrayal is not accidental. Within our current legal procedure, it is inevitable. This book attempts to show why.

More particularly, this book is about our adversary legal style, a pre-Christian hand-me-down by which modern American judicial process is inextricably shaped. It is about how the requirements of that trial-by-battle procedure—historic product of a simplistic thinking-system—ultimately contradict, subvert, and nullify our highest judicial intentions.

This book urges our discard of adversary procedure. It urges that we design instead a system responsible to the entire electorate, administered by nonlegal personnel and summoning the educated, creative participation of every adult citizen. It suggests that we reconceive and restructure the functions of lawyers, judges, and juries. It proposes a system that forbids the battle now requisite; that seeks illumination through informational breadth rather than victory through information's exclusion. It advocates a system whose goal would be individual and societal welfare, rather than one person's "win" at society's expense.

Public confidence in our system of justice is at low ebb. The collapse of that system, a noted lawyer writes, is now.[2] I believe I have

13

learned why. My explanation is not among those commonly given.

Legal journals, popular magazines, and books complain of administrative delay, procedural inefficiencies, and archaic technology. They decry justice's cost to the middle class, its unavailability to the poor, to the consumer, to minority group members. They criticize the narrowness of legal education and the failure of ethical indoctrination; a Bench ill-chosen and ill-prepared; laws out of date; inequitable criminal sentencing; and the consigning to the courts of matters (such as injury cases and drug offenses) that should be handled in other ways, elsewhere. The left calls our legal system a device in the exertion of power by one class against another. Citizens write bitter letters to the editor complaining of loopholes in the law.

These plaints—all true—are nevertheless peripheral. The heart of our judicial crisis is the adversary ethic: the values and conceptual system it represents, together with those antisocial behaviors it confirms and inexorably proliferates.

Consider this: In July of 1973, in upstate New York, two girls separately disappeared. Susan was twenty-one, Alicia sixteen. Shortly afterward, Susan's twenty-two-year-old camping companion, Daniel, was found—murdered. Of neither girl was there any trace.

Several months later, Susan's father, hearing that a man had been arrested and charged with murdering an eighteen-year-old boy in the same mountainous region, flew to New York to talk with the accused's lawyers. The lawyers gave Susan's father no information concerning his daughter. Alicia's parents, meanwhile, thinking her a runaway, continued through subsequent months to advertise in the newspapers, begging her to come home.

Neither girl could come home. Both were dead—and the lawyers had long known it; known it when Susan's father asked their help; known it all that following period during which Alicia's parents had publicized their pleas. In fact, the lawyers themselves had seen (and photographed) the mutilated bodies where they lay, one at the bottom of a well, one in the wooded brush of a cemetery—to which spots they had been directed by the girl's killer: their client.

The lawyers did not tell the victims' parents what they knew; neither did they tell the police. For six months the lawyers kept silent. Nor was it they who finally talked. Instead, their client blurted the truth from the witness stand during his trial for murdering the eighteen-year-old boy. Had the murderer himself not spoken, his further crimes might have remained forever hidden.

What kept the lawyers silent? Nothing less than the ethic of their profession. Had the attorneys done otherwise, stated Dean Monroe Freedman of Hofstra University Law School, "it would be a serious violation of their professional responsibility."[3] The adversary ethic, which insists that the lawyer's first duty is to his client, required two officers of the court to conceal a killer's culpability—though that concealment might have returned the killer to our midst.

The case raised a public uproar about the ethical dilemma involved. The dilemma stems from a central adversary legal tenet: the inviolability of lawyer-client confidences. That tenet—like the 5th Admendment privilege against self-incrimination—aims at guaranteeing the accused a fair trial. Yet at the same time, both tenets block the emergence of information. In their service, Dean Freedman observes (with the unblinking directness that has intermittently upset some of his colleagues), the lawyer has "a professional obligation to place obstacles in the path of truth."[4] Our legal procedure must serve individual welfare at the cost of truth—and too often, of public safety as well. The problem, many legal professionals hold, is probably unsolvable.

Freedman attempts a solution. He holds that the adversary process "has its foundations in respect for human dignity [and therefore] the high value that we assign to truth-seeking . . . may on occasion be subordinated to even higher values":[5] in effect, to the system of justice, and its tenets, which uphold that dignity. The trouble with Freedman's argument is, for me, its premise. Adversary values, whatever their intent, relentlessly diminish human dignity. The problem *is* unsolvable—within an adversary frame. Other and better ways can be designed.

Among patriotic fictions rooted marrow-dear is that which equates America's legal system with truth and justice. In court, we tell ourselves, the truth will come out. "With liberty and justice for all," we recite (hand upon heart) from kindergarten to coffin. These are fine ideals, for which many have fought and died. Hence, when trial victors cry "The system really works!", we are grateful to have our faith confirmed. Critics may mutter and losers weep. Clutching our faith, we reject them both, reminding the loser that his grapes are sour—while at the same time ignoring the *process by which* the winner has prevailed.

Few who go to court, however, maintain for long that luxurious innocence. Through a series of coincidences over a five-year period,

I found myself abruptly thrust into our trial system in a spectrum of unrelated matters. During that time, I experienced every courtroom role except that of the professional, serving variously as witness and character witness, defendant, plaintiff, and juror, in cases both civil and criminal; and in many courts observed scores of cases in which I had no part. I had begun with belief that our legal procedure searched for truth—or, at very least, for information.

I found instead a system in which truth is incidental; in which information is avoided or suppressed as eagerly as sought, and justice is largely accident. I found a system that, because it demands intensely partisan behavior of attorneys and clients alike, gives high priority to selective representation and misrepresentation (revered jurist Roscoe Pound politely called it "exertion to get error into the record"[6]). I found a legal system that promulgates and then rewards those very behaviors it is constituted to oppose: too often making liars of litigants, tricksters of the Bar, and hypocrites of the Bench. Many who enter the legal profession, and many who remain, wish to promote society's welfare. Some manage, against all odds, to do so. Nevertheless, no one directly involved (including the lay person) can remain for long untainted by those adversary means which even the best of legal ends require. Such is, perhaps, no one's purpose, but it is unavoidably the essence of our win-or-lose trial procedure.

At the start of my court journey, I had barely heard the term "adversary system," nor had any idea of its practical implications. By the end of my travels, I had become an adversary of adversary procedure. Subsequently, seeking the reasons for that method of dispute settlement which on its face made so little sense, I began a search through legal texts and journals. My discovery of what was missing, together with shock at what was there, convinced me that my experience, though personal, was less exception than rule; and was due less to any venality or inadequacy of the legal professionals than to the intrinsic nature of the adversary ethic itself. This book details what I found.

That fight-ethic, however, serves not only the lawyers and judges who directly administer it, but society's power holders down the ranks. For adversariness is a mode that singularly advantages power. Most of its beneficiaries therefore worship adversary procedure "like motherhood itself"; [7] and either remain blind to its defects, hold (like Freedman) that despite those defects it serves a higher good, or actively work at screening its fraud from public gaze. Yet fraud it is. For *by its nature* adversary approach to dispute settlement disserves the rest of us—almost totally. That is this book's bias. My case is based nearly entirely upon evidence provided by the legal professionals themselves: their words, writings, and actions; their public claims and private straight-talk.

This book is *not* about individual laws, nor their philosophical, moral, social, or political implications. It *is* about the legal style from which trial decisions emerge.

Supposedly, in our courts, laws, or rules held to embody principles, are applied to "facts" in cases. Those facts selected out of the conflicting array urged by each side come to be called *the* facts. But *the* facts are merely those which, among many possibilities, one of the lawyers has succeeded in selling judge or jury. And until the time when specific laws, statutes, and precedents are brought together with specific facts in a particular litigation, and there selected, combined, interpreted, and embodied in the court's official pronouncement—those laws are no more than abstraction on paper. Good, bad, indifferent—still abstraction.

This book is about the *method* that gives that paper-abstraction its daily, life-consequential reality; the method that, in the United States, determines choice both of the facts and the law held most applicable to them. This book is about the cohesive system of legal techniques and personal behaviors that guides the choice of fact and directs the Procrustean stretching and lopping of laws to fit them (and facts to fit law)—giving paper law the meaning that matters. It is about the adversary procedural *stance* that deforms the selection and fitting: its genesis, underlying conceptual system, and rationale. That stance mocks the best of our laws and clips the wings of highest theory. Above all, it kills respect for lawyers, judges, and lawfulness itself.

"Law" may be what is supposed to happen. This book is about what *does* happen, to you and to me. It is about the practice, rather than the claims, of our trial machinery.

Finally, a legal system is the nexus of a society's assumptions, emphases, and values. Bipolar attitudes infect our culture. They have helped deliver us to racism and sexism, to neglect of our young, weak, old, and poor; to Vietnam and to violence ever rising. They helped lead to a President so obsessed with a phantasm of "enemies" that his impeachment for acts "subversive of constitutional government, to the great prejudice of the cause of law and justice and to the manifest injury of the people of the United States," became finally inescapable; and his resignation forced. Those cultural attitudes are perhaps most clearly operative and explicitly stated in our adversary legal approach. That approach—centered in a primary cultural institution (supposedly exemplifying our "best")—instead ceaselessly recontaminates the social fabric from which it springs. This book is thus necessarily also about those attitudes: what they are, whence they derive, and what they mean for anyone who enters litigation.

I believe that within that attitudinal framework, no amount of patching, tinkering, or stop-gapping will significantly ameliorate our legal ills. I believe that only a new legal system, based on new assumptions, will do. This book tells why. It considers at the same time our adversary society—and suggests a direction for change.

2

OUR ADVERSARY SYSTEM

"Adversary system" is likely to be one of the first phrases heard by anyone who, willing or nilling, tangles with our courts. When, in your attorney's office, you either[1] express dismay at the brutality of the initial blow struck by the other side, or[2] express shock at the brutality of the blow your side is about to strike, your attorney will say, "Well, you see, we have an adversary system of law...."

When, as your case is being prepared, you first say to your attorney, "But *that* story isn't my story...," he (she) will reply, "Ah, but you must understand, we have an adversary system of law...." And if you persist, with: "But that story isn't my *truth*...," your attorney will reply (with an attempt at patience), "But the Court isn't *interested* in *your* truth! In an adversary system..."

What is this "adversary system"?

It is Roscoe Pound's "contentious procedure." It is a method of dispute settlement that requires all persons who go to law to settle differences, to behave as enemies. They must fight—generally the harder, the better.

A judge explains, "The Anglo-American system of law currently pins its faith on its adversary method ...[which] holds that in the ensuing courtroom scrimmages the right will prevail."[3]

"I don't have to tell you," wrote a lawyer in a journal for the select eyes of other lawyers, "that a law suit is not a disinterested investigation but a bitter adversary duel."[4]

19

"The worst client you can get," states attorney F. Lee Bailey, "is the guy on a dream cloud who says, 'I'm innocent so I'm sure to get off.' That attitude shows a lack of understanding of what a big modern trial is—a battle of gladiator-lawyers."[3]

Out of that battle, adversary rationale maintains, the truth will be revealed. This is sometimes called the fighting theory of justice, and it underlies both the conceptual framework and the procedure of our law. Each side must present not all it knows, but only its own "best case"; must assail the opposition; must attack and counterattack, "discover" and avoid discovery.

Nearly all members of our legal profession hold this adversary method to be desirable; in truth admirable—in fact, a very jewel among the world's judicial systems. Yet there is little evidence that either its sources or its claims, its underlying assumptions or its implications, have been much examined at all.

Ever.

For example: The University of Southern California Law Library holds over 270,000 volumes (as of October 1995). Of these, eleven books are listed under the heading "Adversary System." Only one of them is devoted to that system's genesis, its evolution, rationale, and criticism: this book. (Until 1977, there were none.) The UCLA Law Library holds over 450,000 volumes. Only one book is devoted to a full-scale discussion of the adversary system: this book. (Until 1977, there were none.) The Los Angeles County Law Library, with its eight branches the largest public law library in the country, holds over 700,000 volumes. Six books are listed under "Adversary System." Only one of them is a full-scale critique: this book. (Until 1977, there were none.) *Law Books in Print*, which lists its material by subject as well as title, contains 6503 subject categories, from "Abbreviations" through "Zoning." "Adversary system" is not among them.

Of the country's twenty-three top law schools, fewer than half, according to a 1977 publication of the Association of American Law Schools, offered any course devoted to the adversary system. An equivalent statistic is not available today.

At UCLA, twenty-six texts are required or suggested for first-year law students. Twenty-three of these texts make no mention of "adversary system" in either chapter heading or index. Three do: *Legal Reasoning and Legal Writing* by Richard Neumann, devotes five paragraphs to the adversary system; none of those paragraphs offers a critique. *Federal Rule of Civil Procedure* by Stephen Yeazell, et al., lists

"Discovery in An Adversary System" as an eight-paragraph section heading, but neither discussion nor critique of that system follows. *The Killing of Bonnie Garland,* the third book, is a paperback novel that, referring to "adversary system" eleven times in its pages, devotes no single paragraph to it. A previously required text, *Civil Procedure, Cases and Materials,* by Cound, Friedenthal, and Miller, contains two pages in which "adversary system" is touched upon, in a book of 1,048 pages.

And yet, according to these authors in their opening chapter,

A distinctive element of the procedure for resolving legal controversies is the adversary system. This element is indeed central to the whole subject, and unless it is understood it becomes well nigh impossible to explain, much less to justify, most of our procedural law. (my italics)

In three more paragraphs they are done with it.

I believe that our adversary legal system, its assumptions and values, is one of the major taken-for-granted, practically never questioned institutions of our culture. More, I believe it is an anachronism, relic of a primitive way of seeing and thinking about the world. Indeed, our commitment to adversary approach demands that we refuse much of the best knowledge and behavior of our twentieth century, and go backward—centuries back, to ordeal and to magic. For it is from the customs of judicial ordeal and magic that our legal style in large part derives.

PART TWO

To The Advantage
of the Unscrupulous

The elasticity . . . with which the [judicial] duel lent itself to the advantage of the turbulent and unscrupulous had no little influence in extending its sphere of action.

—*Henry Charles Lea*[1]

3

"JUSTICE" AS ORDEAL

Once upon a time, before written laws, judges, and courts, the administration of justice in disputed cases was inexpensive and direct. If evidence was inadequate or too evenly balanced, or an issue sufficiently hotly contested, the accused was made to undergo some physical peril. His survival or demise was interpreted as the verdict upon him of the all-knowing gods. Did he live? Ah, innocent. Oh, he died? Guilty, obviously! That tidy episode was trial, judgment, and punishment in one. Such was judicial ordeal.

That technique did not stand alone in early Western legal procedure. From area to area, era to era, people to people, it existed in varying prominence alongside other judicial methods. Disputes between individuals were commonly settled by fines, or the measured physical retaliation of injury for injury; while exile and death might be solutions for broader antisocial crime. But where decision was difficult—where information was lacking, where culpability was unclear, where accused denied a charge or litigants were backed by equally bellicose family groups so that feud threatened, ordeal was usually the resort. Clan chiefs, feudal lords, or kings handed the problem, with a sigh, up to heaven via ordeal.

There were a variety of ordeals. The commonest were those of water, fire, food, and poison; of oath and trial by battle. All shared a single premise: belief that the best way to end a controversy was to place at least one of the disputants in grave danger and thus force the omniscient spirits to take sides in rescue. "Right" would manifest itself in minimum of injury—or survival. Ordeal contributed largely to the first fruition of western legal ideas. [2] More particularly, it is the spiritual parent of our adversary legal approach.

Our concept of "equal justice" was no part of that early legal model. Though the gods rescued him who was "right"—he was generally right who was deity's friend. Culpability, in other words, was relative to status. For although anyone might be subject to ordeal, it was preeminently the weak who were called upon to furnish such proof of worthy origin, and thereby of a right to life and safety. Aliens, outsiders, and particularly women and children were most often that "discarded class." [3]

Thus, a frequent case in the legends is that of the woman whose illicit pregnancy reveals her misconduct. Though pariah if she had introduced into her group of relatives a child of lesser blood, she was praised if she had been intimate with a scion of the gods. But she must prove her claim of a celestial visitor. That proof would consist in the god's rescuing her and their child from mortal danger: from drowning at sea, for example, in one variation of water ordeal. In the legends—he ofttimes did. To know a god (one way or another) was useful indeed.

The ordeals of fire, food, and poison similarly required the accused to demonstrate the solicitude of some all-powerful spirit. In ordeal of fire, a man might be made to walk over glowing coals, thrust his hand into boiling water or oil, or hold a red-hot iron. Guilt or innocence rested upon the degree of injury sustained—as judged by the medicine man. In ordeal of food, an accused might be made to swallow bread or cheese over which prayers, subject sometimes only to the presiding priest's imagination, had been incanted. If, throat constricted in terror, the victim was unable to swallow, he was promptly held guilty and condemned. With poison, the result depended somewhat on the accused's constitution, but perhaps more on the motives of that infinitely influential medicine man-priest who mixed the dose.

Peril, then, was the essence of ordeal. And exculpation (in practice if not in theory) was very much a matter of high birth, sheer luck, or sufficient clout with heaven's representative, the friendly neighborhood shaman.

Political motives, however, eventually began to alter notions both of the gods and of the justice they dispensed. Morality entered the picture in a formal sense. Nations declared their wars just, looked to their gods for victory, and considered virtuous those deities who granted that success and who had, at the same time, often become associated with governments in "lawgiving." As the gods came to represent virtue, the meaning of divine judgment in judicial ordeal changed formally, too. That "judgment of God" was now seen as heavenly ruling on the moral justice of the claim, rather than lineage or status of the claimant. According to that judgment, the omniscient beings would never forsake the innocent; never permit the wrong to triumph.

In other words: high connection and lucky chance might still be "right"—but they were now called "justice." Our adversary ethic still calls them justice today.

In one form or another, an oath always accompanied ordeal. Here and there it came to be a kind of ordeal in itself. Such oath was a self-curse (or "conditional curse"[4]) calling down upon the perjurer heaven's vengeance. For instance, "If faithful, may much good come unto me; if false, may evil come in place of good."[5]

Skillful perjury, however, soon became a hallmark of the judicial sophisticate. ("Sophistication," defines Webster's: ". . . misrepresentation or falsification in argument. . . .") As early as 1000 B.C., in Greece, it was considered "meritorious to be skillful in profiting as much from the false oath as from a theft. . . ."[6] Five hundred years later, the rhetoricians and sophists served as a "manual of perjury"[7] at the service of the litigant. The object was to preserve the letter of the oath, while evading its spirit.

For example: A sly fellow, accused of refusing to restore a sum of money held in trust, hid the money in the hollow of his staff. Just before taking the oath of innocence, he handed the staff to the plaintiff to hold. Thus he could "truly" swear he had delivered the funds to the plaintiff—and yet keep it all, "even the favor of the gods!" Or, goes another tale, a man who stole a fish in a market slipped it into another's basket and swore with clear conscience that he "had it not, nor knew of any other person who took it." And then there was the judge who, technically faithful to his judicial oath, cast his own vote for the death of a guilty friend on trial—but persuaded his two colleagues to vote for acquittal.

It was against this state of affairs that Plato inveighed: ". . . the law, if intelligently framed, should not require the oath from either party . . . we cannot for a moment doubt that perhaps a half of our citizens are perjurers, who nevertheless do not hesitate to sit at table with the rest nor to associate with them in public assembly and private homes. . . ."[8] Plato was not heeded.

Eventually Christianity, attempting to add sanctity, brought the oath into church. There the defendant was made to swear innocence with hand upon the altar or some heavily blessed relic. When perjury persisted, the number of altars requisite was multiplied. The Anglo-Saxons, for instance, in certain cases allowed the plaintiff to substantiate his charge in four churches, while the defendant could rebut by swearing an oath of denial in twelve. When such altar-arithmetic got out of hand, emphasis shifted to relics as means of perjury control. This led to an increasingly complex religio-legal account-juggling. For example, perjury on a consecrated cross required three times the penance requisite for perjury on an unconsecrated one; but seven times the penance was necessary to absolve perjury if the oath had been taken on an altar with relics. If, however, no priest had officiated at the original ceremony, the false swearer was home free—the oath void and perjury without penalty![9]

Nevertheless, neither churchly sanctity, altar, nor relic deterred the determined. Over one thousand years after Plato, complaints still rose. About A.D. 700, a section of the Burgundian code deplored, "Many we find, are so depraved, that they do not hesitate to offer an oath upon things uncertain, and to commit perjury upon things unknown to them."

It has been suggested that this plague of perjury accounted for the rise of that most famous of ordeals, trial by battle.[10] Unlike the false oath, whose evil consequence might not immediately fall, battle brought down prompt and dramatically unequivocal divine retribution upon the perjurer.[11] Certainly Charlemagne in the eighth century post-Christ (some 1,100 years after Plato's plaint) considered battle a practical remedy for the prevalence of perjury. and certainly, too, outraged litigants increasingly took the law into their own hands and settled matters with violence; while the authorities, in order to maintain some semblance of control, began to structure rules for conduct of the carnage.

In any case, judicial battle was a bilateral ordeal: one to which both sides had to submit. And, however it developed, ordeal appears to be a Western ancestral institution. "Trial by battle," says Holdsworth, "is almost universally found among the barbarian tribes from whom the nations of modern Europe trace their descent. . . . It was accompanied by a belief that Providence will give victory to the right. Christianity merely transferred this appeal from the heathen deities to the God of Battles."[12] Another historian suggests, ". . . the Church found in [ordeal] a powerful instrument to enforce her authority, and to acquire influence over the rugged nature of her indocile converts."[13] In other words, religion's blessing helped institutionalize Battle as an acceptable legal technique in the Western world.

Oddly, the Anglo-Saxons seem to have been almost the only people who did not initially possess the ordeal of battle. But in 1066, William the Bastard (son of Robert the Devil) brought trial by battle to England. Here, with the conquerors' backing, it took fast hold, superseding those other ordeals that were native custom, and lending itself increasingly to the "advantage of the turbulent and unscrupulous."

Explains Lea, ". . . The strong and the bold are apt to be the ruling spirits in all ages, and were emphatically so in those periods of scarcely curbed violence. . . . It is no wonder, therefore, that means were readily found for extending the jurisdiction of the wager of battle as widely as possible. . . ."[14] In Europe as well as England, one of the most fruitful expedients was the custom of challenging witnesses. If, for instance, your case were going badly, you simply challenged an inconvenient witness to defend his veracity. If your swordsmanship was good, this generally took care of both the witness and the case. Such tactics quickly became a favorite method of escaping legal condemnation. Witnesses, in fact, were finally required to come into court armed—and to have their weapons blessed on the altar before giving testimony. One of the Frisian tribes actually enshrined in legal code a handy variation of this technique: A man, if unable to disprove an accusation of homicide against himself, was permitted to *transfer the charge* to *anyone else he wished*; and then decide the question between himself and the hapless by-stander, by combat![15]

Eventually, no dispute existed that might not be submitted to the decision of sword or club.[16] Between the 10th and 13th centuries, ju-dicial battle was so integral a part of the ordinary law, civil as well as criminal, employed habitually in the most everyday affairs, that only infants, women, ecclesiastics, and those over sixty could avoid it. (The guardians of women and minors, however, were required to give battle in their behalf.) Anyone suffering certain physical disabil-ities might likewise decline. But such disabilities were codified with the utmost nicety: the loss of molar teeth, for instance, did not per-mit disqualification; while the absence of incisors, considered im-portant weapons, did.[17]

Nor did even death assure escape. A North German law provided that the dead, when prosecuted, might appear in the lists by substi-tute. A Scottish law firmly ordered that if the accused should die be-fore the appointed time, his body must be brought to the battlefield, "for no man can essoin [excuse] himself by death."[18]

Women, though usually exempt from compulsory combat, were permitted to fight if they wished. This was now and then regulated with tender care. Under a German law, "The chances between such unequal adversaries were adjusted by placing the man up to the na-vel in a pit three feet wide, tying his left hand behind his back, and arming him only with a club, while his fair opponent had the free use of her limbs and was furnished with a stone as large as a fist . . . fastened in a piece of stuff. . . ."[19] Not everywhere, how-ever, was such fastidious adjustment made. The Frankish kingdoms of the East reserved a special atrocity for women, or at least for those who preferred to hire champions to fight for them. When a woman's champion was defeated, she was promptly burned to death no matter what the crime for which the combat occurred. This was one of the numerous instances in medieval law of "the injustice ap-plied habitually to the weaker sex."[20]

Defeat, then, generally involved a triple risk: loss of the suit, pos-sible death on the field, or—if the loser survived—conviction of per-jury often punishable by death or dismemberment. A vanquished combatant was classified with perjurers, false witnesses, and other infamous persons.

Nevertheless, persons exempt from combat still sometimes

wished to contest a matter. Champions, again, were their means to battle. In theory, the champion was a witness, "swearing" through arms to the justice of the disputant's case. But in practice he was often simply a hireling-fighter. Gradually, toward the 12th and 13th centuries, the ablebodied too began to seek ways of appointing substitutes. One such way turned to advantage the custom of challenging witnesses, and at the same time affirmed the contradictory duality of witness-champion. The litigant would hire, ostensibly to testify but actually to disrupt, "some truculent bravo who swore unscrupulously"[21] and whose false evidence would bring down upon him the wrath of the adverse party. The bravo, forced out of court at sword's point, would then turn and in one swoop demolish the adverse litigant and the litigation, too. Eventually a class of professional champions arose. These were permanently retained by landowners, churches, and sometimes entire communities—all wanting, of course, the best fighters money could buy.

Through such devices the profession of champion became before long almost synonymous with "false witness." That synonymity was in fact often demanded by the legal codes themselves, which required the champion to assume the position of someone who had witnessed the action at issue.[22] In England and Normandy, for example, this curious legal fiction required the plaintiff's champion to swear that he had heard and seen the matters alleged in the claim; while the adverse champion dutifully swore the opposite.

Thus, ultimately, the exigencies of bilateral judicial ordeal created a kind of schizophrenic ethic. That legal ethic caught the professional battler between conflicting obligations: to the appearance of truth on one hand, and the practice of deception on the other. Both were his duties. They still are.

When the champion lost, however, he suffered heavily. Publicly revealed as a liar, he became a scapegoat for the community's complicity in his deceit. Thus, while the losing principal in criminal cases might possibly escape with a fine or imprisonment, the hired ruffian was hanged, or at best lost a hand or foot, as punishment for perjury.[23] "With such risks to be encountered, it is no wonder that the trade of champion offered few attractions to honest men who could keep body and soul together in any other way."[24] Indeed, champions came to be classed with the ". . . vilest criminals, and with the unhappy females who exposed their charms for sale . . . the extraordinary anomaly was exhibited of seeking to learn the truth in affairs of the highest moment by a solemn appeal to God, through the instrumentality of those who were already considered as convicts of the worst kind. . . ."[25]

Finally, in Western Europe judicial battle was

> . . . so skillfully interwoven through the whole system of jurisprudence that no one could feel secure that he might not, as plaintiff, defendant or witness, be called upon to protect his estate or his life either by his own right hand or by the club of some professional and possibly treacherous bravo. This organized violence assumed for itself the sanction of a religion of love and peace, and human intelligence seemed too much blunted to recognize the contradiction.[26]

It was not until 1819 that trial by battle was (with belated official rectitude) officially outlawed in England.

4

ORDEAL AS MAGIC

Trial by ordeal was more than peril. It was also a magico-religious process that turned popular magical and religious beliefs to legal purpose; a variation, directed at legal ends, upon themes of purification and divination. Thus an aura of the unknowable surrounded judicial ordeal, and at the same time swelled the power of those medicine-men-priests whose administration was necessary to its efficacy. That aura lingers on. It infuses our courtrooms today and bestows upon our legal professionals the magician-priest's cloak, in addition to the bravo's sword and club.

Magic, like most religions, has two predominant external features. First, a spell: the uttering of words according to a formula in some set order. Second, a rite: a series of actions (again usually in some set order) whose primary function is to convey the spell to that object one wishes to affect. The spell is generally believed to have been handed down from antiquity, and the inflexibility of its verbal pattern is deemed critical to its result. Magical features characterized much of early legal behavior, and stamp our procedural strictures still.

In ancient ordeal some time-honored gesture, nearly always in relation to a significant external object, was integral in the oath-taking ceremony. The Romans clutched a sacred stone, the Athenians stood upon one. The Greek oath-taker stretched an arm toward heaven, or sometimes placed one hand upon an altar "as if touching the god. . . ."[1] Late into English history there survived a ninefold oath that had to be repeated before nine altars without varying a single syllable.

As for legal language, from the beginning verbal inflexibility was often judicial essence. Thus, in the Legis Actio Sacramenti, parent of all Roman laws and ancestor of ours, you could not sue for injury to your vines and call them vines; you would fail. You must call them trees, because the Twelve Tables of Roman Law (the first written collection of Roman Law in 451 B.C.) spoke only of trees. Similarly, according to an ancient collection of Teutonic legal formulas, the Malberg Gloss, you could not sue for a bull (and win) by calling him a bull. You must call him "leader of the herd." Likewise, the forefinger must be the "arrow-finger" and a goat not a goat but a "browser upon leeks."

Judicial battle demanded of all combatants the absolute assertion by each of the justice of his case, "confirmed by a solemn oath on the Gospels, or on a relic of approved sanctity,"[2] together with a declaration by each party of the absence upon his person of charm or Devil's device to influence the divine judgment.

For example, in the case of *Low v. Paramore* in 1571, this pledge was made: "This hear you justices that I have this day neither eat, drunk, nor have upon me either bone, stone ne [sic] glass nor any enchantment, sorcery or witchcraft wherethrough the power of the Word of God might be inleased [sic] or diminished and the devil's power increased, and that my appeal is true, so help me God and his saints and by this book."[3]

Where judicial ordeal was fully developed, its procedural strictures, both physical and verbal, were often as numerous as they were minute. In the days of ordeal's decline, a finicking formalism frequently provided the element of risk that was ordeal's essence: one slip and the victim's race was run.

But risk was not formalism's only judicial function. Formalism also served to make legality obvious by an external appearance. It lent to legal process the look of a divine institution, not subject to human manipulation or will; while to the magician-priests who officiated, it lent immunity from popular censure.

We have come a long way from trial by ordeal; but not nearly far enough.

PART THREE

Every Primitive and Barbarous People

Every primitive or barbarous people has made use of that mystical expert testimony known as the Ordeal in which human life seems almost like the stake in a game of chance or skill.

—Gabriel Tarde[1]

5

BATTLE STILL

Trial by ordeal is alive and functioning in the United States—under a pseudonym. Stripped of sword but still murderous, judicial ordeal is now called "adversary system."

"People think," attorney Jake Ehrlich said, "that a trial is a courtroom investigation of all the available evidence, an investigation so conducted that it will enable the jury to ascertain the truth. This is not the case. The legal profession's current conception of a fair trial is a battle. . . ."[2]

And much as in the bilateral ordeal of battle, says another lawyer, the verdict is still "to be reached, sentence pronounced, in terms of bloodshed, mutilation, slaughter, with justice favoring the stronger brute . . . or the one better equipped and trained to kill."[3]

There are dozens (at least) of books written by attorneys for each other, instructing how to win the battle. In them, terms of weaponry, of injury, and of extermination appear with notable frequency:

"By our manner toward a witness we may have in a measure *disarmed* him . . . but it is only with the matter of our cross-examination that we can hope to *destroy* him."[4]

". . . to *demolish* the effectiveness of the key witness. . . ."[5]

". . . by *annihilating* the key witness. . . ."[6]

". . . the . . . double-edged *sword*—cross-examination."[7]

37

"Cross-examination is the most *potent weapon* known. . . ."[8]

"To *destroy* the witness it is necessary to. . . ."[9]

". . . it is best to *attack* indirectly. . . ."[10]

This behavior another lawyer has termed "trial by *ambush* and trial by surprise. . . ."[11] (all italics mine.)

In *The Art of the Trial,* Norbert Savay puts it plainly: "A student of the art of advocacy and of the legal contest can profit immensely by a deep and protracted study of war strategy. . . ."[12] He adds, "In the original meaning of the word, 'strategy' is the art of planning a military campaign with a view of achieving a termination of war in one's favor. . . . Our definition of legal strategy is identical with that of military strategy. So, too, is our conception of many of the basic principles underlying each. . . ."[13] For example, quoting *Science of War*, Savay elucidates, ". . . the trained strategist bends all the powers of his intellect and the resources of his knowledge to deceive, to surprise, to overwhelm . . . a military commander . . . falls upon the hostile army . . . and makes an effort to annihilate it."[14]

Small wonder that Justice Learned Hand was moved to comment that ". . . as a litigant, I should dread a lawsuit beyond almost anything else short of sickness and death."[15]

Lawyers tell us they do not mean such terms literally. And of course today in trial bodies remain intact. But hearts and feelings do not. Physical health suffers. And beliefs—beliefs in courts and truth and our legal system—are murdered as surely as bodies ever were.

Cross-examination, examination at the hands of the opposing attorney, is the concentrated essence of adversary behavior. It is also the unique pride of the legal profession. Called a necessary art aimed at trapping the unwilling or dishonest witness,[16] cross-examination theoretically reveals material hidden or undeveloped under prior direct examination by the witness's own attorney. That material may be either "qualifying circumstances of the subject of testimony" or "facts which diminish and impeach the personal trustworthiness of the witness."[17]

An authority on evidence elaborates: the witness's

   . . . motives, his inclinations and prejudices, his means of obtaining a correct and certain knowledge of the facts to which he bears testimony, the manner, in which he has used those means, his powers of discernment, memory and description are all fully investigated and ascertained, and submitted to the consideration of the jury, before whom he has testified, and who have thus had an opportunity of observing his demeanor and of determining the just weight and value of his testimony.[18]

Cross-examination has also specifically tactical goals. These include obtaining helpful testimony and discrediting harmful; discrediting the witness; laying a foundation for impeachment of the witness; and laying foundation for an objection to "incompetent" testimony.[19]

However, cross-examination claims higher purpose. *American Jurist,* a descriptive index of legal concepts and terms, categorically states, "the test of cross-examination is the highest and the most indispensable known to the law for the discovery of truth."[20] Wigmore, "greatest of the exponents of the laws of evidence,"[21] declares:

> Not even the abuses, the mishandlings and the puerilities . . . found associated with cross-examination have availed to nullify its value. It may be that in *more than one sense it takes the place in our system which torture occupied in the medieval system. . . . Nevertheless, it is beyond any doubt the greatest legal engine ever invented for the discovery of truth* . . . there has probably never been a moment's doubt upon this point in the mind of a lawyer of experience. . . .[22] (italics mine)

Indeed, adversary cross-examination has joined both ordeal and torture (often held substitutes for each other[23]) in receiving the sanction of the "wisest lawgivers during the greater part of the world's history."[24] And the stated aim of all three has ever been "truth."

Is truth, in fact, the cross-examiner's quest? Replies one lawyer, "An advocate's quest is for victory . . . there is no reward for fighting a brilliant battle but coming in second."[25] Truth is subordinated to that drive for victory—wherever and whenever occasion demands. Cross-examination, far from being "the one and only efficient instrumentality for the *guarantee* of truth"[26] (emphasis mine), is instead the opposite: chief truth-slayer in the fight.

The manuals of forensic instruction make truth's role clear. "These books," Ehrlich states in one of them, "advise the lawyer that he has a duty to give the jury, if possible, a false impression of testimony unfavorable to his side. . . ."[27] And the manuals set forth, in repeated detail, the techniques for doing just that.

SURPRISE AND CHARACTER ATTACK

"The use of surprise," Munkman writes in *Technique of Advocacy*, "may be as effective in the tactics of litigation as in warfare."[28] Savay explains, "the effect of a well-engineered surprise on the jury is tremendous, especially if, until the shock is delivered, the other side has been making a better headway, or even if the showing was evenly balanced. . . . The psychological meaning of a surprise in the trial of a lawsuit is that the reaction which follows, tends to operate as an immediate conviction that the side which has achieved [it] is right."[29] Further, a trial lawyer lectured to a bar association gathering, " . . . surprise elements should be hoarded . . . the traps should not be uncovered. Indeed, you may cast a few more leaves over them so that your adversary will step more boldly on the low ground believing it is solid."[30] If the leaf scatterer is lucky, his opponent will not have time to seek out and interview witnesses or summon evidence to rebut that surprise testimony.

Of course, "One of the best known methods for achieving strategic surprise is by crushing character attack on the credibility of a witness or his character."[31] *Goldstein's Trial Technique* agrees: "Sometimes there seems to be no way of attacking or destroying a witness's story. In that event, if . . . the witness has a poor reputation among his reputable neighbors, then that method of impeachment is positively indicated."[32]

THE SETUP QUESTION

A basic query recommended by most of the manuals, and aimed at discrediting those who testify adversely, is, "To whom have you talked about this case?" (Indeed, that question "should be put to practically every witness that takes the stand. . . ."[33]) Cornelius, in *Cross-Examination of Witnesses,* says: " . . . this question has discredited more individuals on the stand than any other. Especially is it effective where the witness is not of a higher order of intelligence or experience in court. . . ."[34]

The trap, of course, is that the witness has necessarily talked at least with the attorney who called him. But he may believe that talking to others about testimony is forbidden or invalidates the testimony. Or else he assumes that the question reasonably excludes the calling attorney. His "No one" therefore permits the cross-examiner to pounce. The witness has been caught in a lie, the lawyer cries, and his entire testimony must be discounted—whatever it may be.

Another basic setup question erects and attempts to capitalize upon the myth of perfect recall. For instance, of an event that occurred some twenty years before: "In what month was that?"— "Oh, you *think* it was May or June. You mean you don't *know*?"— "Well, which was it, then?"—"Ah, you're *not sure?* Your testimony is, then, *you don't remember?*"

The point, Goldstein instructs, is that "the more times . . . the lawyer can make the witness say 'I don't remember,' the better will be the psychological effect."[35] For, explains Ehrlich in *The Lost Art of Cross-Examination,* "It is impossible in a court of law to place confidence in the evidence of a witness who can be reduced in cross-examination to saying 'I do not remember.' "[36]

SILENT CROSS-EXAMINATION

The lawyer is generally adept with a bag of tone and mime skills that aim at converting his argument into the judge's or jury's "fact." "Ridicule and sarcasm," Cornelius points out, "may be used with telling effect in cross-examination."[37] The approach may be verbal, tonal, or silent altogether. A grin, eyebrow lift, or "listen-to-that" shrug toward Bench or jury box may invite emotional conspiracy. The dismissing of a witness with "That will be all!" in triumphant tone, may pretend that damaging testimony was instead a coup. Another device is to address a witness as "Sir" or "Madame" in a heavy sneer that, if verbalized outside the courtroom's permissive ground, would approach slander.

Such techniques are particularly useful in that they do not appear in any written transcript of proceedings. Thus, an Appeals Court, which rules only upon matters of law and accepts the lower court's version of fact, has no clue to any emotional aura that may have influenced the court in that ascertainment. The examiner's manner is often more important than the substance of his question.

Cornelius writes, "Counsel may use silence effectively in cross-examination by rising slowly as if to question the witness and then with a tolerant smile toward him and an attitude that seems to say 'Oh what's the use, this witness is of no importance anyway,' take his seat with the statement 'I believe I do not care to cross-examine.'"[38]

Wellman, in *The Art of Cross Examination*, offers a variation:

> If the witness happens to be a woman, and at the close of her testimony-in-chief it seems that she will be more than a match for the cross-examiner, it often works like a charm with the jury to practice upon her what may be styled the silent cross-examination. Rise suddenly, as if you intended to cross-examine. The witness will turn a determined face toward you, preparatory to demolishing you with her first answer. This is the signal for you to hesitate a moment. Look her over good-naturedly and as if you were in doubt whether it would be worthwhile to question her—and sit down. It can be done by a good actor in such a manner as to be equivalent to saying to the jury, "What's the use? she is only a woman."[39]

For "woman," of course, substitute any other put-down the examiner might guess will match the fact-finder's prejudice: "clerk," "black," "banker."

(The manuals, as a matter of fact, with almost uniform alarm advise against cross-examining women. "Let me give you my dying advice," said a dean of legal jousters. "Never cross-examine a woman."[40] "No man has yet lived," another declared, "who could fathom the depths of a woman's mind."[41] " . . . The average female witness is the most subtle, clever enigma that was ever offered for analysis."[42] "The man who knows how to handle a woman witness should be paid double."[43] "They are mentally quick . . . positive in their statements . . . operate upon the shifting basis of intuition . . . will change their minds elusively . . . skip from one conclusion to another . . . answer inaccurately . . . their reasoning has great gaps of inference. . . ."[44] "They are quicker-witted than men, and some of them seem to know intuitively what your next question is going to be. . . ."[45] "A female witness is evasive in her answers by nature. . . . She is not a natural-born reasoner, is not logical, but relies almost entirely upon intuition. . . ."[46] "Cross-examining women is as simple as understanding them."[47] "Yes, the cross-examination of a woman has been the rock upon which many a trial lawyer has wrecked his case. . . . Have your armor in good shape and your visor down, otherwise you may be the most seriously wounded when the combat is over."[48])

Silent cross-examination, which offers the witness no opportunity to refute the examiner's clear but unspoken slur, is (for the lawyer) the safest way of doing battle. But if the lawyer has foregone that prudent technique, or placed upon the stand a witness who despite all has bested him, there is still one trick left: "Failing to make a point on cross-examination, and especially when the witness has scored against you, dismiss him with some remark that will provoke a laugh—at his expense, not yours."[49]

THE HONEST WITNESS

Yet what about the honest witness—the one who speaks that truth the cross-examiner seeks? He presents for the law-men a particular problem.

Ehrlich suggests, "Whenever the witness is apparently honest and has tried to give his best recollection of an occurrence, any cross-examination undertaken should be pursued only to the point of obtaining some favorable limitation of . . . his direct testimony. Then he should be dismissed with an air suggesting that his entire testimony lacks importance."[50]

Cornelius suggests a diversionary tactic (my italics):

> . . . if the witness is an honest one and tells a clear straight-forward story, do not cross-examine him upon the main story, he will only emphasize it. Cross-examine him for lack of memory, for distances, for marks of identity, for religion, for politics, for anything but his story . . . . In other words, if you are cross-examining a clear-headed honest witness, never give him a chance to repeat his story, but *pull the attention of the jury away from it.* . . .[51]

And Lake, in *How to Cross-Examine Witnesses Successfully,* urges the maxim: "No matter how clear, how logical, how concise, or how honest a witness may be or make his testimony appear, there is always some way, if you are ingenious enough, to *cast suspicion on it,* to weaken its effect."[52]

INFORMATION

What then about cross-examination's search for "fact": for those "qualifying circumstances of the subject of testimony"? Replies an attorney, ". . . advocacy requires a lawyer to start with something to be proved. . . . He will waste a lot of time if he goes with an open mind. . . . He fixes on the conclusion which will best serve his client's interests, and then he sets out to persuade others to agree."[53] The basic axiom, echoed and re-echoed in the manuals, is "never ask a question unless you know just what the answer will be,"[54] or "will aid your cause."[55]

In *Trial Evidence,* Reynolds advises, "Never ask for explanations unless you are perfectly *sure* they cannot be given. It is always much better to point out the improbabilities and contradictions in a witness's testimony, in the argument to the jury, than to let him explain them away upon the stand."[56] Often, he adds, "the best method to deal with an adverse witness is to decline cross-examining him at all, which, if done with a rather supercilious air, will frequently impress the jury with the idea that his testimony is either totally untrustworthy, or else has little or no bearing upon the case."[57]

Reiterates Wellman, "David Graham . . . once said, 'A lawyer should never ask a witness on cross-examination a question unless in the first place he knew what the answer would be, or in the second place he didn't care.' Certainly no lawyer should ask a *critical* question unless he is reasonably sure of the answer."[58] "Listen," I heard one judge shush a persistent attorney, "you keep on asking questions, you may get an answer you don't want!" In other words, information that is not ammunition must be shunned as the vessel shuns the fatal reef.

Reynolds elaborates the danger:

The principal things to be guarded against in a cross-examination are, first, permitting the witness to supply any omis-

sions which he may have made in his testimony in chief;
second, getting from him explanations of any apparent in-
consistencies that he may have fallen into; . . . and finally,
giving the opposing counsel the opportunity of bringing out
on re-examination some unfavorable testimony which
would not have been admissible but for some injudicious
question put during the cross-examination . . . . Upon
perceiving that a witness has omitted some important point
in his testimony, do not allude to it, but keep him as far from
it as possible, that he may not have the opportunity to repair
his blunder.[59]

Corollary to the techniques of avoiding information are those of
creating misinformation. The question that begins, "Is it not a fact
that . . ." is almost guaranteed to introduce not fact but fiction.
This, and others like it ("So you tell us that . . .") are leading questions. They attempt to slip into the witness's mouth words that represent neither his facts, feelings, or beliefs. The leading question is
not permitted one's own attorney on direct examination. (It is in that
context considered coaching, and coaching is frowned upon in public view—though of course prestand coaching in the privacy of your
attorney's office is understood to be a large part of what you pay him
for. Once upon the courtroom stage, however, judicial delicacy requires that the witness be line-perfect.) The leading question is, on
the other hand, freely allowed to the opposing attorney on cross-
examination. The more critical of such snares are usually laid near
the end of an interrogation, at a point where the weary and addled
witness may accept the examiner's words as his own and fatally answer "Yes."

There are several variations upon this approach; frowned upon
perhaps by the Code of Professional Responsibility, but frequent all
the same. "Lawyers," says one of them, "sometimes ask questions
that they never expect to have answered because they know that
either the judge or the opposing attorney will not allow them
. . . . The only purpose of the question is to bring to the attention
of the judge and jury certain supposedly damaging facts that otherwise cannot be proved . . . as a sort of parting shot."[60] Or an examiner may accuse a witness of wrongdoing, or of having made a
contradictory statement, "without having proof of either fact."[61]
The witness who (if he is inexperienced with our legal procedure)
does not expect an officer of the court to lie, may deny the lawyer's

accusation—but with a degree of confusion in direct proportion to the certainty of the examiner's tone. It is the witness who will appear the liar.

DEMEANOR

What, then, of the claim that cross-examination, by exposing the witness's demeanor for observation, permits the Court to determine the weight and value of his testimony? More often, the witness's demeanor is made another weapon against him.

It is, said a professor of law, "ethical for defense counsel to cross-examine a prosecution witness to make him appear to be inaccurate or untruthful, even when the defense attorney knows that the witness is testifying accurately or truthfully."[62] Ehrlich maintains that tangling up most witnesses by such means is fairly easy.[63] And Mr. Justice White, speaking from the height of the Supreme Court Bench, noted: If defense counsel can "confuse a witness, even a truthful one, or make him appear at a disadvantage, unsure or indecisive, that will be his normal course."[64]

The scenario may go like this:

ATTORNEY (leading question): "And when you went to San Diego, with whom did you go?"

WITNESS (definitely): "I didn't go to San Diego."

ATTORNEY (pantomimes eyebrow-lifting surprise, then, rubbing an ear, the possibility of a hearing impediment): "Excuse me, Your Honor" (adroitly catching the judge's wandering attention and at the same time subtly engaging him on the attorney's side), "but I don't think I caught the last answer."

JUDGE: "Will the court reporter please read back that last question to the witness?"

COURT REPORTER: "And when you went to San Diego" (twice now, judge and jury have heard that the witness "went to San Diego'), "with whom did you go?"

WITNESS (impaled now on the eyes of the entire courtroom—jury, judge, lawyers, reporter, clerk, bailiffs, witnesses, and a gaggle of off-the-street gapers): "I (swallowing)—didn't go to San Diego."

ATTORNEY (openly, hugely incredulous): "You didn't *go* to *San Diego*?"

WITNESS (hesitating just a fraction too long): "No."

ATTORNEY (eyes ablaze, voice a-bellow): "Do you mean to tell this Court that you have *never* been to San Diego?"

WITNESS (whose own attorney has warned him never to say "never" in the witness box, but who in fact has never been to San Diego): ". . . Uh . . . Yes."

ATTORNEY (smiles, reaches for his briefcase. In dumbshow he searches through it, removes a file folder; "accidentally" drops it, thereby assuring it as a focus of attention; finally retrieves it and meaningfully waves a sheaf of papers which suggest reams of incriminating material—but which are actually absolutely blank): "You're *quite sure* of that, are you?"

WITNESS (hypnotized by the menacing papers and now certain that he must, during some amnesiac period or astral life, at least have passed *through* San Diego—but still unable to recall it): "Um . . . Uh . . . (weakly) . . . Yes."

ATTORNEY (triumphantly slams papers down and barks in a fierce tone of utter contempt): "*That* will be all!" (He lifts his hands and brows to judge and jury, silently miming "What can you do with such a liar?")

Neither the glares, vocal tones, incriminating-papers-trick, nor eyebrows will appear in the transcript of proceedings.

The witness stand has been called by both Roscoe Pound and John Henry Wigmore, "the slaughterhouse of reputations."[65] The decimation of witnesses remains a favorite modern trial tactic. ". . . the attorney is *obligated*," said a law school dean, "to attack, if he can, the reliability or credibility of an opposing witness whom he *knows to be truthful*."[66] (italics mine) This technique is officially called "discrediting" or "impeachment."

For example:

A twenty-two-year-old girl, daughter of a local bank president and engaged to a promising young minister in town, has allegedly been raped. The man accused of the crime admits to his attorney that the charge is true. However, there is a rejected suitor, "Jones," willing to testify truthfully that he frequently had intercourse with the girl and that she "behaved in a scandalous way towards strange men."[67]

Ask the legal theoreticians: Should the defense attorney use these facts to impeach the girl and, if necessary, call the rejected "Jones" as witness? The lawyer knows that his client is guilty and the prosecutrix truthful. He has "one purpose, and one purpose only, in using the suitor's testimony to impeach the girl: to destroy her credibility before the jury and thus to make it appear, contrary to fact, that she is lying about the rape."[68] Should he proceed?

Yes, say the seekers of truth.

The case is hypothetical. But the answers are not. The question was put to a symposium of the Federal Bar Association in Washington, D.C., on September 9, 1966. There were four papers presented, and a panel discussion followed.

Stated the deputy director of the Legal Aid Society for the District of Columbia, Addison M. Bowman, "I would tender the witness Jones. His testimony is not false, although, given my knowledge of the facts, I am aware that there was no consent and Jones' testimony creates the impression that there was consent."[69] Stated the U.S. attorney for the District of Columbia, David G. Bress, "Even though defense attorney may know that a government witness is telling the truth, it is nevertheless entirely proper to cross-examine for the purpose of showing the limited weight to be given to the testimony of that witness."[70] George Washington University professor of law James E. Starrs asked, rhetorically, whether his client's confession of guilt should "in any way affect the ardor" of defense counsel's cross-examination of an adverse witness who happens to be telling the truth. "Not one whit," he answered, "unless ours is a system which makes the search for truth preeminent. In that event anything which obstructs that search is impermissible. But, as we know it, cross-examination merely puts the weight and sufficiency of the prosecution's case to the test. This is perfectly acceptable even though the truth may be dimmed in the doing."[71]

The fourth participant, concurring, stated that "The function of an advocate, and particularly the defense advocate in the adversary system, is to use all the legitimate tools available to test the truth of the prosecution's case [and] the testimony of bad repute of the complaining witness, being recent and not remote in point of time, is relevant to her credibility."[72] According to Professor (now Dean) Monroe Freedman, this last participant was "even more explicit in the question period following the panel discussion: he considers it ethical to cast doubt on the girl's credibility by destroying her reputation, even though the lawyer knows she is telling the truth."[73] Who is this last participant? He is Warren Burger, then judge of the U.S. Court of Appeals, and now chief justice of the Supreme Court of the United States of America.

In other words:

Jones' testimony "is not false," says Bowman, and should there-fore be used, although all that it implies and is intended to imply *is* false. It is entirely proper to cross-examine, says Bress, for the pur-pose of showing the "limited weight" to be given the victim's tes-timony—even though it is the truth to which limited weight will be given. It is ethical, says Burger, to attempt to destroy both the girl's reputation and the truth of the case, because the testimony of her "bad repute" (a "legitimate tool") is recent and therefore "relevant to her credibility"—even though that impression it gives of her cred-ibility is a lie. Surely the sophist who slipped his stolen fish into another's basket and swore he "had it not, nor knew of any other person who took it" was no greater charlatan than these moderns.

And the result? If the legal con-game is successful, the finder of fact is misled, the guilty defendant is freed; while the victim suffers an additional and this time public outrage at the hands of a procedu-ral system to which she looked for help. Meantime, that exposure of her most personal history may have irreparably damaged her rela-tionship with her conservative family and fiancé. Of course—the case is hypothetical.

This case is not: (Identifying information has been altered.) In 1975, a woman in her forties, "Mrs. Wilson," a widow employed in a responsible position as an educational consultant by the school system of one of our Western states, was accosted by a man in an unguarded municipal parking structure. He forced her at knifepoint into his car, poured rum down her throat until she was sick, and raped her several times. Finally a scream attracted the attention of a passerby, who called the police. The rapist was caught in flagrante, and the victim driven to a hospital where she remained for one week. When she recovered, Mrs. Wilson was summoned by the State as a prosecution witness against the accused.

Mrs. Wilson expected the trial to concern itself with examination and determination of those facts alleged in the charge. She expected arguments based upon those facts. She expected that she herself would be treated with, at very least, the courtesy of a citizen who had information to offer. Victimized once by the rapist, she did not expect to be victimized again by the legal system that had called her as witness. Mrs. Wilson had never been to law before.

The defense attorneys chose an entirely permissible battle strate-gy. They decided to attack. (Though a number of jurisdictions are now limiting the extent to which the rape victim's sexual history may be pursued, a defense attack upon the victim is still too common in rape, and in other crimes, almost standard.) A newspaper article describes the approach:

> Unless she is atypical—an exceedingly sympathetic victim, very young, very old, badly beaten—it becomes [the woman's] duty to prove she didn't consent to the rape, didn't entice, lure, or otherwise reap the fruits of whatever she sowed. At the hands of an adroit defense attorney . . . she must publicly defend her personal morality, exposing the most minute, often irrelevant details of her sex life, made to feel somehow ashamed if she doesn't emerge chaste.74

Thus the defense attorney queried as follows: Was it not a fact that Mrs. Wilson had solicited the defendant's attentions? ("No," she said.) Was it not a fact that she had voluntarily entered his car? ("No," she said.) Had she not willingly gotten drunk with him, indeed given him a $10 bill to purchase the liquor? ("No," she said.) Had she not deliberately failed to call the attention of the parking structure's exit-guard to her plight? ("No," she said.) Had she not, at three separate opportunities, avoided possibility of rescue by police cars cruising by? ("No," she said.) Was it not true that, as a widow, Mrs. Wilson was "hungry for male companionship"—and now and then purchased it? ("No," she said.) Was it not, in fact, Mrs. Wilson who had actually seduced the man she now called her attacker, and who was so much younger than she—a boy, really! ("No," she said.) Was she not, actually, a sometimes prostitute? ("No," she said, and wept; and could not stop.)

Two years later, the rapist (who eventually pled guilty and was sentenced to twelve months) is one year free. But Mrs. Wilson is not. The scene in her car and the scene in the courtroom are fused in her nightmares. She continues to weep. Her health has deteriorated: she has developed high blood pressure and a heart condition. She lost her job and, under medical orders, cannot take another. Her financial situation has grown precarious, her personal prospect grim. Though the defense failed to discredit Mrs. Wilson—the Court's verdict was still reached, figuratively and in a sense literally, "in terms of bloodshed, mutilation, slaughter." (Mrs. Wilson was "lucky": According to a news report in 1972, " . . . almost overwhelmingly the woman loses. . . . In Los Angeles, of those 3490 rapes reported . . . the district attorney won 320 convictions—less than 10% of the original number. . . ."[75] Since then, though rape reports have risen, convictions have gone down.)

Mrs. Wilson was brutalized as surely by the men of law as by the lawless rapist. (The "men of law" may often be women. The canny rapist hires a female attorney.) But the legal professionals, unlike the criminal, perform their deed as normal course: in public view, within the ethic, employing the skills, gilded by the approbation, of one of the land's most eminent callings.

The criminal is charged and (now and then) jailed. The legal professionals become judges, mayors, governors, Supreme Court Justices, and Presidents of the United States.

Character assassination is a tactic used not only by the defense. It is equally employed by plaintiffs in civil and prosecution in criminal matters; in fact, almost wherever cross-examination occurs and victory beckons.

In criminal law, the rationale which justifies this savaging is that, since the defendant must be presumed innocent until proven guilty, his attorney is entitled to "put the government to its proof"[76] by (among other things) making the prosecution witness appear to be lying. Under this theory, for example, the defense attorney is privileged to withhold evidence, while his client (guilty or innocent) may not be forced to take the stand.[77] Stated Supreme Court Justice Byron White, ". . . as part of our modified adversary system and as part of the duty imposed on the most honorable defense counsel, we countenance or require conduct which in many instances has little, if any, relation to the search for truth."[78]

The prosecuting attorney, on the other hand, represents not a private citizen but the power of the state. Thus the prosecution is theoretically supposed to refrain from those same practices of evidence-withholding and character defamation. Conduct perhaps tolerable in individuals (because it aims at protecting them *against* the state) may be reprehensible when done on *behalf* of state. This "double-standard"[79] is meant to give the citizen equal weight in contest with government.

There are, however, certain tactics to which the prosecution, simply because it *is* state's arm, has unique access. These tactics are not set forth in the legal instruction manuals. Nevertheless, in the profession they are taken-for-granted facts of daily life and in the law journals are freely discussed . Character smear is one of them.

CHARACTER DEFAMATION AS COERCION

The state is singularly privy to individuals' private dossiers, including criminal records and even, in many jurisdictions, arrest reports—despite findings of false charge and dismissal of the case. (Some states forbid the use of arrest reports, though conviction history may be allowed—even if, theoretically, merely to impeach the witness's credibility. In the federal and some state courts, limitation upon use of conviction history has begun; a limit which depends upon judicial discretion and is as yet rare.) The prosecutor may use such material in cross-examination, just as the ancients once invoked a victim's low status against him.

For example, the prosecution, in order to intimidate either a defendant or his witness, may threaten to expose a prior arrest or conviction. In such circumstance, even an innocent defendant with a record has the Hobson's choice of remaining mute (which is, of course, highly prejudicial) or of taking the stand and having the prosecutor reveal his past to the jury[80]—also prejudicial. As one prosecutor put it, "I prefer to use [past convictions] as heavy weights affixed to an object I intend to sink in deep water."[81] Within that bind, defense counsel may well advise his client to plead guilty and forgo his right to trial.

Sometimes a "kill" is made by association. In one case, the prosecution made much of the criminal records of certain defense witnesses, not to discredit the witnesses—but rather the defendant whose friend they were. The prosecutor urged the jury to consider the defendant's character in light of those with whom he fraternized.[82]

SUPPRESSION AND FALSIFICATION OF EVIDENCE

The prosecution is supposed (again under the double standard) to refrain from that suppression of evidence which is permitted the defense; and certainly to abstain from any falsification of evidence.

Nonetheless, the temptation both to suppress and to falsify is too often irresistible. For (in the words of a law professor), ". . . the criminal trial, as we know it in the Anglo-American system, is not a search for truth, but rather the occasion for the prosecution to prove the accused's guilt beyond a reasonable doubt."[83]

Thus for instance, in the sex-murder case of *Miller v. Pate*,[84] the prosecutor produced as evidence a pair of man's undershorts found about a mile from the scene of the crime. These, he repeatedly alleged, were the accused's, and were heavily stained with blood of the very same type as the victim's; an allegation which a chemist, testifying for the state, swore was fact. Since the defendant denied the shorts were his at all, the alleged bloodstains were a vital link in the circumstantial chain connecting the defendant both to the shorts and to the victim (the contention was that he had discarded the shorts *because* they contained the victim's blood). The jury convicted him. He appealed, and the prosecution, countering, waved the "bloodstained" shorts in litigation all the way to the Supreme Court—zeal undaunted by fact, it later developed. At the Supreme Court hearing, in which the prisoner petitioned for a writ of habeus corpus, a chemical microanalyst appearing for the petitioner testified that the dramatic reddish-brown stains of which the prosecutor had consistently made so much, were not blood at all—but paint. The prosecution admitted having known the stains were paint all along (a detail previously unknown to the defense, however, for defense request to examine the shorts had been successfully resisted by the prosecutor at trial). This second expert found "no traces of human blood." The State did not dispute that testimony, counsel contenting himself with the chemical microanalyst's unwillingness to swear there had *never* been any blood on the shorts (though the witness pointed out that "blood substances are detectable over prolonged periods," substances identified as blood even having been extracted from Egyptian mummies). The Supreme Court, granting habeus corpus, noted that the "gruesomely emotional impact" upon the jury of the "blood-stained shorts" (an exhibit "seen with our own eyes") was incalculable; and that the prosecution had—deliberately—misrepresented the truth.[85] According to Dean Freedman, numerous such instances of prosecution behavior could be cited.[86]

PLEA BARGAINING

Of all those adversary practices the state may summon, one of the most disreputable is perhaps that "combination of duress and trickery"[87] known officially as plea bargaining, and unofficially as "copping a plea." Plea bargaining is held necessary to speed the backlog jamming our courts. Without it, "the courts couldn't function for a day."[88] (A Superior Court judge comments, "The trial courts are obsessed with backlog. You never see much about justice."[89]) Indeed, the plea bargain concludes over 90 percent of criminal cases in the United States, but *without that trial* our Constitution supposedly guarantees.

In plea bargaining, the prosecutor may multiply charges by breaking up what is essentially a single accusation into numerous parts, and charging each as a separate offense. Or he may add conspiracy counts. Or he may overcharge: perhaps charging felony (entailing sentences from a year to life) when only a misdemeanor (with maximum sentences of less than a year) would actually hold up in court. The defendant, overwhelmed by the mushroomed threat against him, is (even if innocent) thereby coerced into settling as follows: If he will forgo his right to trial by pleading guilty to one charge of the many, or to the lesser misdemeanor—the prosecutor will drop the rest.

Once such bargain is privately struck between the attorneys, usually with the Court's collusion, the accused, his lawyer, and the prosecutor stand before the Bench. (In the federal courts, the promise which has elicited the plea must be on the public record.) Here the three truth seekers join in requiring from the defendant some variation upon the following well-rehearsed litany:

PROSECUTOR: "Have you received your attorney's advice in this matter?"

ACCUSED: "Yes."

PROSECUTOR: "Do you understand that you have a right to trial by jury?"

ACCUSED: "Yes."

PROSECUTOR: "Do you understand you have a right to take the stand in your own defense?"

ACCUSED: "Yes."

PROSECUTOR: "Do you understand you have a right to cross-examine witnesses against you?"

ACCUSED: "Yes."

PROSECUTOR: "Do you voluntarily give up all these rights?"

ACCUSED: "Yes."

PROSECUTOR: "Do you understand that you have a right against self-incrimination, and that by pleading guilty you are incriminating yourself?"

ACCUSED: "Yes."

PROSECUTOR: "Has anyone made any promises to you, to induce you to make this plea?"

ACCUSED: "No."

PROSECUTOR: "Has anyone threatened you or anyone near and dear to you to make this guilty plea?"

ACCUSED: "No."

PROSECUTOR: "Are you entering this plea freely and voluntarily?"

ACCUSED: "Yes."

PROSECUTOR: "With no promises made to you?"

ACCUSED: "Yes."

PROSECUTOR: "Did you in fact do this act with which you are charged?"

ACCUSED: "Yes."

PROSECUTOR: "How do you now plead?"

ACCUSED: "Guilty."

Under the thumbscrews of the Inquisition, such result was called voluntary confession. It still is.

Nonetheless, with this obligatory recital before an augustly approving Bench and a busily recording court reporter (so that everything is clear and above board and absolutely unappealable) the case is concluded. Practically everyone is happy. The state has saved itself money. The defense attorney has been paid for doing nothing. The prosecutor has spared himself the work of putting a case together—plus the risk of losing if it went to trial. Police departments and mayors' offices add one more statistic to their swelling conviction graphs. The guilty come out ahead.

Only the innocent lose—together with all the rest of us. For under plea bargaining, the innocent always receive punishment without warrant, while the guilty receive less than the law, applied, would require. Even the most vicious killer may, through that means, return to our streets in less than four years.[90] In California recently, a first-degree murderer plea-bargained his way into an even softer sentence. The killer admitted to firing seven bullets into his victim's head and stuffing the body into a car trunk. He was eligible for parole within six months.[91]

As the plea bargain serves the violent criminal well, equally well does it serve the influential civil criminal, to whom it may grant a stunning leniency. It was so used with bargain-basement abandon in the Watergate prosecutions. There those entrusted with law and order at the highest level got off—at worst—with lighter sentences than an auto thief might expect. Former United States Attorney Richard G. Kleindienst, for example, who admitted to having been "less than candid" under oath to Congress, was charged not with perjury but with a misdemeanor. He received (together with judicial praise for the "too loyal heart" which had prompted his lie) one month in jail plus a $100 fine—both suspended.[92]

PUNITIVE PROSECUTION

Punitive prosecution is another gambit in which the prosecutor holds all the cards; one of them a joker. That joker is the mutually back-scratching relationship between prosecutor and police. Thus, a prosecution that has been dropped for lack of sufficient basis may sometimes be abruptly reinstituted when a defendant complains against police misconduct. The prosecutor's duty is, after all, ". . . in addition to prosecuting criminals, to protect the police officers. . . ."[93]

For instance: Valuable personal effects (such as binoculars) may be taken from a prisoner in an arrest in order "to prevent its use as a weapon"; may be held for "safekeeping" or as "evidence"—and eventually become "lost." The owner who pursues the matter too stubbornly may find the charges against himself geometrically multiplied. If he is smart, he cops a plea and forgets the glasses.

As the prosecution explained in one matter, "Three months later he comes in and makes a formal complaint. So we said, 'If you are going to play ball like that why shouldn't we proceed with our case?' I had no reason to file until he changed back on his understanding of what we had all agreed on. *That is done in many criminal cases.*"[94]

In another situation, six prosecutors were prepared to testify that they were unfamiliar with the case, that they considered it unmeritorious, and that they would not care to pursue it. Nevertheless, the case was prosecuted because of the probability that the defendant would file a civil action against the police department.[95]

Essentially, then: In adversary ordeal, equity reduces to ". . . the duty of the prosecutor as an adversary to seek a conviction . . ."[96]

or that of the plaintiff to win his case; and defense counsel's duty to prevent him—by whatever means each of them can. Despite claims of "only . . . fair and honorable means,"[97] few holds are barred. "Enemies" is what our legal system is all about. Little more. The Watergate lawyers were only doing what came naturally.

6

MAGIC AGAIN

Antique words and inflexible rites: out of these, like every primitive and barbarous people before us, we shape our legal procedure. Lawyers and judges have replaced the magician-priest. But mystery remains basic to their power. That mystery is both verbal and procedural. And for the lay person, both words and procedure still hold risk.

LEGAL LANGUAGE

Legal language, while not literally Greek, is—for the layman—practically everything but: Lawyer talk is rich with archaic English ("pray the Court"), obsolete French ("*voir dire*"), Middle French ("*estoppel*"), archaic English descended from obsolete French ("*oyer*," "*trouver*"), Middle English from Latin ("*certiorari*"), and Latin ("*mens rea*," "*pendente lite*," "*res adjudicata*," "*assumpsit*"); together with terms that, though composed of familiar words, have special meanings ("fee simple," "equitable title," "proximate cause").

"The only trouble I have," replied a prospective foreign-born juror when the prosecutor questioned his ability to follow the pending case, "is with some of the phrases you use. If you use plain English, I understand."[1] The native-born may be equally muddled.

Particularly for members of cultural subgroups, even terms of commonest usage may seem a foreign tongue. But the problem cuts both ways: subculture speech (and the customs it reflects) may be incomprehensible to those narrowly selected members of the larger culture who find themselves, as legal professionals or jurors, in our courtrooms.

Consider, for example, the case of *The People v. Young Bear Tracks*. Bear Tracks (who was black) responded inaccurately to prosecution questions concerning his prior convictions and incarceration—because, it was afterward learned, he did not understand the legal terms "felony" and "misdemeanor," nor the formal words "correctional institution." Conversely, the basis of Bear Tracks' defense was lost upon the jurors. Bear Tracks was accused of first-degree murder (which in California required some appreciable process of premeditation). He pled not guilty on grounds of self-defense. In support of that plea Bear Tracks stated that, immediately prior to the homicide, the deceased had "put him in the dozens": a ghetto ritual involving mutual escalation of increasingly intolerable insult. The prosecuting attorney, however, cut off the witness's attempt to define "the dozens," objecting that Bear Tracks was not a "semantic authority."[2] The Court upheld the objection. Subsequent to their verdict of guilty, jury members stated they had found the greater part of the testimony in the case incomprehensible. More, because Bear Tracks (unfamiliar with "felony," "misdemeanor," and "correctional instituion") had appeared to misrepresent his record—the jurors, deciding Bear Tracks and his witnesses were "morons or liars," disbelieved what testimony they *did* understand. (In *The People v. Basher*, Basher—also black—continually lapsed into "jive talk." Those mannerisms, the district attorney argued, "bespoke his guilt."[3])

The merit of legal terminology lies supposedly in its precision. That precision is said to mirror the conceptual exactitude of judicial principles and render legal terms analogous to those of science—that "exalted and noble *science* of jurisprudence."[4] (emphasis mine) But legal terms and scientific terms are of essentially different orders.

The specific language of the sciences is largely denotative, specific, descriptive. It refers with high frequency to particular objects available to eye, ear, touch, smell, instrumentation. Femur and crankshaft are particular parts, respectively, of a human leg and an automotive vehicle. A cell is demonstrable beneath a microscope. An atom is the name we give a hypothesis; but a hypothesis we make from a group of phenomena all observable, describable—and predictable. Legal language, on the other hand, tends to be connotative and general: heavy on opinion, light on description, and lighter still on predictive accuracy. Legal terms refer largely to relationships between abstract ideas ("interference with freedom of contract") or to value judgments ("willfully," "maliciously"). A contract is an agreement about future behaviors. Interference and freedom are concepts that can be defined only in terms of other concepts. Neither interference, freedom, nor the terms of a contract can be apprehended by senses, measured by instruments—nor counted on to guarantee anything. Such words as "willfully" and "maliciously" provide more information about the speaker than about the perpetrator of the act. Without access to the interior of another's head, I cannot *know* whether an action is willfully or maliciously done. I can only with greater or lesser accuracy *infer*. That inference is no more than my *opinion*; opinion derived from always partial selection and perception of information, filtered through my preconceptions and altered by my biases. Yet the lawyer, as a matter of procedural technique, objectifies opinion—his own or one strategically assumed—and then proceeds as if that opinion were the other's objectifiable fact.

Such behavior is reminiscent of the magical assumption that naming actualizes or reifies the named; that whatever is named is somehow "really" there. In medieval times, for instance, when a philosophical structure had incorporated such magical beliefs, men seriously searched for the element "heat" and the substance "nothing." Similarly, the terminology and conceptual representations of our law, though held in grave regard, are about as substantial as "nothing." Actually, the ambiguous, interpretive, and projective emphases of legal terminology bring it closer to sorcery than to science.

For the legal profession, however, those characteristics are highly functional. Professor of law Fred Rodell says, ". . . the chief function which legal language performs is not to convey ideas clearly but rather to so conceal the confusion and vagueness and emptiness of legal thinking that the difficulties which beset any non-lawyer who tries to make sense out of The Law seem to stem from the language itself instead of from the ideas . . . ."[5] And at the same time, legal pyrotechnic so intimidates the layman, so dazzles him with the law's abstruseness and complexity, that he accepts its inaccessibility to all but initiates. Thus the lay person is not only kept, in Rodell's words, ". . . from finding out that legal logic is so full of holes that it is practially one vast void,"[6] but worse: he is left entirely dependent upon his lawyer for interpretation of both logic and language. The strategem has historic precedent:

Between the 6th and 9th centuries A.D., Irish lawbooks were, by virtue of deliberate verbal scramble, made unintelligible to those unfamiliar with their code. So obscure in fact were those writings, that deciphering some of them took later discoverers over fifty years.[7] Comprehension of some modern legal writing might take only a little less long.

Read (if you can) the words of a Justice of the United States Supreme Court:

> Disregarding form and labels, and looking to substance, it is, I think, crystal clear that this is a transparent direct imposition upon the Government's property interests (as distinguished from the lessee's leasehold estate) in this real estate of the general ad valorem real property tax commonly assessed on, and against the owners of, all real estate in Michigan, but under the guise of a tax upon the lessee for the *privilege* (as construed by the majority)—granted by the Federal Government, not the State—*of using* (though it will be noted the statute does not in terms tax "use," but, rather, taxes "real property," sec #1) the Government's property, and, thus, the statute seeks to accomplish by indirection that which the State is constitutionally prohibited from doing directly.[8]

Consider (if you are able) the words of a *Chief* Justice of the United States Supreme Court:

> Coming to consider the validity of the tax from this point of view, while not questioning at all that in common under-

standing it was direct merely on income and only indirect on property, it was held that, considering the substance of things it was direct on property in a constitutional sense since to burden an income by a tax was, from the point of substance, to burden the property from which the provision as to apportionment of direct taxes was adopted to prevent. . . . Moreover, in addition the conclusion reached in the Pollock case did not in any degree involve holding that income taxes generically and necessarily came within the class of direct taxes on property, but on the contrary, recognized the fact that taxation on income was in its nature an excise entitled to be enforced as such unless and until it was concluded that to enforce it would amount to accomplishing the result which the requirement as to apportionment of direct taxation was adopted to prevent, in which case the duty would arise to disregard form and consider substance alone and hence subject the tax to the regulation as to apportionment which otherwise as an excise would not apply to it. . . . From this in substance it indisputably arises . . . that the contention that the Amendment treats the tax on income as a direct tax although it is relieved from apportionment and is necessarily therefore not subject to the rule of uniformity as such rule only applies to taxes which are not direct, thus destroying the two great classifications which have been recognized and enforced from the beginning, is wholly without foundation since the command of the Amendment that all income taxes shall not be subject to apportionment by a consideration of the sources from which the taxed income may be derived, forbids the application to such taxes of the rule applied in the Pollock case by which alone such taxes were removed from the great class of excises, duties, and imposts subject to the rule of uniformity, and were placed under the other or direct class.[9]

"A learned class of very ignorant men," Erasmus called lawyers in the 16th century.[10] Unfortunately, the lay person confronted with such legalese usually assumes that the marbles are not in the attorney's mouth, but in his own inadequate lay head. Rather, they are in the attorney's skull, and it has taken much study to put them there. Not until students have learned to talk the jargon, Rodell says, have they become "in the most important sense, lawyers."[11]

Professor Rodell disrespects legal precepts as bluntly as he does legal language and logic: ". . . the principles on which [the law] is built are so vague and abstract and irrelevant that it is possible to find in those principles both a justification and a prohibition of every human action or activity under the sun."[12] So vague are legal precepts, that the United States Supreme Court (supposedly applying them) was, in the judicial year 1970-71, able to reach unanimous opinion only 23 out of 122 times.[13]

THE OATH

The trial oath, too, retains its magical function: insuring that no matter what perfidy witnesses present, justice will triumph and right prevail. In court today we raise our right hand (it must not be the left!) and affirm the self-curse, "I do solemnly swear to tell the truth, the whole truth, and nothing but the truth, so help me God!" Technically, that rite and spell are no longer requisite. The witness has the legal option of forgoing the oath and instead "affirming" that he intends to tell the truth. But only the rare witness knows he has such choice; it is not offered to him. And of those who do know, few dare risk through the oath's rejection that suggestion of impiety which might offend the good opinion of judge and jury. The oath remains custom, to the point of implicit demand. The consistency with which that oath is shattered, however, might have scandalized even Plato.

Your attorney may well explain (as one I overheard) that "the court's decision usually turns on deciding who is lying least." In *You May Cross Examine,* Herman and Goldberg state, "It is no exaggeration to say that in the ordinary trial court, perjured testimony is introduced in almost every proceeding."[14]

But it is our legal system itself that provides deception's model. It is our Supreme Court that has officially smiled upon the judicial lie of the plea bargain.[15] It is that Court's chief justice who endorses the defense's right to misrepresent a witness's credibility. It is adversary method which, bearing "little if any" relation to the search for truth, mandates that endorsement.[16] It is the adversary lawyer's ethical duty to represent his client zealously which prompts him to coach the client in behaviors that would, in other contexts, be held reprehensible. In the legal trade, however, such behavior is called only "putting your best foot forward," "doing the best for yourself," or "putting the burden of proof on the other side." ("Lawyer," Ambrose Bierce defined in his *Devil's Dictionary*, is "one skilled in the circumvention of the law.")

The client learns, for instance, to what questions he must respond with memory failure. Conversely, he learns that it is safe to invent any conversation or action to which no third party, nor any material evidence, can bear contrary witness. He learns how to swear (and escape charge of perjury) that the return of monies borrowed was actually a "gift" to the lender: "Well, that's how I *thought* of it. I only borrowed the money in order to help him out with the interest!"—at the same rate as any savings and loan. He learns how to append to any answer the qualification "to the best of my memory"; which sounds both stickler-for-accuracy and humbly aware of the frailties of recall—but is at the same time an automatic loophole for any lie in which he may be caught. "I'd hate," I heard one candid attorney say, "to have us be the only ones in the courtroom who *weren't* lying!"

And then there are those ringing words, "NOT GUILTY!" that follow the vow to "Tell the truth . . . so help me God!" Do they mean what they say? Lewis Caroll's Humpty Dumpty would have known better. " 'When *I* use a word,' Humpty Dumpty said, in rather a scornful tone, 'it means just what I choose it to mean . . . neither more nor less!' "[17] So too in lawyer land. Professor of law John T. Noonan, Jr., explains: "The plea of 'Not guilty' as used in the context of a court proceeding, is understood by everyone to mean, 'I cannot be proved guilty of the charge by ordinary process of law.' "[18] In other words, another lawyer implies, the legal mind distinguishes between not guilty in "law" and not guilty in "actuality."[19] The two are not synonymous. Translated into language the rest of us use, not guilty does not mean "I did not commit the crime you have charged me with"; but only "Yah! Go prove it!" The plea of not guilty is, in other words, no more than a ritual gauntlet thrown in challenge of battle. Thus the oath is itself a form of "built-in perjury"[20]—but a perjury that constitutes the adversary path to "truth."

An executive assistant in the United States Department of Justice states, "The right of the defendant to plead not guilty in law, and thereby to make the government prove its case, lies at the heart of our system of criminal justice."[21] However, the justice assistant assures, "only the right to raise legitimate factual issues" is involved. A defendant's right to plead not guilty (when he *is* guilty) "does not and never has authorized either defendant, or his counsel, to offer *false* testimony to prove innocence."[22]

But the injunction against offering false testimony does not extend to the proffering of "true" testimony in order to falsify a larger, and central, issue—such as the crime victim's (or any witness's) credibility. That deliberate falsification is not called "lying" any more than the criminal's plea of not guilty is called perjury. Both rather are called "testing the prosecution's case"[23]—a test from which, despite its contaminated ingredients, truth will magically emerge. Indeed, says Professor Noonan, "Only a moral absolutist would say that a criminal's plea of not guilty is a lie."[24]

"Innocent until proven guilty" is a principle high on the scale of humanist evolution. But it is a principle that the adversary frame degrades. For the presumption of innocence requires a commitment that overarches partisan ambitions: a mutual commitment to information, wherever it leads. A partisan commitment to victory, on the other hand, must preclude the revelation of any information endangering that victory. Thus adversary approach reduces "innocent until proven guilty" to no more than another weapon in the fray. Perhaps worst of all, that reduction tars truth-teller and liar with the very same brush—because under adversary procedure, no one who swears innocence can be believed.

Though the oath is often, with the profession's blessing, the initial perjury, its hallowed convention divests the professionals of responsibility in the matter. The witness has called upon God. It is God Who will police the adversary arena; the buck passed, once more, to Heaven.

PLEADING AND PROCEDURE

Our modern legal formalities are called "pleading and procedure." They serve the same purpose as the rigidities of ancient times, providing for our judicial process once again both an element of risk and the forbidding appearance of a divine institution.

Pleading and procedure cover, technically, those tactical moves by which the lawyer conducts his case. They include the timing and order within which he must serve and file papers, and the phrases he must use. They include the words with which each disputant must plead his claim or defense, and the sort of evidence the courts will accept or reject. Those procedural requisites are called by the profession "adjective," "dependent," or "subordinate." They compose the machinery via which the mill of justice grinds, and as such are theoretically distinct from and subordinate to the "real" or substantive law. Substantive laws, contrariwise, supposedly embody principles; they represent those "primary," "independent" rules handed down from heaven, precedent, or the Olympus of legislatures, which declare what persons may or may not legally do.

Procedural and substantive law are theorized as different, described as different, and taught in law schools as different. They are in effect the same.

In *Procedure, Its Theory and Practice,* William T. Hughes writes, "The history of our law has been stated [by legal historians] . . . to be more than anything else a history of forms and methods of procedure. Almost every practical lawyer must concede that the attempted distinction between the substantive and the adjective law, is illusory."[25] Yet, Professor Rodell comments, with the procedural courses officially set aside as "technique" in our law schools, "The big empty words and the vague abstract principles of the other courses assume a more credible aura of depth and reality to the newcomer."[26] This separation camouflages the fact ". . . that *all* the legal principles . . . amount to no more than tricks of the trade and that *all* the courses . . . are courses in Pleading and Procedure."[27] For example: "The original burden of proof is on the plaintiff" is a principle of pleading and procedure; while "If the defendant's action was not the proximate cause of the injury then the defendant is not legally responsible," is a principle of substantive tort law. But, says Rodell, "All that a student ever learns about either of these principles—or about any other principle of either division of Law—is how to say them and when and where it may be useful to say them."[28]

The point, Jerome Frank suggests in *Courts on Trial,* is that all the rules, including the substantive, are in effect procedural, in that they are all ultimately weapons in the courtroom fight.[29] A legal decision is as likely to hang on a procedural rule as on a substantive one. "All too often," Rodell notes, "not only 'justice' but also the regular principles of 'substantive' Law are thrown out the window because some lawyer, in handling his client's case, has forgotten or violated a 'procedural' rule.''[30]

For instance: A fourteen-year-old girl, on her way home from school, was struck by a car and her leg fractured in several places. It healed imperfectly, so that after long and expensive treatment she was left with a permanent limp. Her parents hired a lawyer, and through him sued the car's driver for $25,000. The matter went to trial, where the essential question resolved into one of contributory negligence. If the girl had been crossing at the corner when hit, she would not be contributorily negligent and would win. If instead she had been crossing in the middle of the block (jaywalking) she would be held negligent and would lose. Upon that issue hung success of the suit.

There were only two witnesses: the girl herself and an older boy. The girl testified that she had crossed at the corner. The boy declared himself absolutely certain she had not. He based his certainty on his memory of her position in relation to a peculiar spot or indentation in the street.

Because of the boy's testimony about that spot, the jury was so impressed (one of them later reported) with the exactitude of the boy's visual recall, that they ruled against the girl. The girl's attorney, who believed his client, was less impressed. Deciding to do some further investigating, he discovered that the critical spot upon which the verdict had turned had actually been made—as the result of underground utilities repair—not until six months *after* the accident occurred. This was new evidence; and grounds for a new trial.

Under procedural rules, the motion for a new trial must be filed within ten days after entry of the original judgment. The girl's lawyer began to prepare such a motion. But he was interrupted. At that critical juncture he fell sick with hepatitis and found himself, seriously ill, in the hospital. He was young, not yet in partnership with anyone, with no one to take over for him. Ten days passed. On the eleventh morning he was released from the hospital. He finished drafting the motion and rushed to court to file it. He was one day late.

The Court denied the new-trial motion. The attorney filed again, asking relief from the denial. His Honor arbitrarily (but within his allowable discretion) refused that also. There would be no new trial. Substantive issues, merits, new evidence, all were rendered subsidiary to procedural failure; and ultimately meaningless. Because of that procedural tardiness resulting from circumstances beyond her control, the girl, permanently crippled, received not one cent.

Whenever he can, of course, an attorney must under adversary ethic turn a procedural lapse on his adversary's part to his own advantage. For example: A lawyer who was on malpractice retainer for a major medical association was called to defend a case. The defendant, a brain surgeon, had mismanaged an operation. In making entry to a critical point in his patient's skull, he had found the delicate tool obligatory to such procedure not at hand. Unwilling to delay matters (he had a full day scheduled) he used the nearest substitute: an instrument of grossly inappropriate dimension. Irreparable damage was done to the patient's spinal cord, rendering him paraplegic.

The case was considered open and shut. Everything—evidence, circumstance, testimony—appeared overwhelmingly against the doctor. Everything indeed except the victim's own attorney, who seemed in no hurry to pursue matters at all. (One can charge more for a long haul than for a short one.) So little pressed was he, in fact, that two years passed without the case coming to trial. Now, in the state where this case arose, a section of the civil code provides that if a plaintiff has not taken action on a suit within a two-year period, the case may be dismissed. At the expiration of that two years, then, the surgeon's attorney, hardly daring to believe his good luck, dashed into court. He cited the civil code proviso and pled for dismissal. Dismissal was granted.

The victim, because of his own attorney's procedural dereliction, was left paraplegic and unrecompensed. The surgeon was home free; and free to "operate" as before.

"Listen," the doctor's lawyer confided to me, "in my opinion that man wasn't just guilty of malpractice—it was more like murder! But he was my client, my duty was to him. My job was to take advantage of anything I could!"

Lawyers of course are aware of the risks offered by pleading and procedure. Their clients are not. But it is the client who must live, and often suffer, with the result.

Unfortunately, the arcane intricacies of pleading and procedure cow the lay person as successfully as does legal language. Indeed, the procedural strictures of our legal system *are* a kind of language. Professor Rodell states, ". . . the *whole* of The Law is nothing but a technique to be mastered, an adroitness to be achieved. That technique, reduced to its simplest terms, is the technique of using a new language. That is all the law student learns in his courses in pleading and procedure. That is also all the law students learns in his courses in 'substantive' law.''[31]

But from that special knowledge, to which he alone holds the key, derives the law-man's primacy.

PART FOUR

The Iron Tread
Of Progress

Universal history often requires the individual to
be . . . sacrificed: the iron tread of progress tramples
thousands underfoot.

Kocourek and Wigmore[1]

7

DIRECT FROM 3000 B. C.

"In the examination of a witness, the first essential is to know his type. For a timid witness may be terrorized; a fool outwitted; an irascible man provoked; and a vain one flattered."[2] One more excerpt from the legal how-to manuals? Not this time. Rather, counsel offered by a Roman at the beginning of the Christian era, but still praised today—some 2,000 years later. A prominent modern trial attorney comments, "No text-book of 10,000 pages on the Art of Cross-Examination could say more than does that bearded capsule of advice."[3] That sameness, holds the profession, is testament not to petrifaction but rather to the timeless validity of those principles and the uniqueness of the legal consciousness that employs them.

A legal historian writes (my italics):

That the legal consciousness is in some respects unique may be inferred from a historical coincidence of more than usual interest. Where other systems of ordered knowledge are concerned . . . in different ages the same set of feelings will not be evoked by the same set of stimulus. . . . In poetry, the modern lover does not express himself like the unknown bard of the Ramayana. In this, one of the most fundamental of human relationships, enormous changes have taken place in the course of the ages. . . . To turn

73

from art and poetry to the sciences. Euclid clearly could not have understood the calculus, still less the formulae of Minkowsky and Einsten. . . . In Philosophy . . . it is obvious that Aristotle could not have employed the logic of Mr. Bertrand Russell. And so one might proceed from one aspect of human activity to another. *Law seems to stand alone in this respect.* The recent discovery of Hamurabi's code makes it clear that the Sumerian and Semitic judges arrived at principles *in every respect identical* with the corresponding principles in modern law. The Code has been forgotten for thousands of years; there was no opportunity for its rules to influence systems from which the Civil Law and Common Law have sprung, yet the principles are the same.[4]

That theme echoes through legal writing. One author declares, "Every jurist whether he has been some leader of savages at the time of the dawn of civilization, or a modern judge sitting in a court of last resort, has sought for the principles which should determine his judgment in something apart from and above the experience of the race."[5] Another states: the law is "the breath of God, the harmony of the world."[6] A third explains, the law's "great fundamental principles . . . are gifts from on high. . . . They are for all time and parts. . . ."[7]

According to Roscoe Pound, "The American lawyer, as a rule, still believes that the principles of law are absolute, eternal and of universal validity."[8]

What other profession so boasts? Not science, surely! Yet the boast is not empty. Legal principles and behaviors past and present *are* often similar to the point of identity. That identity derives, however, from something other than either historical coincidence or "uniqueness" of legal consciousness. The claim of uniqueness is in fact blind to the obvious: a historic and philosophic continuity unbroken from 3000 B.C. That continuity lies in the doctrine of divine law. Divine law's implicit perspective is the conceptual thread connecting our Western legal-political beginnings to our American legal-political present; a perspective that helps limit our legal and societal options now.

Divine law—initially the dogma of absolute rulers—ordained in political, religious, and legal matters a single and certain "right" given from above. In effect, its doctrine forbade men to question laws.

legal procedure, or those who ran the Establishment show. Under
divine law, "Yes, but . . ." became heresy, single perspective became orthodoxy, coercion the legal model. And fear became one of
the chief means by which legal systems served political power.

En route to divine law's emergence, critical changes had occurred
across the social and political board. As tribes merged into nations
and nations into empires, religion and law—initially relatively undifferentiated—complexified into separate structures and developed
into official arms of state. Tribal gods (once chiefly concerned with
matters of food supply, propagation, safety, and shelter) were
joined into state pantheons:[9] justifying regimes, hallowing wars, and
bonding men in holy brotherhood against whatever enemy their rulers declared. At the same time, law began to represent not merely a
means of settling individual quarrel, but watchdog against social dissent.

Tribal law, for instance, had been largely private law: misdeeds
tended to be considered a problem between individuals, families, or
clans, with financial sanctions, often calculated to a nicety, privately
negotiated in order to avert intragroup feud. (The Welsh codes, for
example, rated loss of eyelashes at a penny per hair,[10] and the Salic
codes with notable practicality provided a fine of 24,000 denars for
killing a woman of childbearing age, but reduced the sum to 8,000
denars if she had ceased reproducing.[11]) Even ordeal, employing
jeopardy and often physical pain as a means of judicial inquiry, was
only intermittently used in early days, and had aimed ultimately at
feud prevention. Here, a legal historian notes, ". . . it must be tak-
en into consideration that the sacrifice of the individual secured the
peace of society; . . ."[12] Where nations came into being, however,
the notion of what constituted that "peace of society" changed.
Much of theretofore private dispute settlement went public: crime
came to include not just interpersonal quarrel, but apostasy against
the state, and law was aimed not merely at feud prevention, but at
maintenance of the religious-political status quo.

Fear was a means of that maintenance—and government-con-
trolled legal procedure was very much a means of inculcating fear.
Eventually, in civil as well as criminal matters, legal procedure became a kind of official morality theater: a way to remind all concerned of the mystery and might of governments and those who run
them. Threat had become integral throughout legal process. It still
is.

Divine law was essentially the manifesto of the new religious-political-legal partnership. That manifesto relied on, enlarged, institutionalized, and eventually spread throughout the West certain concepts once specific to ordeal: namely, the beliefs that disputed questions would be solved with absolute certainty and by nonhuman sources.[13] Over the years, laws themselves had come to be seen as of "a higher power, realized in a worldly existence,"[14] and at last under divine law, that higher power became explicitly earthly Authority—embodying divinity, "giving" the law, and rendering absolute decisions.[15]

Divine law authority took varied forms. Rulers claimed to be either gods on earth (Egypt from about 3000 B.C.), the representatives of gods on earth (Mesopotamia, about 2000 B.C.), or to become gods on death (Rome, about 27 B.C.).[16] Consequences, however, were in effect the same: not only divine right to rule, but divine mandate for those political, religious, and legal institutions that each ruler declared one with himself. Where such authority arose, special codes of law were also often claimed to have been divinely given. The Egyptians, for instance, believed their laws came from the god Thoth.[17] The Persians believed theirs came from Ahura Mazda via the prophet Zoroaster.[18] King Hammurabi of Babylon in Mesopotamia announced his legal code given him by the sun-god Shamash. "A motif," the Britannica suggests, "undoubtedly connected with the legend of Moses and the revelations of the Decalogue (Ten Commandments) from Yahweh on Mt. Sinai"[19]—probably about 1200 B.C.

The doctrine of divine origin of law significantly shaped the philosophies and institutions of our Western world. Basing authority for laws in one particular god and manifesting that authority in a divinely ordained ruler provided models for monotheism in religion and oligarchy in government. Representing law as god-given rather than mere human-craft provided a basis for subsequent legal theory. The entrenchment of a priesthood possessing magical-seeming powers, exerting political influence and often interpreting the law, provided a prototype for our present legal profession. Above all, by positing fixed heavenly principles reflected in man's major institutions, divine law validated beyond cavil or question those institutions and the rulers, priests, and law-men who ran them. Dissent now affronted heaven as well as earth. In most practical result, governments remained untouchable, while laws and legal procedure were in the clouds, safely beyond men's reach (or reason)—which is largely where they rest today.

Indeed, so deeply and pervasively does divine law's heritage suffuse our Western world, that its imprint is perhaps as taken for granted as our adversary method itself. Yet those primordial tracks are plain down the years.

Divine law entered our Judeo-Christian mainstream from its Mesopotamian source through two main channels: Greek-Roman Christian, and Judaic-Christian. In the 4th century B.C., the Greek ruler Alexander the Great conquered Egypt and Persia (which latter had previously conquered Babylonia). Those Greek conquests encountered divine-rule ideas; there is even some tradition that Alexander himself demanded to be worshiped as a god.[20] Greece in turn was conquered by Rome, which (beginning with Augustus about 27 B.C.) also produced divine-rule concepts. Meanwhile, Mosaic law had similarly incorporated that vision from its Mesopotamian genesis and given it into Christian doctrine. About A.D. 380, Rome made Christianity its official religion and disseminated it as a compulsory faith throughout its Western European empire.[21] Thus, divine-law tradition passed into Church law which, for many centuries, was almost a "universal constitution" through Europe.[22] That Church law became a chief root source of the English law from which ours directly stems.[23]

Not merely was Mosaic Law embodied in the Old Testament and passed therefrom into Church law; more immediately—and with special relevance to American legal stance—that ancient law of Mesopotamian peoples was planted on American shores, in Massachusetts Bay Colony, by Calvinist settlers.

Mosaic law had been from the beginning very much a political as well as moral instrument. Moses was born into the divine-law tradition of the Egyptian god-kings. About 1200 B.C., shortly after exodus from Egypt, Moses announced receipt of his own set of laws from Yahweh and with those laws forged a straggle of desert wanderers into a nation. That constitution of the Jewish law called the Torah[24] was eventually embodied in the first five books of the Old Testament.

In addition to ethical and spiritual norms, the Torah inescapably reflected much of the attitudes, values, and temporal law of the various peoples inhabiting the Mesopotamian Fertile Crescent and adjacent areas. Some of those temporal customs were directly retaliatory—particularly where financial sanctions were limited and courts of law and prisons nonexistent. A legal scholar says of the Torah, "The conclusion is inevitable that a great part of the law is merely Jewish tribal law written down at a time when the Jews were still in a state not very far advanced from the primitive; and some was assimilated from contemporary peoples."[25] The Britannica states, "Even the earliest code of laws in the Bible (Ex. xxi–xxiii) is simply a local and national form of the civil law common to Babylonia, Assyria and the Hittites. . . ."[26] According to one historian, at least thirty-five provisions out of fifty are similar.[27] Resemblances between Old Testament and Babylonian law are in fact clear. And "revenge psychology"[28] is among them.

For example: Hammurabi's code commanded that when a house falls through its builder's carelessness, causing the death of the owner's son, then the builder's son must likewise be killed.[29] When a man strikes a pregnant (free-born) woman, causing her death through miscarriage, then the culprit's daughter must also die.[30] Similarly, the Old Testament declares, ". . . for I the Lord am a jealous god, visiting the iniquity of the fathers upon the children unto the third and fourth generation. . . ."[31] In both codes, two wrongs make a right: Required Hammurabi, "If a man destroy the eye of another man, they shall destroy his eye." "If a man knock out a tooth of another man, they shall knock out his tooth." "If he breaks a man's bone, they shall break his."[32] The Old Testament directs, ". . . thou shalt give life for life, eye for eye, tooth for tooth, hand for hand, foot for foot, burning for burning, wound for wound, stripe for stripe. . . ."[33]

Explains the Jewish Encyclopedia, ". . . the popular thought, as reflected in Talmudic sayings, imagined that God punishes nations and men with sufferings nearly identical with those which they have sinfully inflicted upon others. The principle that 'with what measure ye mete it shall be measured unto you' is solemnly asserted to underlie the divine law. . . ."[34] In other words, he who retaliated in kind (*lex talionis*) was merely helping the Lord out a little.

Some writers (such as Karl Menninger) see *lex talionis* as an attempt to limit the revenge[35] of endless blood feud. It may perhaps limit revenge—but surely at the same time guarantees it. Indeed, in one instance, the Old Testament specifically forbids the ancient custom of financial compensation for injury and substitutes death instead.[36] Orders Numbers 35:31: "Moreover ye shall take no satisfaction for the life of a murderer, which is guilty of death, but he shall surely be put to death."

Mosaic law had served originally to bond the wilderness wanderers against their enemies and give them national backbone. Two subsequent crises confirmed that law as a bonding agent: the conquest and deportation of the Jews by Assyria in 722 B.C., and by Babylonia in 586 B.C. Judah's prophets turned those defeats to the positive purpose of national solidification. The Jews, they claimed, had been idolatrous, absorbed heathen practises and neglected their law, for which lapses the captures were punishment and purification. Though Jewish law by this time incorporated additional temporal strictures absorbed from captor-peoples, the prophets instead represented those ideas as merely "interpretation" of the divinely given original law,[37] now infused with fresh moral and political force.

In the 17th century, divine law's conceptual perspective received new life once more. Calvinism rooted that absolutism in New England's Massachusetts Bay, the largest and most powerful colony in early America, where, under the "exact and precise law" of the Old Testament[38] selected attitudes of Babylon and Judah again became political instruments. Church and state were one, conformity to orthodoxy requisite, toleration an evil.[39] The Colony's first governor, John Winthrop (a London lawyer) claimed for his magistracy direct stewardship from God. Spoke he, "Whatsoever sentence the magistrate gives, the judgment is the Lord's though he do it not by any rule prescribed by civil authority."[40]

The religious-political-legal model Calvinism established in America was, in effect, the "patriarchal, heiratical, tribal system of a primitive Jewish tribe in the wilderness."[41] Though Calvin had rebelled against established Church-ways, his new model only substituted a new either-or for the old. In that model, vengeance stood superior to love.[42] Through Calvin, Ezekiel's voice still spoke: "Therefore will I also deal in fury: mine eyes shall not spare, neither will I have pity: and though they cry in mine ears with a loud voice, yet will I not hear them."[43] (Nor had the New Testament entirely abandoned that message. Matthew: "And these shall go away into everlasting punishment; but the righteous into life eternal."[44] Thessalonians: "In flaming fire taking vengeance on them that know not God, and that obey not the gospel of our Lord Jesus Christ; Who shall be punished with everlasting destruction from the presence of the Lord. . . ."[45] Jude: "Even as Sodom and Gomorrhah . . . are set forth for an example, suffering the vengeance of eternal fire."[46]) Righteous versus Damned was the conceptual rock upon which those Puritans landed, and upon which shortly Americans of many persuasions began breaking open Indian heads.

Calvinism's Righteous versus Damned struggled in America with more libertarian influences, of course, just as from the beginning a gentler ethic had contended with the politics of vindictiveness. As far back as the Mesopotamian Hittite system, near Hammurabi's time, mutilation was completely absent. Jewish cults such as the Essenes had foreshadowed Christ's teaching of brotherhood and peace, frowned on the growth of a landlord class, and forbidden usury. The ancient Jewish courts had practically abandoned capital punishment; crucifixion was strictly a weapon of Roman power.

Similarly in this country, Pilgrims, Quakers, and countless others took stands for liberty against divine law's absolutism. Men like Thomas Hooker and Roger Williams directly challenged the Bay Colony's divine-right premise. Hooker held any sovereign only a servant of the people; Williams opposed slavery of black man or red and argued that the colonists had stolen their land from its rightful owners, the Indians.[47] Ultimately, Massachusetts became intolerable to both men. Hooker left for Connecticut. Williams, tried and found guilty of "newe and dangerous opinions against the authoritie of magistrates,"[48] fled the Bay Colony to the protection of Indians in what is now Rhode Island. There he founded a new colony.

Where power reached, however, where nationalism puffed and conquest spread, Authority lifted blame and revenge into political arsenal; while legal systems reflected the governments they served. In New England, Puritan righteousness produced torture and mutilation: branding, ears hacked off, tongues bored through; and death beneath the weight of slow-crushing rocks.[49] *The Story of Religion* states, ". . . a careful inquiry must reveal . . . that . . . 'eye for eye and tooth for tooth' is the guiding spirit of more existing legislation than is inspired by the principles of the Sermon on the Mount."[50]

In America, that ancient retributive thunder, coexisting beneath the same religious wrap as the principle of universal brotherhood, helped provide emotional and conceptual justification for violent interpersonal habits. And in our legal procedure, Calvinism's "against" joined peculiarly new-world sociological conditions to exaggerate adversariness beyond England's parent version.

Today's courtroom Grand Guignol still aims at striking fear: thus cabalistic tongue, looming bench, black robe, and procedural peril. "We must realize," a legal scholar says, "that our modern criminal procedure also demands thousands of innocent victims, so liable to error are our methods of proof and conviction."[51] Lawyers may hurl with impunity the grossest attack. For instance, a woman appearing as a state witness in a murder case was asked, on cross-examination, whether she used narcotics.

ANSWER: No sir, not now.
QUESTION: You don't use any at all?
ANSWER: I was ill for ten years and the doctor gave me morphine at the time I had operations.
QUESTION: You don't use them at all anymore?
ANSWER: No.

Whereupon in his summation to the jury, the defense attorney argued,

> Did you watch her? . . . The mind of a dope
> fiend . . . she was full of it when she testified; she showed
> she was an addict; why, she's a dope fiend . . . she's a
> hophead; her whole testimony is imagination and delusion
> from taking dope . . . she testified she had taken dope for
> ten years, and you may well know that she is still taking
> it . . . she's a dope fiend . . . she is lower than a rattle-
> snake . . . a rattlesnake gives you warning before it strikes,
> but this woman gives no warning. . . .[52]

Such misrepresentation should, and often may, backfire, antagonizing the judge and jury who hear it. Yet often enough, damage is done. This witness sued for defamation without success. The doctrine of "sovereign immunity" protects the state against legal action—unless government deigns to allow the suit—giving the vilified no recourse against calumny by officers of our courts. As under divine law still, the state can do no wrong.

Recently, the Supreme Court even ruled that a defendant cannot sue a prosecutor for malicious prosecution, though the prosecutor used false evidence to win a conviction.[53] In another case, a citizen named Davis sued the police officials who had labeled him an "active shoplifter" in a widely distributed brochure which, containing the names and photographs of several hundred persons, made no distinction between those convicted and those merely arrested. Charges against Davis had in fact been dropped. Nevertheless, the Supreme Court dismissed his suit, ruling that those officials who had publicly branded him a criminal had not violated his rights of due process by imposing on him a "badge of infamy" without giving him a chance to defend himself. Loss of reputation alone, the Court held, is insufficient cause for suit—against government.[54]

Finally, in our courtrooms, the litigant is reduced to the status of a child: forbidden to speak except when spoken to, left abjectly dependent upon those who casually settle lives, fortunes, and sacred honor.

"May I say something, Your Honor?"

"No you may not! Your attorney will speak for you!"

Your attorney's mind may be already upon his next case.

8

TUNNEL VISION ENTHRONED

Divine law, requiring a single perspective—its own—as a conceptual orientation, crystallized and passed into Western legacy a particular thinking-system, as well as a doctrinal orthodoxy. That thinking-system is simplistic and limiting. Its captive sees largely what he already believes. Unable, within those conceptual blinkers, either to see or consider other points of view proceeding from other premises along different paths, he is precluded from fresh choice and trapped in unquestioned habits: hooked and had.

All conceptual systems involve a cluster of generally unexplicated corollaries that flow from central, usually nonconscious premises and form the lenses through which we see our world. Under divine law's edicts, in most public matters only two possibilities were assumed: Authority's position and heresy; Right and Wrong. Insofar as such a model is internalized, certainty is the attainable goal, and toward that goal thinking habits are bipolar, predominantly classificatory, absolute, and closed. To that degree do we claim righteousness for ourselves and require an "other," an opposite (religious, political, racial, national, sexual, name-it), a nonself who embodies evil. To that degree does blame become a basic behavior and revenge a solution.

Such polarity not only implies superior-inferior; as it denies complementarity, it also invites battle. For superior tends to become pitted *against* inferior (head versus heart, spirit versus flesh, man versus nature). An educator says, ". . . the two-valued orientation . . . may be regarded as an inevitable accompaniment to combat. If we fight, we develop the two-valued orientation; if we develop the two-valued orientation, we begin to want to fight."[1]

More important: A conceptual system premised on certainty sets its conclusionary parameters *in advance.* Since within those boundaries only two possibilities exist, the bipolar model precludes the dialectic play of opposites that may produce revelation or change. Trial by battle, for instance, did not ask "What happened?" Battle inquired only which of two disputants was right—a question whose answer was limited by the terms of the question itself. From it, nothing new could emerge.

Thus, where judicial inquiry used this dichotomous model, issues must be black or white, responses "yes or no," and any story have only two sides. Largely unthinkable and therefore unseeable were the infinite shades of gray *between* black or white. Unconsidered were those possibilities *in addition* to yes or no, such as yes *and* no, maybe, sometimes; or the versions of any story held by those other than its principals. Battle usually divided the quick from the maimed or dead, no further questions asked.

Where man used that conceptual model, his problem-solving techniques emphasized classification as an end in itself. In order, for example, to discover the "correct" answer that certainty assumed, he tended to choose one particular characteristic of a person, thing, or situation, and with the name of that single aspect (ignoring all else) classify the whole. Such methodology, Bertrand Russell notes, is based on "the notion that . . . the proper pigeonhole will be found for everything. Once we have found the proper place and with it the proper name . . . we are somehow held to be in control of it."[2] Thus victory in judicial battle simultaneously classified the virtuous and discovered, punished, and controlled the wrongdoer.

Where man used that either-or model, his categories were absolute. Since certainty conceives only one correct answer for a question, that answer must be *entirely* and *absolutely* right. Any alternative must be entirely wrong. There are again no possibilities in between. Qualifications such as partially right, sometimes right, right to a certain degree, something *other* than right or wrong, are not tolerable. They vitiate the rightness of the answer, permitting uncertainty to enter. Thus judicial ordeal "unconditionally" solved disputed questions.

Reliance on those orientations, on polarity, classification and absolutes tended to ignore not only differences and uniqueness but also context: circumstances external and internal, including motivation. Obscured, for instance, were those differences between an "enemy" who deliberately did harm; an "enemy" who unwittingly did harm; and that person who took an action which its recipient interpreted as harmful but that might equally be innocuous or helpful if seen with open possibility. To subdue a swimmer in order to rescue him from heavy surf is not the same as subduing him in placid water in order to drown him. Yet both are "subduing him in the water." Combat's trial technique asked only "Who won?"

Finally, an inevitable product of the certainty premise was blame. To the extent that man was captive of his own one-way perspective, he was unable to see himself. He was unaware of himself as interpreter of that which his senses brought him; unaware that it was to his perceptions of the world he reacted, rather than directly to "reality" itself. What he felt was for him *the* truth. More particularly, he was unable to stand at one remove and observe himself as *part* of the context, at the same time both affecting and interpreting it. When things went wrong his first response was apt to be "Whose fault? Whom do I blame?" The certain rightness of his own position meant the unquestioned wrongness of the other and the "justness" of revenge.

Blame is two-valued (his fault *or* mine); absolute (extenuating circumstances, motivation, differences, are not considered); ignores context and self as interactive. Not prevention, but retaliation, becomes all. Indeed the Greeks had a story for it: blame, self-righteousness, and vengeance weave the tale of the House of Atreus, that oddly revered nightmare of the classics. Tantalus' initial atrocity of serving his hacked-up son to the gods for banquet generates a cycle of family cannibalism and murder maintained through following generations: Atreus, Agamemnon, Clytemnestra, Electra, Orestes, and Aegisthus too. Or, in other words: blame isn't very particular. A culprit other than the self must be found; but if the culprit isn't around, anyone else will do. Thus, in judicial combat, challenging innocent witnesses was a favorite mode of escaping a charge—as was outright transfer of that charge to another.

The Far East, meanwhile, had tended to see law and order differently; a difference derived in part from another world view. Although that view created its own orthodoxy, it resulted at the same time in social and legal emphases dissimilar to those of the West.

The Chinese, for instance, did not envision the social order as based in essence on the rule of law, but rather as reflecting a total harmony inherent in nature.[3] China therefore preferred the notion of law as consensus to that of coercion's "supreme command";[4] and conceived legal procedure as a "regrettable necessity," indeed an "institution for barbarians,"[5] instead of one of civilization's highest achievements (as the West imagined). In general, the Far East abhorred blame's black-and-white classification of one party to a dispute as right and his opponent as wrong, since blame retards the "swift restoration of broken harmony."[6] Thus, Chinese dispute settlement relied to a great extent on mediation's voluntary accord as opposed to adjudication's threat of force.[7] In Korea, also, mediation is still usually preferred to adjudication; while the taking into account of so-called "non-legal considerations" is paramount to any body of rules.[8] Koreans, applying no rigid rules of evidence, try to view the individual in total context. Further, since Koreans emphasize the particular (believing no two cases the same) they have unlike us no *stare decisis*[9]—that theory of precedent that holds it ". . . essential for the law to be certain, and . . . to attain that certainty it is worthwhile to sacrifice justice in occasional cases."[10] Likewise, they conceive our idea of "telling the truth and nothing but the truth" as meaningless, because they believe no man can tell objective truth.[11] (Similarly, do the people of a Mexican Zapotec Indian town consider important to dispute settlement not what is "objectively so" but rather the parties' perception of what is so. Here, too, are fault-finding and fact-finding in general played down.[12]) Such approaches are nonclassificatory, relative instead of absolute, and multireferrent.

There are today preliterate non-Western societies without courts or courtlike institutions, without judges or arbitrators, societies that abjure the threats of force in settling disputes.[13] There is at least one literate, industrialized modern Western society (Norway) in which the either-or, coercive legal model of dealing with interpersonal relations and conflicts has lost ground to models such as psychology, economics, and other disciplines.[14] (At the same time, Norway has seen a relative decline in the legal profession's numbers, political eminence, and ". . . perceived usefulness in public and private administration. . . ."[15])

* * *

In most of Western thought, however, divine law's single-reference, bipolar frame persisted as a formative understructure. From it evolved a series of fashions in religion, philosophy, morality, politics, and law. The most significant of those fruits for Anglo-American legal theory was perhaps the idea of "natural law."

Natural law, a kind of disembodied Big Daddy (Divine Reason) in the sky, was first introduced by the Greeks about 400 B.C. and thereafter intermittently resurrected. The theory of natural law posited a proper fixed place and function for every person and thing in a "natural" wordly order. While divine law was known through revelation, natural law (like conscience) was supposedly "written on men's hearts." The two inventions were disparate in emphasis, direction, and general product, yet they shared a common core: belief in absolute precepts given earthly form in government, religion, and law—and ideally unvaryingly applied.

In the 18th century, economist Adam Smith wrote of the "invisible hand" which could be counted upon to order society's welfare through the individual's pursuit of his own economic self-interest. Somewhat later in that same period, British jurist William Blackstone declared, "The law of nature . . . is binding all over the globe in all countries, and at all times; no human laws are of any validity if contrary to this; and such of them as are valid derive all their authority . . . from this original."[16] The *Britannica* comments, with a rare quiet smile, Blackstone ". . . evidently regarded the law of gravitation, the law of nature and the law of England as different examples of the same principle."[17] A British civil servant declared in this century, "One of the principles of the Rule of Law, fundamental to the British way of life and an indispensable part of any system of British administration, is that the law should be certain."[18] Certainty, according to an anthropologist, is an Anglo-American legal credo.[19]

That theme has shaped also the roles of lawyer, judge, and jury. Because, for instance, certainty has no doubts, the lawyer's purpose tends to be affirmation rather than discovery. Thus Francis Bacon, seventeenth-century attorney general of England, complained of a clergyman he was prosecuting: "Peacham was examined before torture, in torture, between torture, and after torture; nothing could be drawn from him, he still persisting in his obstinate and inexcusable denials and former answers."[20] For Bacon, the inexcusable lay not in torture, but in Peacham's refusal of Bacon's *a priori* Truth. So still our judicial investigators. The man of law begins with "something to be proved." His leading question assumes a truth already known.

Ultimately, divine law's legal logic is circular. Since Heaven supports right, only right will win, and therefore any means toward victory is justified—since whoever wins has been right. Hence the certainty system's tunnel-vision had seen no paradox in cloaking judicial battle with Christianity's love and peace[21]—nor in battle's claiming to be a means to truth and justice. We see no paradox today in adversary procedure's claiming the same.

9

TUNNEL VISION STILL

Divine law's conceptual print remains explicitly manifest in our legal procedure. Bipolarity's classification, absolutes, and blame infuse much of the English common law from which our American method emerged, and form the skeleton upon which our adversary legal approach is fleshed.

The common law, *Black's Law Dictionary* explains, is a body of principles deriving their authority "solely from usages and customs of immemorial antiquity." That reasoning and doctrine of remote ages was nowhere initially set down nor embodied in any written code of law. Rather, through early centuries, cases were decided on the basis of local custom, and reflected the personal prejudices, thinking modes, and social conventions of particular judges and communities. From those decisions, following generations extracted precepts used as precedent in later cases. Thus the folkways of a society long gone became transmuted into many formal legal principles we currently enshrine: some still highly functional, some obsolete—but few rarely considered afresh. The common law is simply ancestral habit sanctified. Though the Old Testament shaped many significant themes of our jurisprudence, it is the common law to which we continue to make official obeisance. Revered as the "gathered wisdom of a thousand years,"[1] its premises are hailed as "fixed stars [from which] the law . . . is reckoned."[2] So, for instance, legal scholar William T. Hughes wrote in *Procedure, Theory and Practice* of "those great maxims, forty in number, which are the condensed good sense of the ages, and are therefore applicable to all coherent systems of procedure."[3]

What is the chief maxim, the central jewel in that string of antique gems? States Hughes, ". . . all systems of procedure . . . are shown to rest largely upon . . . an application of the maxim, *De non apparentibus et non existentibus eadem est ratio,* which liberally translated means that where a court cannot take official notice of a fact, it is the same as if the fact did not exist, or, in other words, facts must be made to appear in some juridical way, before they can be considered by the court."[4] Facts, that is, either appear in a "juridical way"—or they do not exist at all.

The following thus happens: A plaintiff, suing in a civil matter, has her lawyer introduce and read a document stolen from the defendant (who has until this moment been unaware of the theft). The material has no factual bearing whatsoever on the issue at hand, but extraneously implies the defendant's liberal political activity. The plaintiff and her lawyer accurately predict it will prejudice the conservative judge against the defendant. If the defendant's attorney protests loudly enough, the heisted material is not officially received as evidence. But in fact Her Honor has heard it. And it helps shape her decision—for the plaintiff. Nevertheless, when the issue of illegal obtainment is raised, the Court can avoid considering the matter because the case at trial is a civil dispute, and theft falls in the criminal category. There is no time to bring a criminal charge, because the statute of limitations runs out that day. The theft cannot be made to appear in a "juridical way."

Abracadabra!

Fact has disappeared in a puff of juridical smoke. The thief is not a thief. Nor, in a juridical way, has the robbery even occurred.

Judicial cognizability often rests solely upon the statute of limitations, whose either-or dictate doubtless tempers justice with travesty as frequently as it does with mercy. Though intended to place some protective limit against the eternal threat of prosecution, the statute, in many crimes, is effective not from date of *discovery* of the act, but rather from the date of its *commission*. As a result, since discovery may occur long after that arbitrary cut-off date beyond which no crime "exists," our procedure in effect often rewards the criminal who has most cleverly covered his tracks.

For example:[5] In California, a man named DePalma, found guilty of robbing a savings and loan, was sentenced to fifteen years in federal prison. The single bit of hard evidence responsible for his conviction—evidence at once scientific and apparently incontrovertible—was his fingerprint found at the scene of the crime. Two and one half years after his incarceration, two and one half years after having been torn from wife and children, his life savings gone, his family forced onto welfare and hopelessly in debt for legal fees—that incontrovertible evidence was (thanks to ceaseless private detective work at DePalma's expense) discovered to be a forgery. The forging of a fingerprint is a complex procedure, requiring an expert in fingerprint technique. In the DePalma case, that forger was an expert indeed: he was the police sergeant in charge of the crime lab that had helped prepare the prosecution.

That police officer was now himself brought to trial—but not in the DePalma case at all. He was charged only with the misdemeanor of having offered false evidence in a previous marijuana case; not with the felony of forgery. He was sentenced—not, like DePalma (whose life he had devastated) to federal prison for fifteen years—but rather to one year in county jail on a work-furlough program. Why? Because, although his crime against DePalma was clear, it was not judicially cognizable: *The statute of limitations on the act of forgery was already passed when the crime against DePalma was discovered.* In other words: DePalma had spent two and one half years behind federal prison bars for a crime the conviction of which was ultimately set aside. Yet the man who had at considerable effort *in fact* committed a crime to put DePalma there was in no way held accountable for that act—but instead (in substitute) for a separate, and minor, misdeed. Since the forgery could not be made to appear in a juridical way, it had (for our law) never happened.

Equally either-or are other common-law precepts. For instance, *Expressio unius est exclusio alterius*: "The express mention of one thing implies the exclusion of another."[6] This maxim, says Hughes, is a "great universal, fundamental principle of logic, reason and law. All must admit that it represents the basic ideas and principles of our jurisprudence . . . without its protective influence not only would certainty fail in government and procedure, but it would fail in contracts as well."[7] But *Expressio unius* denies all psychological thought since long before Freud and all philosophical thought since Hegel's dialectical synthesis of opposites. It denies the coexistent

differences, complementarities, and complexities of material, biological, and emotional existence: ("So you admit you disliked her.
And yet you ask this Court to believe you loved her?") Applied to
interpersonal problems, *Expressio unius* is about as appropriate as a
hot water bottle applied to a bursting appendix. Similarly, Hughes'
Maxim 15: *Allegans contraria non est audiendus,* or "He who al-
leges contradictory things ought not to be heard."[8] Lawyers may,
for tactical reasons, allege contradictions to the Court ("Well, if you
won't buy this argument, will you buy this one?"). But the witness
who contradicts himself is in trouble—although contradiction examined may not be contradiction at all; though contradiction pursued may illumine motivation, suggest new paths for investigation,
or signal confusion significant and begging for further questioning.
Similarly also Maxim 40: *Falsus in uno falsus in omnibus,* or "False
in one thing, false in all!"[9]—though all else the witness speaks may
be truth.

Hughes declares, "Those who have been taught that all laws have
been mediately or immediately derived from the law of nature or of
the Divine or revealed law of God will be pleased to plainly trace
each of the above principles . . . back into the Holy Scriptures."[10]

In short: for the common law, crime fits strict time- and nomen-
clature-limited categories, or there is no crime. The witness is either
entirely consistent or entirely inconsistent. He has never made contradictory statements or always does—and one contradiction is an
"always." "It is better that the law should be certain than that it
should be just,"[11] held common-law judges. Unfortunately, it is
generally neither. But upon those assumptions, our procedure still
largely rests. Thus:

EITHER-OR AND ABSOLUTES

Adversary process is by definition either-or. Any action requires
two sides: polar, intransigent. "Against" is the only legal posture
possible: "Smith *versus* Jones," "The People *versus* John Doe."
The Declaratory Judgment, which is supposedly a means of clarify-
ing questions of law in advance so that persons may proceed without
legal peril, requires an actual controversy before such Judgment
may be sought.[12]

No third person may enter the legal lists without declaring himself, or being declared by the Court, "for" one side or the other; "friendly" or "hostile." (Even the class-action suit is couched in *versus* terms.) There is no designation in legal language for an impartial witness at the trial court level. *Amicus Curiae* ("friend of the court") appears only at the appellate level—where 99 percent of cases never arrive. There is hence in practical use no witness who speaks for neither side but rather for a totally different point of view, or simply to widen the contextual perspective. Indeed the litigant, witness, or attorney who in the course of trial attempts to do so will be reprimanded and, if persistent, held in contempt and penalized. (A law professor, explaining why the Patricia Hearst trial failed to shed expected light upon human motivation and behavior, said: "One side gets up and yells white and the other gets up and yells black while we're talking about shades of gray. There is no room in the law for the advocacy—or the exploration—of the shade of gray."[13])

Even the expert witness is called not for disinterested enlightenment wherever it may point, but *by* a side, *for* that side: painstakingly interviewed in advance and chosen to assure that testimony given will support *only* the calling side (and/or serve as ammunition against the opposition). In fact, expert witnesses, deftly questioned to bring out specific material and nothing more, are in Roscoe Pound's words "partisans, pure and simple."[14] More recently, psychiatrist Thomas Szasz commented concerning the Hearst case,

> In criminal trials . . . there are two types of psychiatrist: excusers and incriminators. The former, hired by the defense, are paid to offer psychiatric prevarications that tend to excuse the accused. The latter, hired by the prosecution, are paid to offer psychiatric prevarications tending to incriminate the accused. If a psychiatrist is unwilling to offer such testimony, he is not hired.[15]

(Two writers on matters legal say, "The ugly truth is that in many fields the most incompetent is the most glib and persuasive and the most positive in his statements."[16])

Pleas made, questions framed, demand two choices only: "Guilty or not guilty?" "Just answer the question, Yes or No!" *Goldstein's Trial Technique* advises, "The successful cross-examiner is the one who has learned to put his questions in such narrow frame as to permit the witness only to answer 'yes' or 'no.' "[17]

Judges and juries must believe one side *or* the other (no matter that they frequently believe neither); must decide *for* one and *against* the other. It remains impossible that truth ever lie in between or be other than has been heard. "A "win" system must have a winner and a loser. That win and loss must be absolute.

CLASSIFICATION

As adversary process is either-or and absolute, so it remains classificatory. In criminal matters, for instance, the first purpose of requiring that facts appear in a juridical way, as well as of such techniques as character smear and the plea bargain, is classification. That the rape victim had prior sexual experience classifies her as "noncredible." She cannot have been violated—no matter that she has been. Likewise, though the plea bargain may dispense with that due process of law the 5th Amendment guarantees, it supplies a category in no time at all. And category is the means to speedy disposition: the ultimate point. Similarly, misclassification is the essence of pleading and procedure's risk. The surgeon's victim left paraplegic and unrecompensed is benched, not merely for the season, but in judicial perpetuity—unless he is knowledgeable enough to bring a malpractice suit against his derelict attorney, and sufficiently hardy to risk the legal lists once more. Few are.

In civil matters, the plaintiff may not simply state those facts he believes entitle him to relief. Rather, he must tailor his facts to fit arbitrary legal categories and designations.

There is, says a professor of law,

> . . . a complex and confusing array of substantive classifications, concepts, rules and standards through which we channel . . . thinking and by which our approach to justice is limited. There are torts based on assault, battery, false imprisonment, conversion, trespass to chattels, trespass to land—with all the problems of trespassers, technical trespassers, licensees, invitees and attractive nuisances—nuisances, libel, slander, deceit, malicious prosecution, intentional falsehood, intentional infliction of harm, strict liability, and negligence with its conceptual problems of duty, breach of duty, misfeasance, nonfeasance, causation, proximate cause, and damages. . . . Some of these torts can be

committed only intentionally, some only by negligence, some by either, and some without either, at least in the conceptual sense of those words. To such actions, are defenses based on consent, self-defense, defense of property, defense of others and of others' property, public or private necessity, privilege, immunity, no duty, assumed risk, fellow servant, and contributory negligence. One could make a handsome down-payment on Manhattan Island if he had money equal to the going rate times the number of lawyer hours that have been spent in meaningless research—meaningless in so far as the real heart and substance of the parties' problems was concerned—in establishing and defeating the technical requirements of those needless concepts.[18]

It is a wise client who knows his own case by trial time. And equity—once seen as escape from that classificatory impasse—no longer helps much. (By the 14th century, the common law having already become so hidebound that persons unable to fit their cases into the obligatory legal pigeonholes were left without recourse, dissatisfied litigants began to petition the king directly for equity. Petitions seeking such remedy finally became so numerous that the monarch delegated the task of hearing them to the lord chancellor, as "the king's conscience." Eventually the Court of Chancery was created as chief of the courts of equity, among whose mottos were "Equity does not suffer a wrong to be without a remedy," and "Equity will do that which ought to be done." A diverse set of principles, now known as the rules of equity, and affecting mainly the law of property and of contract, arose. However, since equity depended upon the State's grace rather than upon legal right, those remedies it granted were entirely discretionary. This led to the complaint, in the words of one jurist, that "Equity varies as the length of the Chancellor's foot."[19] Though there was no pretense that equitable rules existed from time immemorial, ultimately those rules became precedent as inflexible as common-law rules, and virtually ceased to evolve as a common-law corrective. By 1897, Charles Dickens was moved to write in *Bleak House*,

This is the Court of Chancery . . . which gives to monied might the means abundantly of wearing out the right, which so exhausts finances, patience, courage, hope; so overthrows the brain and breaks the heart, that there is not an

honorable man among its practitioners, who would not
give . . . the warning, "Suffer any wrong that can be done
you, rather than come here."[20]

All equitable remedies, such as the injunction, must still be fought
for within the adversary frame.)

That emphasis upon classification which still prevails, necessarily
excludes contextual material; for circumstantial and motivational
particulars may call into question one's categories—and thus one's
case. Clarity and insights that suggest conclusions alternative to
those which will best serve the client's interests are impermissible.
Therefore the lawyer generally works to isolate phenomena from as
many contextual factors as possible: social, economic, historic, psychological, familial, interhuman. Savay calls that technique "Dispersion." Dispersion, he explains, "is the principle . . . employed
when it becomes necessary to confuse the issue or the adversary.
The Court can sometimes be as easily confused as the jury or witnesses."[21]

There are specific Dispersion-ploys. The lawyer may object or
otherwise interrupt at critical moments of testimony, in order to halt
his own witness nearing contextual quicksand; in order to distract an
opposition witness nearing matter too "hot"; or in order to divert
judge and jury from clues that threaten the lawyer's purpose.
Another trick consists in the lawyer's eschewing a sequential presentation of material in favor of a time-and-sequence scramble calculated to baffle even the CIA's chief cipher expert. Remarked one
judge, "Some counsel do a certain amount of grasshopper-jumping
on cross-examination deliberately. In fact, I can remember several
times I used to begin in the middle of the direct [examination] and
work towards both ends, simultaneously. It's not too easy."[22]

Similarly, I have heard a plaintiff's lawyer misrepresent part of a
defendant's written phrase as the whole: reading to the Court, for
instance, "I am readying the house for rental," instead of "I am
readying the house for rental and sale" (when the defendant's alleged refusal to sell has been the plaintiff's charge). Such gambit,
when brought to the Court's attention by the defendant's lawyer
(who is entitled to require the whole to be read) does not necessarily
redound to the misrepresenter's discredit. He has only, after all,
represented his client "zealously within the bounds of the
law"[23]—as professional ethic demands. And in case the litigant him-

self at some point tries to introduce contextual material, the Bench
will usually emphasize the ground rules: "I've warned you before!
This is a courtroom, and you don't give reasons unless you're
asked—or I'll hold you in contempt! Your attorney will bring out
any explanations you have later!" Your attorney may not. And if he
should, the force and bearing of that information upon the original
question will have been long lost in the hot and dusty wind of legal
brouhaha.

Within the terms of that either-or system, truth cannot emerge
from a wealth of informed and cogently organized data. Rather,
truth remains manifest in victory. That victory—still called
"right"—is achieved necessarily, and at best, through conceptual
and informational oversimplification. More usually it arrives as a
by-blow of exclusion, diversion, distortion, and direct deceit.

It is that partisan approach which, in addition to the law's linguis-
tic and ideational vagueness, renders our jurisprudence a non-
science. For scientific progress has abandoned either-or, absolutes,
and classification as an end in itself. Science has increasingly
reached for inclusion of context and the understanding of parts in
relation to whole. Above all, science pushes for illumination beyond
old boundaries. Adversary search, on the contrary, forbids advance
beyond preestablished conclusionary limits.

BLAME

Blame is also foreign to scientific method. But blame's righteousness and revenge inevitably follow either-or conceptualization. To
offer in court any approximation of the statement, "Well, the fault
wasn't *entirely* hers," can be fatal. ("Christ, are you crazy?" I lis-
tened to one lawyer chide a client. "The judge'll throw us right
out!") Within a polar frame, failure to deny a charge in toto constitutes admission of total culpability.

In accident litigation, for instance, a personal injury attorney
writes, the fault system ". . . tends to advocate an all-or-nothing
approach . . . the slightest bit of fault on the part of the victim
completely precludes a [monetary] recovery. It makes him accept
100 percent of the responsibility for the accident, even though he
may have been only 1 percent at fault. Cases are lost nowadays by
worthy claimants whose only sin is reading a book while a passenger

in a car instead of maintaining a lookout, riding with a driver who had only one cocktail, or not wearing a seat belt."[24]

In personal injury matters, that fault system has begun, within some jurisdictions, giving way to a system of comparative negligence. Nonetheless, the attorney's adversary imperative remains, in general, *deny* all charges and blame your opponent. In a West Coast trial the defense attorney counseled, ". . . in a murder case, try the victim. And if you can't try the victim, try the district attorney."[25]

Such advice is neither scurrilous nor farce. It is simply adversary logic. For within the terms of the either-or game, the very presumption of innocence for the guilty *logically* requires a converse presumption of guilt for the innocent. Another lawyer explains, ". . . if the accused is presumed innocent, the accuser must be presumed guilty—that is, lying. If we accept the first assumption as valid, we must also accept the validity of the second." For instance, he continues, "We may in fact know quite well that the defendant has committed [the crime] and that the victim is telling the truth. But the police, the prosecutors and the courts must act as if the defendant is innocent. . . ."[26] (The role of police and prosecutors is actually somewhat more ambiguous: though they usually believe, and certainly tend to proceed, as if the accused were guilty—still they must to some degree defer to the theory that considers him officially innocent until proven not so.) Via "logical corollary," the same lawyer holds, that presumption of the accused's innocence *must* reversewise presume the victim's lie; however, these are simply "procedural presumptions—safeguards to ensure that we do not punish innocent persons."[27] But in fact the contrary occurs: innocent persons—those known-to-be-truthful victims treated as liars—are punished by the very procedural safeguards that may leave the known-to-be-guilty defendant unpunished at all.

Polar logic cannot (in practice) conceive *equal* presumptive safeguards for *both* parties. Either-or must have a goat: victim-or-defendant, defendant-victim. Polar reasoning has nowhere else to go.

So it is that not only the adverse party but witnesses too are, in Wigmore's words, "set up as marks to be shot at."[28] Suggests the legal aphorism, "No case? Then abuse the opponent's witnesses."[29] The outer limits of such behavior are determined essentially by the lawyer's "utmost zeal" in his client's behalf and his taste for blood—together with his skill in drawing it. The Court seldom intervenes. And when appealed to, the Bench may testily respond, "Well, the attorney's allowed to ask those questions. You can't teach an old dog new tricks. And you just hold your tongue, or I'll remove you from the stand!"

In similar vein, the precedent maxim (*Stare decisis, et non quieta movere*) directs, "Adhere to the decisions and do not unsettle things which are established."[30]

To those things established, conceptual and procedural as well as preceptive, both Bench and Bar remain most singularly loyal. That loyalty is to a method which does not cool fires, but fans them; to a system that by its nature must reopen old wounds, create new ones, and leave scars that sometimes never heal. Our legal system processes disputes. It can rarely settle them.

10

CHILDHOOD'S LENSES

Our bipolar legal framework, though structurally simplistic, is nevertheless embraced by many erudite persons. This is no paradox. For knowledge, necessarily channeled through a thinking *system*, can be no more imaginatively used than that system permits, nor are those locked within a system easily able to consider alternatives. The conceptual-attitudinal lenses through which erudition looks help shape perception, influence response, and determine the purposes to which erudition is put. Indeed, our legal profession's educated bipolarity is curiously similar to orientations sometimes reported as characteristic of children—who must in critical ways abandon them in order to grow up.

Consider:*
Children below the age of eight generally cannot take into account another's point of view. The small child is literally egocentric, a "prisoner" of his own viewpoint in that he lacks "freedom from the limitations of a single perspective."[1] Thus the child finds it "difficult (and even unnecessary) really to exchange ideas with others, since

*All cited statements concerning children in this chapter depend upon Jean Piaget, developmental psychologist and educator, and upon the summary of his work by John H. Flavell.

this demands a focusing on the other's perspective in order to coordinate or contrast it with his own."[2] The child in fact is relatively unaware of others' ideational (and physical) positions. "Only his own point of view—*his* schemas, *his* perceptions, etc.—can really figure in his various activities, since he is unaware that others see things differently, i.e., that there are points of view of which his is only one."[3]

Similarly, the lawyer *must* not share his adversary's perspective, and must (if he can) prevent judge and jury from doing so either.

The child tends to be unaware of relativity of viewpoint, motivation, and context, in favor of absolutes. His "uni-perspective egocentrism"[4] prevents him from grasping the "*reciprocity* existing between different points of view. . . ."[5] Further, ". . . it must be overt consequences alone which count in assessing the wrongfulness of acts . . . not the inner intentions and motives involved."[6] Thus the young child judges the larger theft with altruistic motive as worse than the smaller theft with selfish motive.[7]

Similarly the lawyer *deliberately* denies reciprocity of view, denying or distorting intents and motives where it serves.

Younger children operate under a "morality of constraint"[8] in a context of child as inferior, adult as superior.[9] Within that context, adult prohibitions appear handed down from on high, givens "unquestioned and sacred," while justice becomes whatever the authority figure commands.[10] This leads to the "confusion of what is just with the content of established law and to the acceptance of expiatory punishment. . . ."[11] The younger the child, the likelier to favor such punishment, and, usually, "the more severe the better."[12] But though the child between three and five regards game-rules as eternal, deriving from divine or parental authority, his actual behavior "unwittingly breaks them at every turn. . . ."[13]

Similarly the attorney, ostensibly honoring law's letter as "given," *wittingly* evades law's intent wherever winning beckons.

The younger child tends to ". . . judge a lie which *fails* to deceive (usually because it is so 'big,' so unbelievable) as 'naughtier' than one which succeeds."[14] For instance, suggests Piaget, ask the small child ". . . to compare two lies: telling his mother that he has received a good grade at school when he has not been graded at all, or telling her that he has been frightened by a dog as big as a cow . . . the first seems 'less bad' because one does sometimes get good grades and, above all, because the statement is sufficiently plausible for the mother herself to be deceived!"[15] In fact, a tall tale innocently told "is worse than a more believable untruth told with deliberate intent to deceive. . . ."[16] It is not intent, but "formulation" that counts.[17]

Bluntly declared Richard Nixon's attorney James St. Clair (referring to a preimpeachment case), "It is not necessarily important that you *do* something wrong; it is very important that there be the *appearance* of nothing being done wrong."[18] (emphasis mine)

Not only do young children find every punishment perfectly legitimate, but (for other persons) unequal punishment for the same crime acceptable—in fact, "just" or "fair."[19] Similarly our adversary system.

It is, for example, not our biggest thieves who go to prison. It is our least successful ones. In 1959, out of 502 tax-fraud convictees averaging a $190,000 take *each*—only 95 (fewer than 20 percent) went to prison; and for seven months and less. On the other hand, over 60 percent of burglary and auto-theft culprits (federally convicted)—averaging only $321 in burglary and $992 in auto-theft each—went to prison for periods of eighteen to thirty-three months.[20] In other words, both culpability and sentence length vary inversely with the size of the filch. The judicial message is: "When you steal—steal big."

It helps also, of course, to start with a hefty purse. An attorney writes, "Ninety per cent of the [criminal] cases in California are disposed of on guilty pleas—to lesser charges—because the defendant knows if he goes to trial with this hack lawyer who has been assigned to him he is liable to get stuck with more."[21] But only the impecunious must settle for that court-assigned lawyer. (The public defender is *not* necessarily a hack; in fact, in many jurisdictions such as California and the federal system, he may often be superior to the private criminal attorney. The public defender is, however, particularly in local jurisdictions, usually overworked. In any case, according to one study, defendants with court-assigned attorneys generally served twice as long as those with sufficient funds to hire their own lawyers.[22])

Monetary inequity exists not only in criminal defense. It inhibits equally the bringing of civil complaints. Out-of-sight discovery costs and \$35 to \$75 per hour lawyer fees make legal remedy in effect nonexistent for 90 percent of our citizenry.[23] But beyond costs: the very *nature* of the adversary frame *itself* limits recourse to our courts in disputes, and defeats law's claim of functioning as a behavior guide *in advance*. Problems must appear as fights before they can be heard; while (once again) our procedure's classificatory system severely limits those matters it will term "fights." Meanwhile, alternative forums, such as administrative and consumer agencies, are unequipped to handle, and unresponsive to, many legally noncognizable problems. Even the well-to-do may have no resort.

Contemplate a true-life (middle-class) drama: One day in 1970, the owner of a microwave oven heard via newscast that certain such ovens had been discovered to leak nonionizing radiation. The owner promptly asked the Public Health Service to check her range. Inspection revealed that when the oven door was opened in mid-cooking cycle, there was some slight emission above the Maximum Permissible Exposure Level of 10 milliwatts per square centimeter. The malfunction was, however, easily repaired by the manufacturer, and the owner proceeded to use it as regularly as ever she had before: for breakfast, lunch, and dinner. Not until several weeks later did she idly decide to ask Public Health Service to verify the repair.

The original agent arrived, examined—and backed hastily away. Open-door emission was now over 200 milliwatts per square centimeter! In fact, more precise reading was prohibited by danger to the measuring kit of a closer approach to the oven.

The distressed (and overexposed) owner began research into microwave phenomena and effects; and soon uncovered, in both government and electrical engineer publications, facts omitted by appliance industry literature. For example: Microwave exposure can cause (among other results) eye damage, interference with cellular physiology, and stress reaction.[24] Negative bioeffects can be cumulative, taking possibly three to five years to appear.[25] Microwaves produce, as by-products, infrared, ultraviolet and X rays, while nonionizing microwaves themselves may ultimately prove to be a greater danger than ionizing radiation.[26] More critically, there is insufficient fine-grain knowledge in the field.[27] Even so basic a matter as the safe-exposure maximum remains an open problem: exposure limits established in the Soviet Union are *a hundred to a thousand times lower* than those established in the United States.[28] At the same time, there is no such thing as zero emission.[29] *All microwave ovens leak,* and that leakage increases as the oven ages: the only question is, how much.

Despite those hazards, however, no oven yet sold incorporates any overemission warning device—although the human sensory apparatus, unaided by instrumentation, is totally incapable of detecting microwave energy. The owner in this case, for example, had experienced exposure over forty times the currently permissible maximum, and felt absolutely nothing. Yet a fluorescent light bulb, held within two inches of the oven door, is turned on by overemission. The oven manufacturers do not install them.

What action might the oven's owner take? Her letter to the manufacturer brought only an offer to repair her oven (again); but no response either to her request for standard incorporation of a warning device, or to her request that industry claims of "absolute safety" and "fail-safe operation" be withdrawn. Since she had suffered no immediately demonstrable injury, she had no basis for a damage suit whose financial fruits might attract legal representation on contingency. Similarly, consumer groups resisted spending funds where physical injury was unapparent and monetary reward not foreseeable; while the President's Consumer Action Council failed even to reply to correspondence in the situation. And the owner herself had insufficient funds to bring legal action to compel manufacturer safety-performance.

In brief: A vast and increasing number of microwave appliance owners would continue not simply endangered, but without information permitting them choice in the matter of their own safety—because without a lawsuit, industry regulation was unavailable. For, implicit in adversary theory, is that *there must be a fight before law can speak;*[30] before "law," in practice, exists. No fight? No law—no matter the private or public consequence.

Our law, in other words, is not a moral or performance standard whose application, or even guidance, any citizen may request. It is a victor's prize. While only a relative few can afford the battle, a lesser number still, buying the prize beforehand through on-retainer legal advice or sheer monetary unapproachability, win the battle through bypassing the fight. Our procedure, generally for sale and to the highest bidder,[31] is largely power's tool.

Lawyers are not children. Nonetheless, adversary conceptualization forces childhood's orientations upon them. That conceptual

method requires those who enter its bounds to order litigational experience in essentially single-perspective, polarized terms. It requires them to reduce experience to either-or simplicities—as do
children.

To that reduction, however, the legal profession brings something
extra: the adult's intention, knowledge, and resource. It is a potentially malign combination.

The malignancy is that of propaganda. Adversary behavior is a
manipulative technique that aims, in the worst public relations
tradition, at stimulating not the hearer's thought processes, but his
adrenals; and speaks less to concepts and issues than to prejudices.
According to the Institute of Propaganda Analysis, the forms of
propaganda are "name-calling, glittering generality, transfer, tes-
timonial, plain folks, card-stacking, band-wagon."[32] Under those
headings, a great part of adversary reductionism can be subsumed.

Meanwhile, the rest of us, like children for whom ". . . the concept of what is just is confused with what is demanded or imposed
from on high,"[33] accept our "win" system of law as heaven's fiat.
We have, after all, the best judicial system attainable. Our judges,
legislators, governors, Presidents—lawyers, most of them—they all
tell us so.

By ten or eleven years the child has begun to transform much of
his earlier conceptualization into higher-level, more adequate concepts.[34] After close to five thousand years, our approach to dispute
settlement has yet to do the same.

11

MORAL SCHIZOPHRENIA

What *are* the rationales for adversary ordeal?

A professor of law says, "The underlying hope is that if the law permits the lawyer-gladiators to make the fight, out of the clash and clang of their legal or factual battling, the rights of the case will appear and justice be done."[1]

Another professor adds: ". . . the adversary system permits the tribunal to remain uncommitted while a case is being explored from opposing viewpoints, thus requiring the liability of guilt to be demonstrated publicly to a neutral tribunal. . . ."[2]

A lawyer says, "One of the underlying premises of the adversary system . . . is that the truth is more likely to emerge from the strong pull of self-interests than from a 'neutral' investigation. . . ."[3]

A law text states: "The theory of our adversary system is that each litigant is most interested and will be most effective in seeking, discovering and presenting the materials which will reveal the strength of his own case and the weakness of his adversary's case so that the truth will emerge to the impartial tribunal that makes the decision."[4]

Another text reads,

> The reasons for the prevalence of the adversary system are manifold, but four postulates are certainly among the most important: (1) A truer decision will be reached as the result of a contest directed by interested parties. (2) The parties,

who after all are the persons principally interested in the resolution of the controversy, should bear the major burden of the time and energy required. (3) Although impartial investigation may be better when no final decision need be reached, setting up sides makes easier the type of yes-and-no decision that is thought to be necessary in a law-suit. (4) Since resort to law has replaced the resort to force that characterized primitive ages, the atavistic instinct to do battle is better satisfied by a means of settling disputes that is very much in the hands of the parties.[5]

An article in *The American Bar Association Journal* states, "Only when [the judge or arbiter] has had the benefit of intelligent and vigorous advocacy on both sides, can he feel fully confident of his decision. . . ."[6]

Finally, a legal scholar declares, "In the intellectual history of mankind, the two principal methods developed for securing and testing data have been scientific research and the adversary trial."[7]

In other words: Under adversary procedure right will appear, justice be done, truth emerge. The battling is legal or factual. "Materials" are "presented," the parties are "interested," the case is "explored." The strength of the litigant's case and the weakness of his adversary's is "revealed." From contest will arise a truer decision.

There is no mention, in those judicious tones, of destruction, crushing blows, ambush, annihilation. No mention of those directives we have read: no word of "confusing the Court as easily as the jury or witness," nor of "no matter how honest the witness, there is always some way, if you are ingenious enough, to cast suspicion, to weaken the effect." No mention of "Never ask a question unless you know the answer will be favorable" or "cannot be given." No mention of "No case? Abuse the opponent's witnesses." Nor is there mention of cases like *Miller v. Pate,* where defense's request to make its own examination of the allegedly "bloodstained" shorts was resisted by the prosecution and denied by the judge.

Now and then, nonetheless, some members of the legal profession have seen adversary method differently:
Morgan says,

It is doubtless true that the theory of our adversary system is attractive in statement [but] If it were to operate perfectly, both parties would have the same opportunities and capacities for investigation, including the resources to finance them, equal facilities for producing all the discoverable materials, equal good or bad fortune with reference to availability of witnesses and preservation of evidence, and equal persuasive skill in the presentation of evidence and argument. The case is rare where there is even approximate equality in these respects. . . .[8]

Roscoe Pound comments,

. . . contentious procedure . . . leads the most conscientious judge to feel that he is merely to decide the contest . . . according to the rules of the game, not to search independently for truth and justice. It leads counsel to forget that they are officers of the court and to deal with the rules of law and procedure . . . as the professional football coach. It turns witnesses, especially expert witnesses, into partisans. . . . It leads to sensational cross-examinations to "affect credit." . . . It prevents the trial court from restraining the bullying of witnesses and creates a general dislike, if not fear, of the witness function which impairs the administration of justice. . . .[9]

Two biographers of Sacco and Vanzetti reiterate that, under our adversary system,

Neither party has any obligation to bring forward material which will aid his adversary or will weaken his own case. The theory of the system is that each party will disclose the weakness of his adversary. Thus the truth will emerge to the view of the impartial tribunal. This . . . assumes that each side will be equally intelligent, equally diligent, and equally fortunate in investigation and discovery of pertinent data. . . . No argument is necessary to convince the most unobserving that these assumptions are without any basis in fact.[10]

Thurman Arnold writes,

. . . to summarize the assumptions underlying . . . a lawmaking body which never speaks except to settle a com-

bat . . . the result would be somewhat as follows:
. . . Courts are apt to formulate or apply rules soundly if
the opposite sides are prevented from sitting around a table
together in a friendly conference. Mutual exaggeration is
supposed to create a lack of exaggeration. Bitter partisan-
ship in opposite directions is supposed to bring out the truth.
Of course no rational human being would apply such a theory to his own affairs . . . mutual exaggeration of opposing
claims violate(s) the whole theory of rational, scientific
investigation. Yet in spite of this most obvious fact, the ordinary teacher of law will insist (1) that combat makes for
clarity, (2) that heated arguments bring out the truth, and (3)
that anyone who doesn't believe this is a loose thinker. The
explanation of this attitude lies in the realm of social anthropology.[11]

Fleming James, Jr., finishes, "Adversary procedure presupposes
equality of opportunity, means and skill . . . but these are seldom
evenly matched. It often degenerates into . . . victory to the swift
and strong rather than to the party in the right."[12]

That outcome does not, however, invalidate adversary procedure
in the eyes of adversary loyalists. Though victory may go to the
swift and the strong, loyalists maintain that legal battle's ultimate
virtue lies elsewhere than in outcome: it lies in the satisfaction of
fighting itself.

An attorney says, ". . . the justification of the adversary proceeding is in the satisfaction of the parties. . . . The best way to get
that done is to encourage them to fight it out, and dissolve their differences in dissension."[13] A legal historian writes, "One of the se-
crets of the success of the legal process in replacing the ordeal is
found in the very fact that it provided similar satisfactions to that
offered by the ordeal."[14]

No matter that to "dissolve differences in dissension" is, within
an "enemies" framework and "win" goal, a contradiction in terms,
feeling, and possibility. So long as belief in an "atavistic instinct to
do battle" prevails, battle will be claimed to satisfy. That claim implies: primitive people must have primitive tools.

But battle's satisfaction is less than clear. Satisfaction for whom?
Satisfaction for those who benefit from (and wish to maintain) the
political, economic, and legal status quo? Yes. Satisfaction for the

venal, for the sophistical who enjoy their skills and are likelier to win? Yes. Satisfaction for the law-men who earn their living at combat? Yes. Satisfaction for the rich and powerful who are little subjected to the rigors of legal battle and who can purchase the expert counsel and legal discovery necessary to victory? Maybe. But satisfaction for the rest of us? For the "targets set up to be shot at"? For the witness who has even the most mistaken, long-forgotten, but never expunged arrest record? Satisfaction for Mrs. Wilson, the rape victim? Satisfaction for those of us (there are some) who simply don't *like* to fight?

No.

Indeed, the nonlitigious are emotionally disadvantaged in the adversary courtroom as surely as the impecunious are financially disadvantaged. That handicap, however, is as rarely acknowledged as is the difference between victory for one disputant and equity for both.

French social scientist Gabriel Tarde suggests that the judicial duel could have developed only in a "pugnacious tribe. . . . No pacific-minded people . . . could have devised it."[15] Clearly it could only have been maintained in one. But we are a pugnacious tribe afflicted with monumental provincialism. The Reader's Digest book *You and the Law* states that our Anglo-American legal system "is the only one in the world that tries to give evenhanded justice to all persons. . . ."[16] Even more grandiose: We tend to see our lady with the scales as the best, not just of all existing but of all *possible* legal systems. Unfortunately, that particular lady is a fiction.

Something beyond provincialism, grandiosity, or simple yearning for evenhanded justice blurs our vision, however. We ignore the difference between victory and equity, the gap between legal ideal and legal actuality, because we have maintained to significant degree in our daily lives the conceptual system that helped produce battle as a means of dispute settlement. It is not just our legal profession which functions within polarity's frame. Too often—so do most of the rest of us.

Our either-or habits have become increasingly inadequate to technological and human demands; they are increasingly strained by pressures of a society grown complex beyond our conceptual readiness. Our words are more and more distanced from deeds, our intentions and claims distanced from acts on an overwhelming scale: personal as well as societal. We deny to too many others their hu-

man connection and, failing to see what we do, betray too frequently our declared best values. A kind of moral schizophrenia ravages
our lives. Blindness to that split is, inevitably, single-perspective's
end product. But in today's world, such blindness endangers us all.
For so long as that tunnel vision persists, justice will be inequitable;
personal lives will move from botch to shamble; and "progress"—
polluting air, land, and sea—will disastrously neglect the interdependence of all things natural. Governments will deceive the governed and lives will be expendable—on our streets, as well as in all
those pockets of disadvantage and defenselessness at home and
abroad.

The distancing of man from man is implicit in the bipolar, adversary ethic that permeates our world view.

"Every philosophy," Alfred North Whitehead wrote, "is tinged
with the coloring of some secret imaginative background, which
never emerges explicitly into its trains of reasoning."[17] Western philosophy is colored by our ancestral either-or, Righteous versus
Damned. That imaginative background still tinges—despite modern
awareness of the murkiness of motives and ambivalence of circumstance—our view of man. That view has particular ethical consequence. Within its logic, man is seen as a "free actor": free of social, biological, familial, circumstantial context, free to choose and
thus entirely responsible for his own sin or salvation.[18] According to
psychologist Daryl J. Bem, this concept of man underlies traditional
Christian thought; Western societies rest largely upon it.[19] But the
salient emphasis of a Right-Wrong system is less the free actor's responsibility than it is a vision of the victim as Sinner and (because he
had absolute "free choice") chief agent of what retribution he has
incurred. By the same token, he who imposes retribution becomes
an agent of Right: a sacred executioner.

Yet within that system, the free actor is hardly free at all. Habi-
tuated to bipolarity's superior-inferior frame of reference, he is peculiarly vulnerable both to uncritically accepting authority's claim
of "rightness" and to identifying with that authority. In either case
he considers himself relatively nonresponsible for his acts. His morality will consist in serving Right—any way necessary, and without
much question; for Right, by definition, need neither question itself
nor look to external criteria for validation. Thus, whether obeying
an explicit command or some self-arrogated, internalized directive

seen (under any number of religious, philosophical, or political guises) as authority's will—and therefore "moral"—the process is the same. The sacred executioner is captive of an ethic within which the most odious deeds may find logical consistency and be thought justice.

So assassins may be motivated. So revolutionary groups, operating within the same conceptual system (albeit with different goals) as those they aim to replace, may proceed by the very same means they revile in their enemies. Single perspective, trapped in two-choice polemic, judges the other but cannot see the self. The two are in different fields of view.

For instance: In the 12th century, Church courts proclaimed the equality of all men before the law, but initiated the Inquisition. "The Church shrinks from bloodshed," canon motto declared, but the Church demanded that the civil personnel to whom it handed over its heretics, torture and burn the dissenters.[20] The Church officially prayed that victims' lives be spared, but those lay administrators who did spare lives were themselves liable to be hauled before the Inquisition as heretics.[21] In 17th-century England, although the judicial murder of so-called witches was slowing due to a general disposition to attribute natural causes to happenings,[22] England's lord chief justice once more hanged two women as sorcerers. Stating that witchcraft's reality was unquestionable, he explained first that "the Scriptures had affirmed so much; and secondly the wisdom of all nations had affirmed laws against such persons, which is an argument of their confidence of such a crime."[23] Within single perspective, premise and conclusion are usually the same.

America has its own idiosyncratic version of Righteous-Damned. That version is Winners-Losers. Winners-Losers colors our public and private lives, as well as our law.

Losers, predominantly, settled our nation: younger sons with neither purse nor title; refugees from religious and political persecutions, from slums and ghettos, from hopelessness, from debtor's prisons and famines. With each new wave of immigrants, new Losers came. But they were Losers come here to win. And win they did: not merely, for many, opportunity and wealth; but a continent from its rightful owners. Those who won, however, did so essentially in struggle *against* wilderness and fellow man. Winning was the American dream and ultimate blessedness; losing the nightmare and unforgivable sin.

That imaginative background has poisoned our democratic purpose and Constitutional ideals as effectively as it has negated our judicial intent. Though our government officially declared itself formed to establish justice and promote the general welfare, in practice the American frontier—requiring the conquerors' brutality perhaps as often as bravery—was very much an "each for himself" society. Further, under 18th-century laissez-faire theory (the ideological umbrella of the period) any regulation of behavior was noxious. That ideology, relying upon a "natural order" to produce a balanced social good by means of unfettered individual action, had been in many ways a progressive political instrument. Arguing that each individual is the best judge of his own welfare, laissez-faire was a major doctrinal force in the extension of political franchise, the improvement of judicial procedure, the promotion of liberty of contract, and of religious freedom as well. Nevertheless, underlying that theory was a mechanical view of society as essentially an aggregate of individual atoms each of which, by pursuing without limit its own best interests, would achieve the general benefit. That mechanical view ignores inequities in individual strength, aggressiveness, and even value systems. Liberty of contract, for instance, is a reality only where equality of bargaining power exists—and the bargainers are willing to fight for their advantage. Thus laissez-faire doctrine, embodied in public policy, served to perfection both the preemptor of Indian land and the later robber-baron financial conglomerate as well. "Against," euphemized as "competition," has remained the characteristic stance of American success. "Them as has, gets" (Matthew 25:29) and the shafted deserve their shaft.

Thus, still: Though we call Hitler's death camps foreign barbarity, and dub Mafia violence subculture aberration, we have named our own Indian genocide a form of manifest destiny, and our own wars holy. Death has frequently enough been our own "final solution" for other peoples. Though we fought our most recent war (as always) under the banner of humanist values, yet Marine recruits in military training were "punched and humiliated if they failed to understand that the term 'Vietnamese' was never to be used; only the epithets 'gook,' 'dink,' 'slant' were allowed for friend and foe alike."[24] We disdain the Spanish Inquisition, but have made peace with government-opened mail, telephone taps, and regulations such as Federal Law 91-508, which tacitly sanctions investigation by insurance companies into our "character, general reputation, personal characteristics and mode of living. . . ." From Little League ex-

cesses[25] to the political process by which contestants outspend, out-
sham, outsmear and outmisrepresent each other to power—in our
society, nice guys tend to finish last. Winning is, in fact, an American cultural addiction that even the heaviest pratfall or most arrant
defeat may not cure. On the envelopes of those letters Watergate-
thief G. Gordon Liddy writes his children from prison, he still prints
the same message: "Win!"[26] Losers rarely question the game. They
only plot to play more cannily next time.

Such reaction represents neither lack of intelligence, nor mis-
placed loyalty to a value structure or cause. Rather, within an either-
or orientation, abandonment of criticalness in response to accepted
authority becomes almost automatic. That abandonment may range
from the ludicrous to the murderous.

In Chicago, in 1974, a lecturer appeared before an audience of
fifty-five persons among whom were educators, school administrators, psychiatrists, psychologists, and social workers.[27] The speaker
was introduced as "Dr. Myron L. Fox, an authority on the application of mathematics to human behavior," and his topic was
supposedly "mathematical game theory as applied to physical
education." In actuality, "Dr. Fox" was an actor. And his lecture
was, literally, nonsense. Specifically, it was "pure, meaningless
double-talk." Yet when his listeners were afterward asked their
opinions, at least forty-two people responded that Fox's material
was well organized and had stimulated their thinking. One critic
opined it "too intellectual a presentation." Fourteen thought Fox
had dwelt too long upon the obvious. But of the fifty-five there assembled, not one learned person described Fox's content as gibber-
ish—nor realized the entire performance a hoax.

Social psychologist Stanley Milgram, conducting a different experiment, discovered something more malign: the extreme willing-
ness of adults to go to almost any lengths on authority's command.[28]
Specifically, ordinary people, drawn from working, managerial, and
professional levels, were induced—obeying an experimenter's orders—to deliver electric shocks ranging from 15 to 450 volts to
another human being (an actor who actually received no shock at
all). In *Obedience to Authority,* Milgram reports that many subjects
will obey the experimenter no matter how vehemently the victim
pleads,[29] no matter his shrieks of pain nor even his claiming the le-
thal potential of heart trouble.[30] Out of more than one thousand participants, almost two thirds fell into the category of obedient sub-

jects, and one quarter of those continued to the administration of the highest shock level.[31]

In the process of such behavior, Milgram says, several rationales occur. Most commonly, the subject sees himself as not responsible for his own actions, attributing all initiative to the experimenter, a "legitimate authority"[32] whose agent he is. Another adjustment is one in which the subject denies the human element behind agencies and institutions, and sees himself as serving not the experimenter, but the higher purpose of an abstract science.[33] At the same time, many subjects "harshly devalue the victim *as a consequence* of acting against him . . . [they view him] as an unworthy individual, whose punishment was made inevitable by his own deficiencies of intellect and character."[34]

The Stanford Prison Study, conducted in 1971 by social psychologist Philip Zimbardo, produced similar findings.[35] That study was designed to simulate a prison environment, with volunteer college students, selected for emotional stability and maturity, playing the roles of prisoners and guards over a two-week period. The "guards" were uniformed, provided with mirrored glasses, billy clubs, and whistles, and given permission to exercise control and enforce rules no matter how meaningless. "Prisoners" were dressed in smocks and stocking caps, locked in barren cells, and deprived of most of their rights. Within six days the experiment was abruptly terminated—because it had already created an extreme social pathology. The "guards" were behaving with consistent cruelty, devising ever fresh ways to degrade the inmates; while "prisoners" had suffered psychological breakdowns. The evil, experimenter Zimbardo believed, lay neither in guards nor convicts but rather in the authoritarian relationship itself, and in the roles that relationship—backed by institutional sanction—required.

Our educational system is probably our culture's prime means of imprinting those lessons. Zimbardo calls our schools "prisons of the mind," where we early learn to surrender intellectual autonomy and play out the prisoner-guard relationship.[36] The school's "good" child does not question his teachers, salaams to administrators, and jockeys hard on a grading curve where one person's gain is another's loss. In Milgram's words, the first twenty years of life are spent "functioning as a subordinate element in an authority system. . . ."[37] An anthropologist says,

In a society where competition for the basic cultural goods
is a pivot of action, people cannot be taught to love one
another, for those who do cannot compete with one another. . . . It thus becomes necessary for the school, without
appearing to do so, to teach children how to hate . . . for
our culture cannot tolerate the idea that babes should hate
each other. How does the school accomplish this ambigui-
ty? Obviously through competition itself, for what has
greater potential for creating hostility than competition? . . . The central obsession in education is fear of
failure.[38]

And the result for us all? John Steinbeck described it over a quarter century ago: "It has always seemed to me . . . the things we
admire in men, kindness and generosity, openness, honesty, understanding and feeling are the concomitants of failure in our system.
And those traits we detest, sharpness and greed, acquisitiveness,
meanness, egotism and self-interest, are the traits of success. And
while men admire the quality of the first, they love the produce of
the second."[39] There is the irreconcilable and widening contradiction.

The win-lose model—its values increasingly disparate, its vision
increasingly isolated from contextual variables and interpersonal
connection—ends at war with itself. Two psychologists report,

The American competitive spirit . . . has produced a culture whose children are systematically irrational. Ten-year-
olds . . . repeatedly failed to get rewards for which they
were striving because they competed in games that required
cooperation. In other situations these children worked hard
and even sacrificed their own rewards in order to reduce the
rewards of their peers. . . . They learn to pursue personal
ends and to block opponents in conflict-of-interest situations, even where mutual assistance is required for goal at-
tainment.[40]

Social critics increasingly complain of the "alienation" of man
from man. That alienation is only single perspective's lonely path—
the right hand become enemy of the left. And that split is accelerating at nearly every level. As we are dealt with, so do we learn to deal
in return; diminishing ourselves in the process.

According to a former advertising executive (who might as well have been referring to our government, our industries, our politics or our law): After twenty-five years in the ad business, one cardinal principle emerged—"Don't worry whether it's true or not. Will it sell? . . . The American people . . . are now being had from every bewildering direction . . . the key will-it-sell principle and the employed techniques are the same . . . whether someone is trying to sell us war, God, anti-communism or a new, improved deodorant. Deceit is the accepted order of the hour."[41]

Where polarity shapes thinking and winning is the orthodoxy to which men chiefly adhere, deceit is absolutely justifiable. Where allegiance is at the same time nominally given to such nonadversary values as brotherhood, equity, honor, and interpersonal responsibility, moral schizophrenia becomes inevitable: a social disease that our legal procedure, likewise split between lip-service to truth and practice of deception, neither treats nor cures, but only spreads. Justice Learned Hand remarked, "The administration of justice is a good test of the civilization of the people where it exists."[42] Most often, we fail that test.

Like other "primitive and barbarous peoples" before us, we let single-perspective's blinkers limit our choices—legal and societal—to witches and sacred executioners. Adversary rationale tells us we require primitive tools; yet so long as we have only such tools, we will learn no better ways.

More important: Even those of us who *do* know better ways and most sincerely wish to use them, too often cannot. For within the adversary bind, the hands of the most conscientious lawyer, judge, and juror are largely tied. The bar of justice is a bar indeed.

PART FIVE

The Philosophy of "As If"

The law "is no stranger to the philosophy of the 'As If.' It has built up many of its doctrines by a make-believe that things are other than they are."
—*Benjamin Cardozo*[1]

12

"BASTARDS, ACTORS
AND JUGGLERS"

Though most codes of the 13th and 14th centuries deprived champions and their children after them ("in common with bastards, actors and jugglers"[2]) of all legal privileges such as succeeding to property or bearing witness, the Italians, almost alone among European peoples, saw matters differently. Accepting the existence of champions as a necessity, Italians were disposed to elevate rather than denigrate the profession.[3]

American society incorporates both images: the lawyer as Shyster Penultimate, fixer, finagler, and ambulance chaser; and the lawyer as White Knight, "prestigious, dignified counselor, attractive to women, literate, a pillar of his community."[4] But the Italian view predominates. We elevate our attorneys to many of the most strategic and honored positions our society holds: focal in industry, Wall Street, our chief political parties, government.

Beginning with the Constitutional Convention of 1787, two thirds of our Congressmen and Senators have been lawyers.[5] Of the thirty-seven* men who have occupied the United States Presidency to date, over two thirds (72 percent) studied law.[6] The American legal profession, commented de Tocqueville in the 19th century, is an

---

*Cleveland served two separate terms as twenty-second and twenty-fourth President. Ford is therefore the thirty-seventh man to hold the office.

aristocracy, "the most powerful, if not the only, counterpoise to the democratic element" in our society.[7] Lawyers, in their collective impact, are sometimes held to be a fourth arm of government.[8]

Under a vast guise of job titles, it is the lawyer who makes the deals and breaks them; writes the laws and crafts their loopholes; channels the money and launders it; arranges "deniability" and obscures duplicity's tracks. Shyster and Knight submerge beneath that overarching actuality.

In Washington, where the federal bureaucracy is the power, the most effective lawyers are familiar with at least one government branch. Often the lawyer worked there, or perhaps ran it. In New York, where money is power, the most prestigious firms have solid ties to Wall Street. In Chicago, where politics is power, the 140-man firm of Kirkland, Ellis, Chaffetz and Masters has political connections in both parties.[9]

The lawyer is not merely summoned after the fact of litigation contemplated or quarrel begun. He is increasingly the before-the-fact policymaker for those financial, industrial, and political interests that, together with the military, constitute American's unelected command. In *The Superlawyers,* Joseph C. Goulden calls the Washington lawyer ". . . the man American business depends upon to 'subdue . . . and shape' the federal government. . . . [His] role is that of advising clients how to *make* laws, and to make the most of them."[10] There are in Washington alone five or six hundred attorneys who deal with the federal government as lobbyists or trade association officials; lawyers at all levels from President down through Foreign Service officers and FBI agents.[11] Lawyers stack the advisory committees that shape the policies of Federal regulatory agencies.

Professor Rodell writes, "It is the lawyers who run our civilization for us—our governments, our business, our private lives. . . . It is not the business men, no matter how big, who run our economic world. . . . The whole elaborate structure of industry and finance is a lawyer-made house. We all live in it, but the lawyers run it."[12]

We behave "as if" those lawyers were honorable men: all, all honorable men; even those lawyers who may help their clients "keep on the marketplace a host of consumer products—ranging from pharmaceuticals to pesticides and automobiles—which are gravely dangerous to the American citizen."[13] Within our adversary ethic, they *are* honorable men. They are only doing what all good attorneys (and all good Americans) are supposed to do—win; even the most scrupulous of them. Even attorneys like Samuel Williston.

Once upon a time, Williston, called by a colleague "One of the most distinguished and conscientious lawyers I or any man have ever known,"[14] was defending a client in civil suit. In the course of trial, Williston discovered in his client's letter file material potentially damaging to the man's case. The opposition failed to demand the file; nor did Williston offer it. His client won. But, recounts Williston in his autobiography, the judge in announcing his decision made clear that his ruling was based in part on his belief in one critical fact: a fact Williston, through a letter from the file in his possession, knew to be unfounded.[15]

Did Williston, that "most conscientious lawyer," speak up? Did he correct the Court's unfounded belief, the better to serve both truth and justice? He did not.

"Though," he wrote, "I had in front of me a letter which showed his [Honor's] error," Williston kept silent. Nor did he question the propriety of his behavior. For, said he, the lawyer "is not only not obliged to disclose unfavorable evidence, but it is a violation of his duty to his client if he does so."[16]

The overwhelming majority of Williston's profession agrees with him, in criminal as well as civil cases. Charles Curtis states, "We may share his discomfort, but there is no doubt of the propriety of his behavior."[17] An "eminent panel"[18] of the American Bar Association's Committee on Professional Ethics and Grievances has gone further. The Bar mandates that when a client lies to the judge by claiming no prior record, his lawyer should remain silent though he knows his client is lying.[19] Supreme Court Justice Harlan explained, the lawyer "of necessity may become an obstacle to truth-finding, in fulfilling his professional responsibilities."[20]

But what of the fact that the lawyer is not only, in Harlan's phrase, "half litigant," but is *at the same time* an "officer of the court, participating in a search for truth"?[21] What of the American Bar Association's own Canons of Professional Ethics, whose "plain meaning," according to Justice Department executive assistant Richard L. Braun, "prohibits attempts by attorneys to *deceive, confuse or defraud the court*"?[22] (emphasis mine) How can the lawyer at the same time both conceal and search for truth? He can not, of course.

I maintain that the famous "search for truth" is the major "as if" in the game of legal make-believe. I maintain that the image of the lawyer as participant in that search is the second major "as if." I maintain that the goals of winning on one hand and truth on the other are mutually exclusive, indeed irreconcilable contradictions between which the laywer is caught—in a flat conflict of interest. But in that conflict, winning must take precedence over truth. Winning, Guérard comments, is the profession's "honor, duty, as well as profit."[23] That is the treason of our adversary system.

Conflict and treason are vigorously denied. The legal profession, equating the drive for victory with the search for truth, generally insists that ". . . investigating and presenting the facts from a partisan perspective . . . [maximizes the likelihood] that all relevant fact will be ferreted out and placed before the ultimate fact-finder in as persuasive a manner as possible."[24] Further, law-men deny that withholding of relevant fact either deceives, confuses, or defrauds the court: "Non-disclosure . . . does not mean affirmative participation in fraud. . . ."[25] The legal profession distinguishes, in other words, between the *overt* proffering of false material ("affirmative participation") and the *covert* withholding of true material ("nondisclosure"). Overt is fraud; covert is not. In fact, covert deception is the adversary lawyer's ethical obligation.

Charles Curtis emphasizes, "I have said that a lawyer may not lie to the court. But it may be a lawyer's duty not to speak."[26] Similarly goes the American Bar's recommended Oath of Admission: "I . . . will never seek to mislead the Judge or jury by any artifice or false *statement* of fact or law. . . ."[27] (emphasis mine)

But speech and silence may have the same result. Both may limit that quantity of relevant fact from which the fact finders must draw their "wise and informed decision."[28] Silence as well as speech may alter decision utterly. Silence may do even more: by concealing a client's crime, free him to do violence once more. How then does the lawyer have "a *duty* not to disclose, but not the right *actively* to deceive or defraud"?[29] Why are passive and active deception not equivalent? Why is nondisclosure not fraud? What in the world can the difference be? Simple. "Partisan perspective" is the key.

Within that partisan perspective, the side the lawyer serves *is* truth. Search is unnecessary. Sale is the point. And while overt deception may repel the buyer and lose the deal, covert deception maintains that *appearance* of honesty crucial both to the pitchman's success and the general repute of the legal trade. Further still: since partisan perspective does not see the self as part of context, the "nonaction" of silence allows the attorney more easily to view himself as nonaccountable for silence's result. He has "done" nothing. He can have victory and moral purity too.

In his pitch the lawyer must, of course, vigorously enact the factual purity of whatever Faith has hired him; an adversary theatrical convention in which active and passive deception merge. Purity's role is a partisan essential, expected by client, judge and jury. The jury in particular, "as every trial lawyer knows,"[30] is alert to, and will be greatly affected by, any indication that the attorney believes his client guilty. Thus the lawyer must proceed with every sound of belief, despite any knowledge he may have to the contrary, and despite his coprofessionals' awareness of the obligatory charade. However, as one judge commented, "The manifest appearance of a believer is all that is wanted; and this can be well acted after a little study. . . ."[31]

Besides that requisite "appearance of belief" is another reason for nondisclosure's deception: the "sacred trust of confidentiality." Lawyer-client privacy, the profession holds, must "upon all occasions be inviolable,"[32] or else the client "would only dare to tell his counsellors half his case."[33] The result would be impairment of the "perfect freedom of consultation by client with attorney [which is] . . . essential to the administration of justice."[34]

(Indeed, the legal profession considers lawyer-client confidentiality analogous to that of doctor-patient. But the patient consults his doctor in order to get well, and does not recover at anyone else's expense. Adversary procedure, on the other hand, produces at least one loser for every winner; and, in the persons of humiliated witnesses, usually more.)

For example, the profession maintains, if the attorney (aware via his client's confidences that the adverse witness is telling the truth) fails to try to discredit or destroy that witness, the client may well feel betrayed, and confidence and candor between lawyer and client wither.[35] Our legal system, Dean Monroe Freedman states, "cannot tolerate such a result."[36] Adversary procedure, ostensibly serving truth, must deceive—or collapse.

That paradox, almost universally denied though it be, consistently trips the legal tongue:

Ehrlich, in *The Lost Art of Cross-Examination*, writes on page 57 that "The problem of truth and the search for the accurate, truthful witness is, has been, and will always be the endless occupation of the good cross-examiner."[37] But on page 50 of the very same text he has directed that ". . . if an honest witness is timid, the lawyer should, by cross-examination, play up that weakness in order to persuade the jury that the witness is concealing important facts."[38]

Wellman, in *The Art of Cross-Examination,* writes on page 22 that ". . . no substitute has ever been found for cross-examination as a means of separating truth from falsehood. . . ."[39] Yet 101 pages later he confesses that ". . . the *sole object* of cross-examination is to break the force of the adverse testimony. . . ."[40] (emphasis mine).

U.S. District Attorney David G. Bress declares in *American Criminal Law Quarterly* that ". . . the basic purpose of the trial is the determination of truth. . . ."[41] Two paragraphs earlier he has supported cross-examination as a means of limiting truth's impact.

Noonan, in the *Michigan Law Review,* insists that "An impartial, informed and wise decision presupposes that the person deciding the case has been given the truth. To furnish him with a lie is to mock impartiality, to mislead rather than to inform, and to stultify the decisional process rather than to make it an exploration leading to mature judgment."[42] Two pages later, he defends the ritual plea of not guilty, which may well do exactly what he has just deplored.[43]

Although officially the lawyer's conflict of interest does not exist, now and then (approximately once per decade) some legal maverick violates judicial *omertà* and lets the secret slip. It is a risky act. ("Anyone who preaches what he and his hearers practise must incur the gravest moral disapprobation," a writer once quipped.[44])

In the 1950s, for example, there was Charles Curtis. Curtis, an attorney of more than thirty years' experience, loved the practice of law.[45] But first in an article and then in a book he wrote, ". . . one of the functions of a lawyer is to lie for his client."[46] A lawyer's "freedom from the strict bonds of veracity and of the law are the two chief assets of the profession."[47] The "relations which a lawyer has with his client on one hand and his court on the other are somewhat bigamous. . . ."[48] "I don't see why we must not come out roundly and say that one of the functions of the lawyer is the disagreeable duty of choosing between being false to his client or false to the truth."[49] And finally, "I don't know any other career that offers ampler opportunity for both the enjoyment of virtue and the exercise of vice, or, if you please, the exercise of virtue and the enjoyment of vice, except possibly the ancient rituals which were performed in some temples by vestal virgins, in others by sacred prostitutes."[50]

The chairman of the American Bar Association's Committee on Professional Ethics, Henry Drinker, was not amused. Wrote he, "I read the [Curtis] article with amazement and indignation; . . . indignation that he should publish, to be read by law students and young lawyers, so many distorted and misleading statements as to the lawyer's duty to his clients, to the courts, to the public. . . . A lawyer need never lie for his client."[51] It was Drinker's own Bar Committee which held that, when a lawyer's client lies to the court, the attorney should support that lie with his silence.[52]

In the 1960s there was Monroe Freedman. Freedman, then George Washington University professor of law and codirector of the Criminal Trial Institute of Washington, D.C., presented to the institute a paper that began: "In almost any area of legal counseling and advocacy, the lawyer may be faced with the dilemma of either betraying the confidential communications of his client or participating to some degree in the purposeful deception of the court. . . ."[53]

Professional hackles snapped to attention. Several judges, none of whom had either heard the lecture or read it,[54] complained to the Committee on Admissions and Grievances of the District Court for the District of Columbia, urging Freedman's disbarment or suspension. Only after four months of proceedings, including a hearing, two meetings, and a review by eleven federal district court judges, did the committee announce its decision "to proceed no further in the matter."[55]

Freedman still persisted. The following year he wrote in the *Georgetown Law Journal*, ". . . the role of advocate and counselor in an adversary system may require the attorney to withhold truthful and relevant information from the court in a particular case—even though the search for truth may thereby be frustrated to some extent—because greater injury could be done to the adversary system of truth-finding if clients had reason to be fearful of confiding in their attorneys."[56] Freedman asked, "Is it proper to put a witness on the stand when you know he will commit perjury? . . . In a substantial number of instances, the attorney who recognizes that he functions in an adversary system . . . will be compelled . . . to answer yes. . . ."[57]

The legal journals rumbled again.

Richard L. Braun (perhaps innocent of the import of his phrasing) replied: ". . . I submit it to be a fundamental premise that neither prosecutor nor defense counsel should *affirmatively* participate in deceiving the court or jury. . . ."[58] A lawyer, he said, "should *never* put a witness *other than the defendant* on the stand if he knows that the witness will give perjured testimony. . . ."[59] (last emphasis mine) Three judges, including Warren E. Burger, complained to the dean of Freedman's law school. Burger declared himself unable to believe that anyone who was "law-trained, mature and responsible,"[60] could have spoken as did Freedman. Elsewhere Burger said, ". . . properly understood, the duties of a lawyer to the court can never be in conflict with his duty to his client."[61] ". . . it is no more the duty of defense counsel to win his case at all costs . . . than it is the duty of the prosecution to gain a conviction in every case."[62] And on two subsequent occasions, Burger demanded that Freedman not appear with him on panels discussing legal ethics.[63] It was Burger who would use the testimony of the crime victim's repute to give the lie to that truth she tells.

In the 1970s there is Martin Erdmann. Erdmann, "one of the five or ten best defense lawyers in New York,"[64] was interviewed by a national publication concerning the administration of criminal justice. Asked about the lawyer's responsibility to be honest, Erdmann replied, "My *only* responsibility is to my client. And not to suborn perjury, and not to lie personally. My client may lie as much as he wants."[65] Further, he commented, "I have nothing to do with justice. Justice is not even part of the equation."[66] Appellate division judges he called ". . . the whores who become madams."[67]

Erdmann had gone too far. The judges of the New York State Appellate Division charged him before the Bar Association with "professional misconduct."[68] The Bar obediently rebuked him. Still unappeased, the justices of one department brought charges against Erdmann in another department of the same division—so that while the first department was complainant, its divisional colleagues were judge and jury.[69] Refusing even to hear testimony, those evenhanded justices censured Martin Erdmann once more.[70]

Erdmann's misconduct lay in roasting the judiciary as well as revealing for lay ears the place of truth in the adversary lexicon. But the roast was perhaps the more heinous offense. For while in ancient days the bravos fought each other, in modern battle they are expected to reserve their lances for the adverse litigant and his witnesses. That misconduct the profession directs against the *layman* receives far more casual response. In 1973–74, for example, 4,187 citizen complaints were filed with the California Bar. Of these, less than 50 percent *even reached preliminary investigating committees*; and only 276 (less than 7 percent) produced even the issuance of formal charges.[71]

Ponder, then, the sort of complaint that legal officialdom deems unworthy of notice at all. (Names of principals and identifying dates are changed and extraneous material is deleted.)

Board of Governors
The State Bar of California
1230 West Third Street
Los Angeles, California 90017   May 17, 1973

GENTLEMEN:
On January 7, 1973, I filed with your Los Angeles office a complaint regarding attorney William Blatt. That complaint set forth, in detail, facts concerning Mr. Blatt's use in an adversary proceeding of stolen material (a personal file and correspondence); material taken without either the knowledge or permission of the persons to whom it belonged, nor ever given by those persons to Mr. Blatt or to anyone else.

On April 23, your local Administrative Committee No. Two informed me by letter that "the facts are insufficient to warrant disciplinary proceedings by the State Bar"; a phrase which your Staff Attorney translated as meaning "insufficient basis for proceeding."

May I most respectfully request your reconsideration of this decision, as one seriously damaging to that spirit which is intended to infuse both the law, and that association of its practitioners, the Bar.

First, obviously, in a number of ways the law has attempted to forbid the receipt and use of illegally obtained material: Among those ways, second-hand dealers are enjoined from receiving goods which they have reason to believe, by inference from surrounding circumstance, may have been stolen. The police are enjoined from using material which has been illegally obtained. For anyone, it is a misdemeanor to open and read, or cause to be read, any letter not addressed to himself.

I am aware that none of these points applies, in literal letter, to the situation I have brought to your attention: My litigation was civil rather than criminal. And there is no proof that it was Mr. Blatt himself who opened the correspondence he read. (Indeed he has apparently stated that it was his client who brought him all the material, opened.)

Cleaving to that "letter of the law," your Committee clearly had "insufficient basis" for proceeding. However, the spirit which is intended to infuse that law stands, I believe, equally clear. That spirit stands opposed to theft, and to the profiting, monetarily or in any other way, by another's theft.

Mr. Blatt is an officer of a court system which is meant to represent and embody that spirit. He is likewise a member of a Bar which, in its Code of Professional Responsibility, speaks also for that spirit. For example:

EC 1-5: [the lawyer] "should refrain from all illegal and *morally reprehensible* conduct . . . respect for the law should be *more than a platitude.*"

EC 1-6: [the lawyer should] "strive to avoid not only professional impropriety but also the *appearance of impropriety.*"

Second: I believe there can be little doubt that Mr. Blatt (or indeed anyone of average intelligence, coming into possession of material not addressed to himself, and belonging to persons with whom he is engaged in contest) was in no way, by any reasoning whatsoever, entitled to assume that the material which he received had in fact been intended by its owners either for him, or for his client. I believe it altogether unlikely that the contrary probability did not in fact occur to him: that it had been improperly, and illegally, obtained.

I believe that in the absence of first-hand direction from the rightful owners as to their intention, Mr. Blatt (like policemen, second-hand dealers, or any other citizen) was obliged either to inquire that intention, or to return the material without use.

That he did neither was, I believe, at the very least both "morally reprehensible" and a gross "appearance of impropriety." It was surely a violation of that ethical and moral spirit of which the attorney, "because of his position in society" (EC 1-5) should be prime exemplar.

Third: I believe that for the Bar to refuse disciplinary action in this matter, is to subvert the spirit of that law it has sworn to uphold; vitiate the moral imperative and deny the intention of its own organization. Such refusal lends support to the negative stereotype of the lawyer as cynical evader of legal spirit through sophistical manipulation of the legal letter. Such refusal implies that behavior such as Mr. Blatt's is so widespread in the legal profession that to discipline him would be to reproach all. Such refusal implies that the lawyer is a peculiarly privileged member of society, outside those ethical requirements which apply to all others. Such refusal implies license to theft, and to profiting by theft, so long as the thief or recipient is a lawyer sufficiently versed in the law to avoid legal culpability—with client to serve and fee to be made.

Such refusal can only be one more contribution, by the Bar itself, to that disrespect for the Bar which is becoming pandemic.

If respect for the law's spirit is truly "more than a platitude," I urge reconsideration of your Committee's decision.

Very Truly Yours,
JANET LEWIS

* * *

Janet Lewis
Los Angeles
California   May 30, 1973

DEAR MRS. LEWIS:

This office has received your letter of May 17, 1973, directed to the Board of Governors.

However, despite the eloquent appeal contained in your letter, it is my firm conviction that, without more, the Board of Governors will decline to order Local Administrative Committee No. Two to proceed with a preliminary hearing.

Under the circumstances, I would like to have a State Bar Investigator speak with your ex-husband concerning the matter [of] the attorney's prior knowledge of the file. . . . As soon as I hear further from you, with Mr. Lewis' address, I shall proceed with your case.

Very Truly Yours,
CHRISTIANA G. BRYSON
Staff Attorney
The State Bar of California

Christiana G. Bryson
Staff Attorney
State Bar of California
1230 West Third Street
California 90017   June 28, 1973

DEAR MISS BRYSON:
Your letter of May 30, together with our subsequent conversation, makes it clear that the Board of Governors will
not summon Mr. Blatt to a hearing without definitive information from his client, Mr. Lewis, concerning the manner in
which Mr. Blatt came into possession of the stolen material.
The Board misses the central point. That point is *receipt
and use*. If God Himself had dropped the material into Mr.
Blatt's lap and urged, "Use it, Willie!", the choice as to
whether or not to do so would still have been Blatt's. There
is nothing Mr. Lewis could tell you that might possibly alter
this point. Nor, I believe, would he if he could. Blatt is Lewis' attorney of many years standing. They mutually stood to
benefit from the use of the stolen file. To expect help from
one against the other in the matter is as realistic as expecting
one of Ma Barker's boys to finger Ma.
More important, *it doesn't matter*. Receipt and use were
discretionary decisions. Mr. Blatt, with every reason in the
world to believe, or at very least suspect, the material was
stolen, deliberately chose to accept it and proceed. Mr.
Lewis is not a member of the Bar. Mr. Blatt is. *It is not Lewis' testimony, but Blatt's, that the Bar must hear.*
For the Bar to refuse even the appearance of holding Mr.
Blatt responsible for his freely chosen actions, is irrefutable
Bar sanction of, and complicity in, "legal" theft and tainted
evidence. One can only assume, sadly and cynically, that
the Bar's behavior in such situations was laughably familiar
to Mr. Blatt when he felt free to proceed.
I shall appreciate your forwarding this letter to the Board
of Governors, together with Mr. Lewis' address, which I
enclose. My real thanks for the personal courtesy and help
you yourself have extended me.

Very Truly Yours,
JANET LEWIS

And the upshot? Silence. Silence entire, from that day to this.

* * *

Even the most honorable attorney may prefer to ignore such "as if" worms at the adversary core. According to an anthropologist, people are " . . . self-correcting mechanisms. They are self-corrective against disturbance, and if the obvious is not of a kind that they can easily assimilate without internal disturbance, their self-corrective mechanisms work to sidetrack it. . . ."[72] Even Jerome Frank.

Frank, eminent lawyer, scholar, federal judge, chairman of the SEC, was a prolific critic of legal behavior and attitudes. He called our trial procedure " . . . the equivalent of throwing pepper in the eyes of a surgeon when he is performing an operation,"[73] and declared, "John Q. Citizen should be told of the flaws in the workings of the courts . . . "[74] But Frank, too, wavered in the crunch.

Professor Rodell recounts that when he was first mulling over the notion of writing *Woe Unto You, Lawyers!* (with its "cold truth about the lawyers and their Law"[75]) he outlined his ideas to a lawyer who was "not only able but also extraordinarily frank and perceptive about his profession. 'Sure,' he said, 'but why give the show away?' That clinched it."[76] Rodell published his book in 1939. Although Jerome Frank ultimately contributed the preface to *Woe*'s second edition in 1957, it had been Frank, Rodell revealed many years later, who had originally protested "giving the show away."[77]

That show is simply this: adversary ritual demands of all the same dance. It provides for both the highest and lowest of ends, the very same means. When he enters the lists, the lawyer must reach for the tools at hand. Or lose. The most altruistic attorney on earth, limited to those means, must butcher truth—as the most virtuoso surgeon, required to operate with hammer and chisel, will produce a mangled patient.

Yes, the lawyer can eschew the worst of those tools, *if* his adversary does also. He can to some degree explore, reveal, reason, *if* his adversary does also—and if the Court will tolerate such prolongation. He can (in civil suit) settle amicably, reasonably, fairly, out of court, *if* his adversary will also. But when one side fights, so must the other—or fall. The lawyer may love that game or hate it. It is the only law-game in town.

Gung ho or not, however, the bravo is only doing the job we have sent him on. He/we are a functioning unit. After all, in battle, we want the best gun on *our* side.

* * *

And therein lies the third "as if" in the game of adversary make-believe. The myth is that *at the least*—novice or old hand, all-thumbs or ace—the lawyer *is* a true champion, fighting his client's fight, battling his opposite number to death or draw.

T'ain't necessarily so. The attorney's "win" and his client's need not be synonymous. In fact, they may be antithetical.

With high frequency, the only people *really* fighting are the litigants; spurred to spiraling reach by their lawyers. Unlike olden times, the bravos in modern adversary fray most often only pretend to fight each other. Today's battle is more commonly shadowboxing than substance; a show staged to justify fees as well as embroider that adversary histrionic in which the court personnel collude as supporting cast. For unless the client keeps his champion on business retainer or otherwise represents probability of a financial future, the two will likely never see one another again. Unless the client represents a matter, criminal or civil, which will bring the bravo fame, his value to the lawyer is temporary, marginal, and (aside from the possibility of referrals) most usually weighed as take the money and run.

Thus the lawyer may, for his own purposes, variously promote a lawsuit, swing a plea bargain or refuse a settlement, contrary to his client's welfare or wish. Since perspectives within a polar system remain alienated, interests may approximate, but self-interest rules. Generally, the attorney's interests coincide more closely with those of his fellow champion and even of court personnel than with his client's. Relationships within the court system are after all continuous, and properly nurtured will facilitate the lawyer's professional future. The nonretainer client, on the other hand, tends to be a one shot.

For these reasons, one sociologist calls the practice of law a confidence game. The court organization, says Abraham S. Blumberg, "possesses a thrust, purpose and direction of its own. It is grounded in pragmatic values, bureaucratic priorities, and administrative instruments. These exalt maximum production and the particularistic career designs of organizational incumbents . . . [they] exert a higher claim than the stated ideological goals of 'due process of law' and are often inconsistent with them."[78] While accused persons come and go, the court structure and its professional occupants remain. Close relations between the lawyer and all levels of that court personnel are a means of obtaining, maintaining, and building the lawyer's practice, and are a *sine qua non* in negotiating pleas and sentences as well.[79] They must be preserved at all costs.

The client then, Blumberg writes, is " . . . *a secondary figure in the court system . . . . He becomes a means to other ends of the organization's incumbents . . . .*The accused's lawyer has far greater professional, economic, intellectual and other ties to the various elements of the court system than he does to his own client. In short, the court is a closed community."[80] (emphasis mine)

That community, as an "ongoing system handling delicate tensions, [requires] . . . almost pathological distrust of 'outsiders' bordering on group paranoia."[81] Fearfully anticipating criticism, the court personnel are in effect "bound into an organized system of complicity. This consists of a work arrangement in which the patterned, covert, informal breaches and evasions of 'due process' are institutionalized, but are, nevertheless, denied to exist."[82] Even court stenographers and clerks "are on occasion pressed into service in support of a judicial need to 'rewrite' the record of a courtroom event."[83] I have seen statements of judicial prejudice disappear in transcript, while sometimes the court stenographer "hears" (in good faith or not) that which in terms of legal image *should* have happened—but didn't. That "should" remains the inviolable official record.

The audience for whose eyes the drama is mounted is, of course, the client. His fee is the grease that keeps the whole works going. Both client and fee are easily had. For legal service is largely intangible. Much of it is a lobbyist, brokerage, agent, sales representative sort of activity.[84] Therefore law practice lends itself particularly well to flimflam, in which the litigant is at once gallery and gull.

The following may happen: A defendant, charged with drunk driving, may wish to contest the matter. But some attorneys, carefully billing the client beforehand for consultation and estimated court time, proceed to submit the case on the basis of the police arrest record, without explaining to the client the implication of that act. In fact, such submission, requiring neither preparation nor presentation of defense, is equivalent to pleading "no contest"—which the client could have done himself, for free. The ploy provides the lawyer with quick profit for zero work; a bamboozle understood by the client too late.

All law practice, Blumberg says, involves to varying degrees

> . . . manipulation of the client and a stage management of
> the lawyer-client relationship so that at least an *appearance*
> of help and service will be forthcoming. . . . At the outset,
> the lawyer . . . employs . . . a measure of salespuff
> which may range from an air of unbounded self-confidence,
> adequacy, and dominion over events, to that of complete ar-
> rogance . . . in the larger firms, the furnishings and office
> trappings will serve as the background to help in impression
> management and client intimidation. In all firms . . . an
> access to secret knowledge, and *to the seats of power and
> influence is inferred, or presumed to a varying degree as the
> basic vendable commodity of the practitioners.*[85] (second
> emphasis mine)

The mark must, however, be kept off-balance, "soft" and need-
ful; criticality suspended. Therefore, lawyers seek at the same time
to keep their clients in a proper state of tension and to arouse in
them that "precise edge of anxiety which is calculated to encourage
prompt fee payment." [86]

The private criminal lawyer (whose client may well disappear behind bars) protects himself by demanding his fee in advance.[87]
"Inexorably, the amount of the fee is a function of the dollar value
of the crime committed, and is frequently set with meticulous precision at a sum which bears an uncanny relationship to that of the net
proceeds of the particular offense involved."[88] The private lawyer
indeed conditions "even the most obtuse clients to recognize that
there is a firm interconnection between fee payment and the zealous
exercise of professional expertise, secret knowledge, and organization 'connections' in their behalf."[89] Crime pays—the private legal
community.

Generally, in fact, the bigger the client's take has been, the more
extravagant and protracted the legal show. The entire courtroom
repertory company backs the act. Blumberg explains,

> The larger the fee the lawyer wishes to exact, the more im-
> pressive his performance must be, in terms of his stage ma-
> naged image as a personage of great influence and power in
> the court organization. Court personnel are keenly aware of
> the extent to which a lawyer's stock in trade involves the

precarious stage management of an image. . . . There is a tacit commitment to the lawyer by the court organization . . . to aid him in this. Such augmentation . . . tends to serve as the continuing basis for the *higher loyalty of the lawyer to the organization; his relationship with his client, in contrast, is transient, ephemeral and often superficial.*[90] (emphasis mine)

In that masquerade, the judge as well as other personnel "serve as backdrop for a scene charged with dramatic fire . . . the incongruity, superficiality and ritualistic character of the total performance is underscored by a visibly impassive, almost bored reaction on the part of the judge and other members of the court retinue."[91] There is afterward,

. . . a hearty exchange of pleasantries . . . wholly out of context in terms of the supposedly adversary nature of the preceding events. . . . No other aspect of their visible conduct so effectively serves to put even a casual observer on notice, that these individuals have claims upon each other. . . [which] range far beyond any priorities or claims a particular defendant may have.[92]

Whereas in civil matters the prospect of a higher fee lures the attorney towards litigation, in criminal matters the reverse obtains. Since the criminal fee has been collected in advance, profit here often urges the private lawyer to *avoid* battle; for the less time and effort spent, the greater his gain differential. To this end, Blumberg says, a variety of coercive techniques may be directed against an accused. Court personnel assist in some of these pressures, which include the tailoring of probation and psychiatric reports and the discretionary power of bail among the arsenal of weaponry.[93] The plea bargain may enuse.

That "cop-out ceremony"[94] is, however, only a different *kind* of battle—one in which the defendant may be persuaded, bribed, or blackmailed into taking a dive by his own manager. For it is the defense attorney, more immediately than police, prosecutor, or judge, who tends to twist the screws that produce the plea.

It is at this point that a defendant may first feel betrayed. For "while he had perhaps perceived the police and prosecutors to be adversaries, or possibly even the judge, the accused is wholly unprepared for his counsel's role-performance as an agent-mediator."[95] The lawyer may in fact be a double agent.[96] But as an officer of the court on one hand hand and his client's champion on the other, the attorney is beneficiary of a fund of trust in both camps, out of which his own self-interest banks. (While the plea bargain makes no economic difference to the public defender, it may certainly help speed his processing of backlog.)

Sometimes an additional humbug accompanies the plea bargain. According to an Office of Criminal Justice publication,[97] some prosecutors join with defense attorneys in convincing the client that a valuable service had been performed. Although both attorneys know that the original charges were too heavy to sustain and no real bargain has occurred, the client may be led to feel that a reduction in the charges has been well worth the fee the attorney demands for obtaining it. The client is duped into believing that he has benefited from a genuine negotiation.[98] For both lawyers, however, the case has been disposed of with minimum effort; while the defense attorney, paid for maximum, enjoys a tidy profit on the difference. Client, and truth in the matter, share the deficit.

Once the accused cries "Uncle!", the lawyer again switches hats. He now becomes a drama coach, directing his client in the enactment of penitent whose remorse merits the lesser charge.[99] That compulsory rote by which the defendant swears that he is entering his plea "freely, willingly and voluntarily, without promise, commitment or coercion," not only precludes any change of mind of appeal; it shields the court organization from charges of violation of that due process which has in truth been breached.[100] The sellout is wrapped and delivered—insured.

Likewise in civil suits, the litigant's interests and his champion's are essentially opposed. That opposition, flowing once more from the lawyer's basic identity as entrepreneur, is responsible for many of those behaviors that peculiarly characterize the legal trade.

For instance, attorneys tend automatically (and to the limit of the client's purse) to toss back and forth in prolix legalese as many complaints, replies, amended complaints, demurrers, interrogatories, and what-have-you as may be calculated to obstruct, divert, delay, and generally pad counsels' pockets. One judge calls this "a routine back-scratching operation among lawyers. That is how everyone makes a living."[101] That fee padding requires at the same time a certain routine sales patter. For example, the lawyer may claim to have negotiated over months when the matter has actually been agreed between attorneys in the first week. The lawyer may claim to have wrested an extraordinary settlement ("Believe me, you came out smelling like a rose!") which is in fact less than the minimum a court would have awarded. If the client smells skunk rather than rose and asks a too-pertinent question, the attorney one-ups, "Look, all the ramifications would take me days to explain. You'd have to have gone to law school to understand."

"Chambers" is the scene of many a civil sellout; one motivated perhaps most often by the lawyer's currying (for himself) future favor from the judge, before whom he expects to appear again in other matters. In chambers' off-the-record secrecy, the lawyer may well make an arrangement that scuttles his client's case. But that agreement will appear in court as the Bench's order, against which, the law-man assures his client, appeal is impracticable. Particularly if the case is a one-shot.

Although the profession's ideal client may be "a rich man who is scared to death,"[102] the ordinary litigant has limited financial resource. When that available milk has run out, the champion may take his pail and trot to the next dispenser, leaving his client high and dry despite what appeal or legal recourse may be indicated.

Contrariwise, although the compromise of settlement may be for the litigant far more practical in time, tears, and dollars, it may be for the lawyer very impractical indeed. Settlement forgoes that courtroom big-time which warrants the lawyer's star-pay. Therefore, attorneys may aid and abet each other in a repertoire of settlement dodges. Writing in a legal journal, an author who prefers to sign himself Anonymous calls them *Games Lawyers Play.*

The plaintiff's lawyer begins:[103] He may demand an exorbitant sum to settle, or may oversell his client on the possibilities of gain, thereby prompting the client's refusal of any reasonable settlement offer. In a negligence case (where he gets a percentage of the award) he may declare himself "reluctant to take responsibility for deciding what this paralyzed man should accept." He may use a pretrial judge's unrealistically high recommendation for settlement as a basis for refusing any lesser sums. He may direct antagonistic measures at his opponents neatly calculated to close down communications and preclude settlement negotiations.

The defense lawyer responds:[104] He may sell his client on the necessity of "starting from a good bargaining position" or "position of strength" by "exposing the weakness of the plaintiff's case" before talking settlement. That exposure may, however, require endless hours of between-lawyers make-work ("discovery") such as depositions and accounting—particularly in noncontingency cases. Or the defense lawyer may proclaim negotiation pointless because the plaintiff's attorney is "not to be trusted." He may represent himself as a crusader, opposed on principle to the venality of plaintiffs and their counsel. Or, perhaps empowered by a conciliatory client to "offer up to $150,000," the lawyer may instead offer some scandalously low figure in the knowledge that the plaintiff will be enraged and settlement be forestalled.

In other words, Anonymous explains, each side uses the other's game to play his own.[105] It is a game plan to which only the champions are privy; one whose incentives are strictly monetary; and from which the clients' interests are excluded. Understandably, then, the demand for a retainer is common civil practice—in case the client tires prematurely of the sport, takes his marbles, and goes home.

Usually, however, the experienced attorney calculates to a nicety just how far both his client's patience and boodle will stretch. Only when the goose's golden eggs are gone (and bones picked nearly clean) will settlement abruptly occur. The case, whatever its merits might have seemed, is finished. The champion, replete, fades into the sunset.

Our fourth arm of government takes paths our founding fathers never mapped. Other and better ways can be designed.

13

THE FICTION OF
THE IMPARTIAL JUDGE

British jurist Blackstone called judges "depositaries of the laws, the living oracles. . . . "[1] Martin Erdmann spoke of "whores become madams."[2]

Blackstone's mystique threads judicial theory. It supports the notion of the "impartial judge," exalts the Robe, and is chief among those veils that screen judicial indecency: the indecency of judicial selection, power, and function in adversary procedure. Erdmann's disenchantment has eyeballed the actuality.

The mystique of judicial function as oracular, essentially passive, and bathed in irreproachable celestial light, is archaic. It derives from divination and ordeal; from portents, poison, and battle as legal techniques. More immediately, it derives from Authority's posing as divine law's embodiment, validating whatever political structure was current.

Both that pose and its accompanying mystique require belief in the adjudicator's nonresponsibility. Under divine law, the adjudicator might reveal or interpret the divine ordinance, but he was theoretically responsible neither for its content nor result. There were, after all, " . . . absolute legal principles, existing prior to and independent of all judicial decisions, and merely discovered and applied by the courts. . . . "[3] Through Greek and Roman times, judges were largely mediums of "given" law, while in the Middle Ages they searched "among divine sources for the pre-existent truth."[4] English common law continued to see the judiciary (in a phrase borrowed from Cicero) as the "speaking law";[5] in theory "merely inanimate beings"[6] reiterating eternal principles. Thus it remains a principle of English law that no action may be brought against a superior court judge for a judicial act, even one allegedly done maliciously and corruptly.[7]

Today we no longer consider the judicial verdict entirely Heaven's. We now conceive the judge as an "umpire" between contestants.[8] We call him impartial. (Ordain the Canons of Judicial Ethics: "A judge should be temperate, attentive [sic] . . . conscientious, studious, thorough, courteous, patient, punctual, just, impartial. . . . "[9]) Nevertheless, his role remains officially the same: as in Battle, guilt and innocence will declare themselves; the impartial umpire need only announce the result. His (Her) Honor is nonaccountable as ever.

Thus still in modern combat, each side is allowed "within the rules of the tournament, to fight in its own way . . . . "[10] The judge must (in theory) accept the duel essentially as the adversaries shape it: its premises, its limits, its most gaping holes. The court "has no duty to make an independent investigation, and no facilities for doing so."[11] Though professional opinion has begun to question judicial passivity, interposition by the Bench is still generally deemed an interference.[12] The Bench has no obligation to ask the crucial question ignored—not even when "young lawyer George Bumble is adroitly fumbling his case and failing to make a point that is right there in the contract."[13] Nor is His Honor required to cry "Foul!" upon the bloodshed though here and there a judge may do so. His not to blunt the lance, bait the wolf, protect the lamb from slaughter. His not to censure for contempt of informational process, of sensibility nor of human dignity; but solely for contempt of Court. He is guardian only of that "brooding omnipresence in the sky"—the Law; and himself as its sacrosanct symbol.

In the adversary system of litigation, one judge states, "the State has been relegated largely to the function of furnishing the stadium and the referees; of booking, staging and deciding these civilized fights. . . . "[14] The Court's decision anoints not truth, but merely the winner of the brawl.

Said Justice Learned Hand, "Conservative political opinion in America cleaves to the tradition of the judge as passive interpreter. . . ."[15] That tradition did not persist in America through sentiment alone. It was fortuitously consonant both with the new-world egalitarian ideal and America's competitive spirit.

According to the new-world dream, America offered equal opportunity to all. On these shores, no judicial preference must aid the advantaged. But by the same token, that judicial hands-off policy required that the Bench not aid the disadvantaged either—and there was the rub. For judicial laissez-faire, ostensibly serving equal justice for all, in practice permitted heavyweight to fight lightweight with little interference. Thus, while the judge's passivity left law (once more) largely to "the advantage of the turbulent and unscrupulous," the principle of impartiality claimed that, as ever, Right had won. At the same time, since all men stood "equal" before the Bench, inequality both of class origin and opportunity were by implication denied. Society's loser had again only himself to blame.

"A government of laws and not of men" was that judicial Darwinism's slogan. That slogan—covering, in one phrase, both the new-world dream and the old-world tradition of judicial nonresponsibility—has long swelled American rhetoric. It was incorporated in the solemn Charter of Massachusetts and is inscribed on law library walls: "This library is dedicated to serve those who labor in the faith that ours is a government of laws and not of men."[16] It is dictated by the Canons of Judicial Ethics: "A judge should be mindful . . . that ours is a government of laws and not of men. . . . "[17] It is cited by jurists: "I've always believed we are a country of laws, governed by laws and *not men*. . . . "[18] (emphasis mine)

Still, laws will not apply themselves—that remains the judge's job. Indeed, the judiciary must perform a special conjury: dispense justice equal and impartial, while remaining only "the mouth which pronounces the words of law."[19] And there lies an improbable task. Inherent contradiction exists between duty to equality of justice and duty to passivity in its administration. (Judge Sirica's activist role in the initial Watergate trial highlighted that contradiction and raised increasing controversy on the subject in law journals and press.)

Consider:

The "government" or "rule" of law proposes "the absolute supremacy or predominance of regular law as opposed to the influence of arbitary power . . . . "[20] That proposition dreams of law the same for all persons and no person above the law; law superior both to temporal whim and judicial crotchet; law neither created by Authority, bent nor bought by influence. However: ". . . in order not to become arbitrary, a judge *must not be affected by the particular circumstances of the case before him.*"[21] (emphasis mine) In other words: Although one thief may steal in order to feed his children and another in order to feed his drug habit, the old view requires the trial judge to view both men the same. Although the widest disparity may exist between that ex-vice President whose criminal acts betrayed the trust of an entire electorate, and the private citizen whose similar act touches a relative few, the Court must pretend to see no difference at all. (When sentencing time arrives, of course, attention *is* supposedly paid to such differences; yet still the private citizen will likeliest end in jail, while the public servant goes scot-free.) Nevertheless, hypothetically immune to fear, favor, or bias, His Honor must appear to pluck law off the shelf and apply it without looking. He must award the prize without seeing the race.

The theory-sublime collapses into courtroom farce: judicial blindman's-buff, or pin-the-law-on-the-donkey. The judge supposedly avoids bias by turning his face from circumstance and transcends the arbitrary by closing his eyes to particulars. Where then *may* he safely look? To abstraction, of course! To precepts impersonal, timeless, absolute. He must look to law-in-the-sky, the only alternative polarity offers. Yet even if obedience to that laissez-faire directive were possible, the race would thereby go to the swift and the strong.

Furthermore, bias cannot be avoided by shutting contextual variables from view. On the contary, bias must be presumed a condition of life itself. The mind without bias (i.e., "bent, tendency, trend, inclination"[22]) can only be a mind without imprint at all. Indeed, the most pernicious bias consists in believing oneself to have none.[23] On the other hand, prejudice ("preconceived judgment or opinion"[24]) most surely perpetuates itself by refusing to look beyond preconception. The judge's openness to information constitutes his only hope of dispelling what bias or prejudice he has. There is the catch.

Law that denies man's agency and governs without reference to human context is once more "given" law, accepting whatever exists as meant to be. That law ensures the bias it intends to prevent, the favors it means to refuse. Paradox follows: Government "not of men" not only contradicts the democratic concept of government of, by and for the people, but ultimately ignore's law's object—people and their interactions.

Indeed, the judiciary's supposed blindness to the particular circumstances of the case, known sometimes as the "mechanical theory" of law or "slot-machine justice,"[25] is perhaps more aptly called the "phonograph theory of judicial function."[26] Push goes the button and out spill the precepts, invariable. Calvin Coolidge sang the old tune plainly: "Men do not make laws. They do but discover them."[27] Heaven, in effect, still does the judicial job. The judge merely discovers the decision and passes it down. Or that, at least, is generally represented as the judicial role. Thus trailing clouds of glory, the Bench draws a decent cloak—for the public eye—over adversary carnage.

The theory of judicial impartiality implies, however, somethimg more than that His Honor umpires a fight between equals or even that judicial disinterest keeps the fight clean. The theory implies that the Bench responds to reason alone. The judge is portrayed as empty of opinion in the matter at hand; waiting to be filled and tipped towards judgment by nothing more than the accretion of fact (which will determine the law that applies). As the parties begin theoretically on an equal footing, so is the judge supposed to start off with an open mind.[28] An impartial judge is in fact the adversary trial's "first and most essential element."[29] In the drama, His Honor enacts equity's representative and logic's man. His performance is imperative to the aura of probity that drapes the adversary dodge.

Is the judicial tune unvarying? Does the judiciary apply law to facts with elegant and uniform dispassion? Of course not.

In New York City in the years 1914–1916, The Committee on Criminal Courts of the Charity Organization Society became curious as to what extent a "personal equation" might enter into the administration of justice. The committee began collecting statistics on how different judges handled similar classes of cases in the City Magistrates' Courts. Justice, it soon became apparent, was not entirely "an abstract thing as immutable as the law of gravitation."[30]

For example: Out of 566 persons charged with intoxication, Judge Naumer found 565 guilty and *discharged one person*—less than 1 percent; while his colleague Judge Corrigan, out of 673 persons, found 142 guilty and *discharged 531*—or nearly 79 percent.[31] For disorderly conduct, Judge Simms discharged 18 percent, while Judge Walsh discharged 54 percent. Of vagrancy cases, Judge Simms discharged 4.5 percent, while Judge Fitch discharged 79 percent.

Sentencing ranged as widely. Judge McQuade fined 85 percent and *suspended sentence on 7 percent*; while on the same charge Judge Folwell fined 34 percent and *suspended sentence on 59 percent*.[32] Judge Brough suspended no vagrancy sentences at all, while Judge Conway equitably suspended every *alternate* one.[33] Brough sent 80 percent of his cases to the workhouse; Conway only 17 percent.[34] Marsh suspended sentence in 1.9 percent of his petty misdemeanor cases, while McGuire did so in 72.5 percent. Steers fined 80 percent of his disorderly conduct cases; Folwell only 7 percent.[35]

The investigators panicked—and promptly discontinued their study.[36] Over one-half century later, studies have begun again. Inequity remains the only judicial certainty.

For instance: Defendants from the world of organized crime are let off five times oftener than are ordinary persons.[37] Black criminals tend to receive prison terms averaging nearly one third longer than whites.[38] Poor defendants serve fully twice as long as those with enough money to hire their own lawyers.[39] Suspects brought into New York's overflowing courts receive lighter penalties than those unlucky enough to be convicted of the same crime upstate.[40] A New York policeman found guilty of conspiring to sell half a pound of heroin, can (and did) receive a suspended sentence; whereas an addict who sold only 1/73 of an ounce (but appeared before a different judge) can (and did) receive thirty years.[41] And if you grow up to be President, you may bypass our legal system altogether. Richard Nixon, despite the charge of "repeated violation of the constitutional rights of citizens" (Impeachment Article 2), despite charge of repeated "statements for the purpose of deceiving the people of the United States" (Impeachment Article 1), and despite his admitted withholding of criminal evidence, was pardoned "fully, freely and absolutely" without fuss of indictment or fret of judicial determination at all. John Dean, whose truth was focal in cracking the most scabrous scandal in American governmental history, was sentenced to one to four years.

California's Rand Corporation undertook a local sentencing study. Rand reports,

> In general, consistency in sentencing practices is mixed. Judge 1 in Van Nuys and Judge 2 in Pomona tend to sentence severely. Judge 1 in Pomona and Judges 1 and 4 in Norwalk tend to sentence leniently . . . In some cases, however, a judge tends to sentence severely for one offense and leniently for another. For example, in Long Beach, Judge 2's felony sentence rate and prison rate for burglary are the highest, whereas Judge 1's are the lowest; for robbery the converse is true. . . . One judge imposed felony sentences in only 6% of dangerous drug possession convictions and another in 62% . . . ; one in only 9% of burglary convictions and another in 82% for the same category of cases; one in only 44% of robbery convictions and another in 97% of the same cases and among several judges, the prison rate for burglary varied form zero to 20%, and for robbery, 7% to 57%.[42]

Sentencing, in other words, depends less upon punishment fitted to crime, upon the contextual circumstances of the case, or even upon the particular criminal's history, than (in Judge Marvin Frankel's words) "upon the wide spectrums of character, bias, neurosis and daily vagary encountered among occupants of the trial bench."[43] Similarly innocence and guilt are less a function of law inexorable applied to facts, than they are the uneven results of Authority's thumb upon the scales of justice. Impartiality is judicial myth. The actuality is quite another thing.

The claim of judicial impartiality is the fourth major "as if" in the game of adversary make-believe. That claim masks not only the wide variation of justice-meted, but also the nature and scope—if not the fact—of judicial power.

The Bench's power is unique. While lawyers, as a group, constitute in their effect an unofficial fourth arm of government, the judiciary is the officially designated third arm. In our American system of three-way checks and balances, the judicial branch was conceived as equal with executive and legislative power. It is, however, something more.

All our laws are exactly as effective or useless as those judges who interpret and enforce them.[44] An anthropologist writes that " . . . there are few social roles invested with such power in American society that are yet subject to so little control."[45] His Honor magnifies all the fine print of our daily lives:

> . . . the usury and garnishee laws, the instalment contract laws, speed laws and license laws, laws relating to houses and plumbing and cockroaches, parking and noise abatement, health and advertising and tipping and marriage and divorce—laws that affect the everyday lives of every one of us . . . it is the interpretation and inforcement of such laws—not the passing of them—that measures the extent to which we may impose and be imposed upon, to which we may make use of what we own, to which, in fine, we may own what we have come to think we earned.[46]

The trial judge, Dean Green said, "is the most important officer of government . . . ," and his personality is the largest single factor in law's administration.[47] According to a member of the Bar, "the law of a great nation" means only "the opinions of a half-a-dozen old gentlemen . . . ,"[48] since when those men from a majority of the highest tribunal, " . . . no rule or principle which they refuse to follow is Law in that country."[49] Conversely, if those judges state a rule "discordant with the eternal verities, it is none the less Law."[50]

Until laws are applied to facts, they are paper law only. Until facts are selected out of the variety each side urges, their weight is purely hypothetical. The judge brings both to earth and life. He chooses for belief particular facts; chooses that law which, he states, applies to those facts; and declares his ruling—backed by government's coercive power. Until the Court makes both choice and ruling, nothing happens. Indeed, precedents and principles, codes and constitutions, rights and facts, are all no more than "ingredients for making law."[51] They are strictly Law-Theoretical.

Jerome Frank explains,

> Law is made up not of rules for decision laid down by the courts but of the decisions themselves. All such decisions are law. The fact that courts render those decisions makes them law. There is no mysterious entity apart from those de-

cisions. . . . Rules . . . are not the Law, but are only
some among many of the sources to which judges go in making law out of the cases tried before them. . . . The law,
therefore, consists of *decisions . . . whenever a judge decides a case he is making law.*[52] (first emphasis mine)

It is the *decision* that will be enforced. That judicial decision is Law-
in-Fact. And Law-in-Fact is only what the Court—trial judge or Supreme Court Justice—decides it is. Each time.

In truth, Gray said, "all the law is judge-made law. The shape in
which a statute is imposed on the community as a guide for conduct
is that statute as interpreted by the courts."[53] Judge-made law is
"real law" though generally presented and described as mere interpretation. Further, "Whatever forces can be said to influence the
growth of the law . . . exert that influence by influencing the judges."[54]

Nevertheless, statutes and rules are on the books. They supposedly represent the popular will. Are they at least first among
those ingredients for making law to which His Honor turns? Too often they are not. Law-Theoretical serves generally as a peg for His
Honor's temperamental hat: post-facto rationale, subsequent to decision made.

The judge, one of their number says, "really decides by feeling
and not by judgment, by hunching and not by ratiocination, such ratiocination appearing only in the opinion . . . [the judge] having so
decided, enlists his every faculty and belabors his laggard mind, not
only to justify that intuition to himself, but to make it pass muster
with his critics."[55] Toward that end, he mentally reviews all those
rules, principles, legal categories, and concepts, that he may find
useful, selecting from them those that will best support his desired
result.

Another judge reports,

> . . . of the many things which have been said as to the mys-
> tery of the judicial process, the most salient is that decision
> is reached after an emotive experience in which principles
> and logic play a secondary part. . . . These considerations
> must reveal to us the impotence of general principles to con-
> trol decision. Vague because of their generality, they mean
> nothing save what they suggest in the organized experience

of the one who thinks them, and because of their vagueness, they only remotely compel the organization of that experience . . . . [56]

After all, explained a third member of the Bench, "The same evidence which to one may be convincing, to another may seem absurd."[57] The law of the land, according to Gray, remains "human opinion."[58]

It is the judge's habits of thought that produce that opinion;[59] nothing less, finally, than "his entire life history."[60] But the bases for his judgment and the law it creates may forever lie concealed—because His Honor is not required to publish the reasons for his ruling. At trial court level he rarely bothers to set forth his thinking. Similarly, the upper courts and even the Supreme Court often rule without any explanation at all.

Even when judicial explanation does appear, however, the light it sheds may be dim. For official judicial opinion ". . . is in large measure an after-thought. It omits all mention of many of the factors which induced the judge to decide the case."[61] Yet because the judge "cannot *appear* to be arbitrary"[62] (emphasis mine) he will at the same time dress his opinion in the most impressive legal garb memory and research can summon. The judge can literally, working backward, figure out and publish facts and rules that will make his decision appear logically sound.[63] Another member of the judiciary contended, if the trial judge "should make it a rule that he would never decide between contending parties except according to the length of their noses, it would always be easy for him to render judgments whose reasonings were perfectly correct according to law and absolutely unassailable . . . . "[64] (Judges are not alone in rationalizing with afterthought a decision based on a host of other, conscious and unconscious, factors. Sociologist Harold Garfinkel contends that most of us invariably construct the rationale for an action after the fact, doing things in ways that will make it easier to construct that post-facto rationale. For example, in a one-way mirror experiment, a group of jurors were watched while they deliberated—without telling them they were being watched. According to the panel that observed them, there was hardly any relation between their observed motivations and those explanations for their decision they reported later.[65] Unique to the legal profession, of course—and unavailable to the rest of us as validation for our rationales—is the law's unapproachable imprimatur.)

Rodell has claimed that "just as the devil can always cite Scripture to his purpose, so can any lawyer on either side of any case always cite The Law to his."[66] And so can any judge. Law-Theoretical will legitimize nearly any ruling the Bench chooses to make Law-in-Fact.

The lawyers are in on the game. They know that His Honor can believe the expert who swears the document is genuine as easily as he can the expert who swears it a forgery. They know that the judge can, as he chooses, believe the single witness, the ex-husband resisting alimony, who swears his ex-wife "held herself out" as the wife of another, just as easily as he can believe the thirty-eight witnesses who all swear she didn't. (Judicial mathematics depends upon His Honor's eyesight. If he sees the woman as "another predatory female"[67] then via his entirely legal calculation her thirty-eight witnesses will add up to zero.) The law against spitting on the sidewalk may be plain as plain can be; but if the fact finder decides the defendant merely coughed, that law does not apply. The law against bribing a policeman may be clear as day; but if the fact finder agrees that the accused was indeed only asking the officer to make change for a thousand-dollar bill, that law is irrelevant.

No matter precepts and precedents. Bother statutes and facts. His Honor is The Law. (And at trial court level, when he sits without a jury, he may be The Facts too—since Appeals Courts may not reconsider those facts the lower courts find.) So long as we conceive the judge as impartial, of course, that power does not matter.

Judicial mystique is at pains to dismiss the idea of judicial accountability in general, and the specific charge of judge-made law in particular.

Judges, Bacon said, "ought to remember that their office is *jus dicere*, not *jus dare*; to interpret law, and not to make law, or give law."[68] Blackstone said that judges "are not delegated to pronounce a new law, but to maintain and expound the old one."[69] Even when they flatly reverse or abandon a prior decision, they only "vindicate the old law from misrepresentation."[70]

Blackstone's editor apparently went even further. He deemed it important that judges should say, and that people should *believe*, that the rules according to which judges decide cases had a previous existence.[71] Commented Jerome Frank, "The lay public, that is, are to be duped."[72] But the trumpery has purpose. It lifts the Bench nearer Heaven, and its occupants beyond charge of mortal motive.

"When men became Supreme Court judges," a historian says, "they were believed to be no longer actuated by the prejudices and passions of common humanity."[73] American tradition has long held that, following appointment to the judiciary, men and women necessarily leave behind their prior personal and political views; at least in the dispensation of justice. Judicial bench and vestment stage-prop the charade.

The bench represents a complex one-upsmanship: both spatial and behavioral. His Honor sits, physically and psychologically, above and superior, "the lord of this quasi-feudal system."[74] All others stand below, look up, inferior. Not only does the bench's elevation imply sovereignty; but surrounding that throne is an invisible moat, demanding the protocol of majesty. Past its borders, neither litigant nor lawyer may step without express permission: "May I approach the Bench, Your Honor?" Documents may not be handed the judge directly—not even by the lawyer "officers of the court"— but only by bailiffs or clerk. These observances are (officially) only "custom"; but custom no disputant nor lawyer is foolish enough to ignore.

Meanwhile the robe's ceremonial uniformity denies the human flesh beneath the threads. Indeed, the robe is a kind of religious cloth. Woven of mystery and magic, it conjures the "lawyer who knew a governor"[75] into a "jurist"—beatified, impregnable. (In most U.S. state courts, judges did not wear the robe until the last decades of the 19th century, when conservative lawyers saw the Bench as a bulwark against rising Populism's threat.)[76] The priestly garment renders its wearer as unimpeachable as the decree he brings from the gods. Below, business continues as usual.

Presidents, like law-men, are in on the game. They know that bench and robe do not exorcise the prior man. Presidents from Adams through Lincoln and Roosevelt to Nixon, have almost invariably appointed (or tried to appoint) to the Bench men in sympathy with their own views.[77] Via such appointment, a President's reach through the years exceeds the brief grasp of his term. The voters may dump the Executive, but till death or retirement of his judicial appointees, the electorate is stuck with that President's policies.

Professor Rodell knows the score, too. He wrote,

> Government by judiciary . . . is . . . far more a government of men, not laws, than of laws, not men. Nor activism

nor self-restraint nor federal-state relationships nor absolute constitutional demand leads a Sutherland to vote against the New Deal, a Brandeis for wage and hour laws, a Frankfurter against state right to counsel, a Black for freedom of assembly—nor do these easy abstract theories explain why each so voted. From John Jay on . . . the vote of each Supreme Court Justice, however rationalized à la mode, however fitted afterward into the pigeonhole of some pretty politico-juridical principle, has rather been the result of a vast complex of personal factors—temperament, background, education, economic status, pre-Court career—of whose influence on his thinking even the most sophisticated of Justices can never be wholly unaware . . . . That, at any rate, has been my maverick approach to the study of constitutional law for more than a quarter century.[78]

On March 15, 1962, in the pages of *The Georgetown Law Journal*, Rodell placed that maverick approach—and himself—squarely on the line. In the United States Supreme Court, a redistricting case was then pending. Rodell wrote, "Let me now risk ridicule . . . by essaying a way-out-on-limb exercise. . . ."[79] Relying on "largely extralegal factors"[80] Rodell proceeded to predict, man by man, the eventual tally. The Court, he said, would order redistricting by a vote of five to four: Black, Douglas, Warren, Brennan, and Stewart, versus Frankfurter, Harlan, Clark, and Whittaker.

Eleven days later, the decision came down. Rodell's score was impressive. He had predicted accurately—seven times out of eight. (Clark joined the majority; Whittaker abstained.)[81]

A significant part of the "science" of law involves the lawyer's attempt to make Rodell's kind of book. The claim that the attorney seeks an impartial judge is the fifth "as if" in the game of adversary make-believe.

In adversary procedure, the lawyer does *not* want an impartial judge. Quite the opposite: it is partiality he seeks. In truth, by adversary definition, the law-man wants as much bias as he can find—on his side. "We actually condone judge-shopping in our courts,"[82] says Superior Court Judge Tim Murphy. The attorney, estimating to a nicety those handicaps and odds the avaliable judicial personalities offer, tries to maneuver his client before the judge likeliest to give him a "win." Canny jockeying to the starting gate is half the courtroom strategy. "Lawyers," Murphy says, "are always trying to psych the judge out, like people at the racetrack trying to figure out the horses. Lawyers make their living trying to figure out how judges will handle discretionary matters. That is what you pay a trial lawyer for—assessing the judge's discretion."[83]

Judicial discretion is compounded of interpretation and choice, representing what His Honor *makes* of law and fact—and what he chooses to *do* about it. Since generally his ruling follows his feelings, discretion represents the leeway sympathy has to flower and bias to swing. It is the very essence of judicial actuality. The lawyer's victory may very much depend on accurate perception and effective manipulation of the Court's leanings—or upon creating them.

An ex-president of the American Bar Association advised, "The way to win a case is to make the judge want to decide in your favor and then, and then only, to cite precedents which will justify such determination. You will almost always find plenty of cases to cite in your favor."[84] A jurist confessed, "I might once in a while be embarrassed by a technical rule, but I almost always found principles suited to my view of the case. . . ."[85]

Beneath the cloak of impartiality and within the limits of those issues the adversaries raise, the Court's discretion operates with little impediment. It ranges from what one sociologist calls "A resourceful judge ['s] . . . subtle domination of the proceedings . . . ,"[86] to action overt and unequivocal.

Dicretion manifests itself in those attorney objections Her Honor overrules and those she sustains. It manifests itself in that evidence Her Honor admits and that she denies. It manifests itself in which information she agrees is "immaterial, irrelevant and incompetent" and which she lets enter. It manifests itself in which testimony she lets the jury hear, versus which testimony she denies them—or which, having let them hear, she gravely instructs they are "not to consider" at all.

Judicial discretion manifests itself secretly in chambers, that privy closet from which disputants are excluded but where adverse attorneys and judge meet. There, ignoring rules of evidence together with niceties of due process, often bandying gossip that its subjects are not there to deny or casting aspersion that its objects are not present to refute—they may make deals no witness audits and no transcript records; deals that cannot be appealed because they do not "exist."

Judicial discretion manifests itself openly in threats against the lawyer who goes further in aiding his client than the Court deems he should. An attorney who preferred to remain nameless said, " . . . a lawyer who criticizes judges—*any* judges—puts himself in extreme peril."[87] Not long ago, a Massachusetts lawyer reports, "one of our leading judges here threatened a defense attorney with contempt of court if he mentioned the Supreme Court once more."[88] Discretion manifests itself clearly, for instance, in the difference between a "Judge King [who] tried to give everyone a break. And Judge Scott—well, in most of the cases she sat on the verdict was guilty. . . ."[89]

The Court's discretion need make no nod to the most glaring signs of justice miscarried: even when, for example, another confesses to the crime for which a defendant has already been convicted and sentenced; even when that crime's victim declares that she originally misidentified the perpetrator. A lawyer described just such a case:

> I took [the victim] to court, and she told the judge she felt as a decent citizen she had to admit her mistake and rectify it. The judge looked her in the eye and said, "I don't believe you." He refused to let the kid out of prison. I went to the supreme judicial court about the case, but they didn't want to embarrass a colleague by reversing him and wouldn't do anything. Finally I persuaded another district court judge to hear the case, and he threw it out and let the kid go. By then, another month had passed, and God knows what happened to him in jail in the meantime.[90]

From the judge's tonal deference towards one witness, to his tonal contempt towards another; from the judge's first words as he sits, to that final charge with which he instructs the jury and poses their alternatives, judicial discretion makes constant choice. The judge is not passive at all. He is very active indeed.

However, unless His Honor has, during course of trial, made some gross error of law, none of those discretional choices are by themselves (in most jurisdictions) basis for reversal on appeal. Not partiality, but "law" is what counts. In a government of laws and not men, partiality is denied to exist.

Thus, even where the most extreme discretional bias is clear, the judge can use a ploy that almost guarantees nonreversal. He simply grants all points of law to that side he intends ruling *against*—in order to be free to award for the opposite side on "fact," without fear of upper-court upset. At its most humane, the method works as follows, one judge explained to a lawyer:

> You see, on the first day of trial, I made up my mind that the defendant, your client, was a fine, hardworking woman who oughtn't to lose all her property to the plaintiff, who had plenty of money. The plaintiff was urging a legal rule which . . . I thought . . . was legally right, but very unjust, and I didn't want to apply it. So I made up my mind to lick the plaintiff on the facts. And by giving him every break on procedural points during the trial . . . I made it impossible for him to reverse me on appeal, because, as the testimony was oral and in conflict, I knew the upper court would never upset my findings of fact.[91]

And then there is discretion less benign: there is Sacco-Vanzetti. In February of 1927, Justice Felix Frankfurter, then professor of administrative law at Harvard, published a critical analysis of the legal proceedings to that date in the case against those Italian immigrants, "the good shoemaker and the poor fish peddlar"—charged with murder and on trial for their lives.

Frankfurter wrote, "By systematic exploitation of the defendants' alien blood, their imperfect knowledge of English, their unpopular social views, and their opposition to the war, the District Attorney invoked against them a riot of political passion and patriotic sentiment; and the trial court connived at—one had almost written cooperated in—the process."[92]

For instance, in the trail of Nicola Sacco and Bartolomeo Vanzetti, Judge Thayer heard Proctor (the ballistics expert) testify that the bullet that killed one of the robbery victims "was 'consistent with having gone through' Sacco's pistol"[93]—and charged the jury that Proctor had in effect testified it *did* go through. But Proctor, in a sworn affidavit, subsequently contradicted that charge. He swore he had meant only that the fatal bullet had passed through *a* Colt—not *the* Colt automatic belonging to Sacco.[94] Indeed, he "*could not* have testified, and did not mean to testify, that the mortal bullet was Sacco's."[95] For, said he, "At no time was I able to find any evidence whatever which tended to convince me that the particular model bullet . . . came from Sacco's pistol and I so informed the District Attorney and his assistant before the trial."[96] On the witness stand,

"Had I been asked the direct question: whether I had found any affirmative evidence whatever that this so-called mortal bullet had passed through this particular Sacco's pistol, I should have answered then, as I do now without hesitation, in the negative."[97]

"The whole meaning of Captain Proctor's affidavit," Frankfurter wrote, was that, by prearrangement with the District Attorney, questions and answers in the matter had been formulated so as "to mislead the jury as it misled the Court [with] terrible harm to the defendants."[98] To that end, "Proctor used language which was true in one sense but false in the meaning it conveyed to those not privy to the arrangement. . . . Formal accuracy was consciously resorted to as a means of misleading the Court and jury."[99] Nevertheless, despite Proctor's "uncontradicted affidavit"[100]—Thayer denied defense motion for retrial. It was within Judge Thayer's discretion to do so.

An impressive body of new evidence now appeared: evidence, wrote Frankfurter, "not only that Sacco and Vanzetti did *not* commit the murders, but also, positively, that a well-known gang of professional criminals *did* commit them."[101] But Judge Thayer chose to ignore that evidence. Another man confessed, as part of that gang, to the crime for which Sacco and Vanzetti had been sentenced to "suffer the punishment of death by the passage of a current of electricity through their bodies."[102] Judge Thayer chose to ignore that confession as well. Independent evidence arose supporting that confession.[103] Thayer ignored that too. Those choices were, each and every one, entirely within Thayer's judicial discretion.

Frankfurter wrote,

> Surely no jury of disinterested and informed lawyers would hesitate for a moment to hold that, if the evidence concerning the Braintree crime and the Morelli gang came before a magistrate, he would be bound to commit for the action of a grand jury; that a grand jury would clearly be justified in presenting a true bill against them; and that on trial a judge would submit such facts for a jury's verdict. The jury that tried and convicted Sacco and Vanzetti had *no such facts before it*. . . .[104] (emphasis mine)

Judge Thayer remained unmoved by the jury's factual deprivation. Though Thayer's duty at this point was only "the very narrow one of ascertaining whether here was new material fit for a new

jury's judgment,"[105] he decided there was not. He refused another
trial to consider that fresh evidence. It was entirely within his discretion to do so.

Sacco and Vanzetti's lawyers appealed to the Massachusetts Supreme Judicial Court. That Court duly considered—and, finding "no
error"[106] in any of Judge Thayer's technical rulings, held that Thayer's decision could not "as a matter of law" be reversed.[107] They
denied the appeal. It was entirely within their discretion to do so.

But, cried Frankfurter, Thayer's opinion "stands unmatched
. . . for discrepancies between what the record discloses and what
the opinion conveys. His 25,000-word document cannot accurately
be described other than as a farrago of misquotations, misrepresen-
tations, suppressions and mutilations. . . . The opinion is literally
honeycombed with demonstrable errors, and infused by a spirit alien to judicial utterance. . . . "[108] Above all, Frankfurter asked,
"Did Judge Thayer observe the standards of Anglo-American justice? In legal parlance, was there 'abuse of judicial discretion' by
Judge Thayer?"[109] That indeed was the crux of the case.[110]

The Supreme Judicial Court soberly replied that it had found "no
abuse of judicial discretion on the record presented. . . . "[111] In
the Boston *Herald*'s translation, "The supreme court did not vindicate the verdict [the court only] certified that, whether the verdict
was right or wrong, the trial judge performed his duty under the law
in a legal manner."[112] In Felix Frankfurter's translation, the court
claimed itself "satisfied that throughout the conduct of the trial and
the proceedings that followed it, Judge Thayer was governed by the
'calmness of a cool mind, free from partiality, not swayed by sympathy nor warped by prejudice nor moved by any kind of influence
save alone the overwhelming passion to do that which is just.' "[113]

The Supreme Judicial Court's finding that Judge Thayer had oper-
ated within proper bounds was—once more—within *that* court's
discretion. (Probability had been with Thayer. To that date, no Massachusetts Judge had *ever* been found to have abused his
discretion.)[114] Thus were Nicola Sacco and Bartolomeo Vanetti law-
fully murdered at Charlestown, Massachusetts, in the year of our
Lord one thousand nine hundred and twenty seven.

"I met Judge Thayer once," Charles Curtis recounted many years
later:

We were in his chambers in Boston settling . . . [a] case
then on trial before him . . . he was standing between me

and the window, so that when I looked out . . . behind him
I saw the top of the Charlestown Jail where the death house
was. . . . I wasn't thinking much about it until I realized
that Judge Thayer was no longer talking about our case, but
strutting up and down boasting that he had been fortunate
enough to be on the bench when those sons of bitches were
convicted. I had a chill. . . . [115]

Who *is* the man upon whose discretion life may hang? He is an
officeholder for whom few requirements exist: not uniform standards of excellence, intelligence, honesty, empathy, self-awareness,
nor even of knowledge. In many jurisdictions he need not even be a
lawyer. He is a man trained within the confines of polarity.'s blame
system, but untrained in discretionary skills: untrained in listening
for sounds of distortion, bias, closure—either in others or in himself. Even in those states where a judge must be "learned in the
law," that command embodies no definite standards, but represents
only a suggestion to the voters.[116]

The Federal Bench, with stiffer standards, tends to be of higher
caliber than state and local benches, where 99 percent of cases
end.[117] Yet the judge, Lewis M. Isaacs, Jr., says, is too often a person "whose ignorance, intolerance and impatience are such as to
sicken anyone who stops to think about them . . . [the judiciary is
overloaded with] bias, intolerance, cowardice, impatience, and
sometimes graft."[118] The man who for twenty-seven years was director of the Federal Bureau of Prisons testified, "That some judges
are arbitrary and even sadistic . . . is notoriously a matter of
record.'

"Most judges," a lawyer says, "are ex-prosecutors, ex-cops, ex-
officials who worked on the hard side of government, or ex-party
workers. Most of them were hacks—small-time lawyers with big-
time friends—and some were crooks the week before they went on
the bench. . . . Most of those men have no respect for the individual and no interest in his character or his future. And many of
them are outright bigots, too."[120] Let us, Judge Samuel Rosenman
said, "face this sad fact: that in many—far too many—instances,
the benches of our courts in the United States are occupied by mediocrities—men of small talent, undistinguished in performance, technically deficient and inept."[121] Another judge remarked, "People
think that alcoholism is the occupational disease of judges. It is not
alcoholism; laziness is our occupational disease. It is terribly difficult to make some judges work."[122]

Rodell states,

> . . . it is out of the acknowledged leaders of the profession,
> who are acknowledged to be leaders because they make so
> much money, that most judges are chosen . . . when a law-
> yer becomes a judge, he no longer has a direct financial in-
> centive to manipulate The Law in favor of the rich people
> and the big corporations. But he will usually have spent
> most of his professional life, before he became a judge, do-
> ing just that. . . . Which means that he will lean toward
> the side where the money lies—and The Law will lean with
> him.[123]

There is curiously little hard statistical information on the judiciary in this country. Judge Murphy writes,

> We do not know much about judges in the United States.
> We are not even sure how many there are. We think there
> are about 15,000 limited-jurisdiction judges [magistrates,
> justices of the peace] but some estimates of the latter go as
> high as fifty thousand. . . . We do know that most of the
> judges and the people who perform judicial functions in the
> United States *are not lawyers*. I suspect that most are not
> even high school graduates. We know that most of them are
> tied in very closely with the local political system.[124] (em-
> phasis mine)

The robe, in fact, is most usually an item of barter in the political
swap-meet: either purchased openly with legal tender, awarded as
payoff for personal or political debts,[125] or acknowledged as IOU toward future favors. "Political rewards, personal friendships, party
service, and even prior judicial experience have been the major qualifications"[126] for appointment to the United States Supreme Court,
one writer notes. "I would like to [be a judge]," Martin Erdmann
said. "But the only way you can get it is to be in politics or buy it—
and I don't even know the going price."[127]

Judge Murphy reports that ". . . in Georgia, a candidate for a
judgeship must pay over three thousand dollars as a filing fee to the
political party. This is not under-the-table money. In Texas, the candidates must pay a four- to five-thousand-dollar filing fee. It is common talk that a judgeship in the lower courts in the city of New York
costs one year's salary to the party."[128]

In California, campaign contributions of $40,000 and $100,000 have been reported coincident with appointment to the Municipal and Superior Court benches, respectively.

Other factors may enter: In Los Angeles, for instance, a certain judge received appointment to the State Superior Court by grace of a governor's secretary—who gave credence to the gentleman's plight of troth. Over ten years later, His Honor remains on the bench—and a bachelor.

Officially, judicial selection occurs with greater propriety. In the federal courts, the judiciary is seated entirely by executive appointment. At the state-court level, the judiciary is seated variously by executive appointment; by partisan election in some areas and nonpartisan in others; by legislative selection in still other states; and in a final group, by executive appointment from a panel nominated by a nonpartisan commission of lay persons and lawyers.[129]

Nontheless, that appearance of propriety is deceptive. On one hand, "executive appointment" is a euphemism for "political plum": both Republican and Democratic Presidents have, for instance, chosen men from their own parties over 95 percent of the time.[130] On the other hand, while popular election is claimed to distribute judgeships equitably, in practice fully 50 percent of "elected" judges (above municipal level) are *actually* appointed. They are seated initially via the governor's right to fill by appointment those judicial vacancies created by death or resignation; and then, as their terms expire, are "reelected" in cyclical voter rubber-stamp until their own death or resignation—when the closed cycle begins again.

Thus, for example, between 1948 and 1957, in four of the nominally elective states, *over 80 percent* of judges at the appeals court level were in fact *appointed*. In ten elective states 60-80 percent were in fact appointed.[131] At the trial court level, similar figures prevail.

Furthermore: candidates in elective states, even when not originally selected to fill judicial vacancies, are still appointed in effect. They are chosen by political party leaders to run without opposition, or on coalition tickets, so that the voters again have no choice.[132] In both cases, the citizenry merely ratifies rather than votes.

Judge Rosenman commented,

> The idea that the voters themselves select their judges is something of a farce. The real electors are a few political leaders who do the nominating. . . . Political leaders nominate practically anybody whom they choose . . . the vot-

ers, as a whole, know little more about the candidates than what their campaign pictures may reveal. . . . For example . . . after the 1954 elections . . . [a poll] showed that not more than one per cent of the voters in New York City could remember the name of the man they had just elected Chief Judge of the Court of Appeals—our highest judicial post. In Buffalo, not a single voter could remember his name. . . .[133]

In Cayuga County in 1954 over 95 percent of persons polled were unable to name *any* of the judicial candidates for whom they had just voted.[134]

Yet, while the judicial elective system's "curse"[135] may be that it turns every elective judge into a politician, nonpartisan election does no better. Two directors of the American Judicature Society write, "Whichever candidate has the catchiest name, the biggest campaign fund or the most appealing profile will win. There is *no guarantee of even minimum competence.* In fact, if a person is good enough as a lawyer there is some probability that he will not run for judicial office . . . this system tends to put on the bench men who have little or nothing to lose if they don't make it. . . ."[136] (emphasis mine) Nor, indeed, does nonpartisan election necessarily guarantee a nonpartisan candidate: for the party machine may easily, sub rosa, fill the prospective judge's campaign coffers. In truth, legal ability and experience on the bench may matter little, while a large campaign fund or strategic spot on the ballot may be the determinants of nonpartisan election.

Ability, according to Judge Rosenman, "has only been an incidental consideration in nominating a candidate for judicial office."[137]

Essentially, meanwhile, the cost of campaigning bars the elective bench, partisan or nonpartisan, to almost all but the rich or the bought. In a large state like Texas, for instance, the cost of running a state supreme court campaign has been estimated up to one million dollars. In smaller states, it may be well over $100,000.[138] A pertinent question, suggests a Missouri lawyer, is "where does all this money come from when the judicial office involved pays, for example, only between $15,000 and $25,000 per year. The rather shocking answer is that in the main *it must come from lawyers and potential litigants of the very court involved*"[139] (emphasis mine)—despite the Canons of Ethics.

Selection of judges by state legislatures is no happier, since the nominee's name usually springs from the party in power. Thus, the man chosen may find, when he sits in judicial solemnity, that there remain a number of backs to be scratched—a number in direct proportion to the number of legislator-votes he received.[140]

Finally, there is the "Missouri" or "Merit Plan" of judicial selection: a relatively recent approach combining the preferable aspects of prior techniques with an attempt to remedy those evils likewise inherent in them. This plan, however, has created certain new and insidious problems of its own.[141] The "combination plan" provides for appointment of judges by the governor from a list of nominees put forward by a nominating commission composed of lawyers and lay persons. But the lawyer members come from heavily status-quo bar associations; while the lay members are appointed directly by the governor—a method flatly incongruous with their purpose.[142] Merit Plan selection, therefore, still rests essentially with the executive, who may, if he wishes, indirectly choose both the candidates for judicial office (via pressure upon the commission) and the judges from *among* those candidates.[143]

In sum: His Honor, however chosen, usually dangles from political strings. Partiality to the manipulators of those strings is a tacit condition of his initial eminence, and of his judicial survival as well. Although political considerations sometimes produce "by accident alone" a first-rate judge, oftener they produce, in Judge Rosenman's words, "mediocrities or worse."[144]

So long as we conceive the Bench impartial—mediocrity will do.

Yet something more is wrong. Our governmental check-and-balance system is ill-checked and unbalanced—not simply because of the judiciary's power, but because the judiciary achieves its seat thanks largely to the executive branch. Judicial and executive interests tend more frequently to merge than restrain one another.

His Honor and the governor not only trade favors at the political swap-meet; ultimately they dine, if from different tables, at the same financial barbecue. They are subsidiaries, in effect, of the same holding company—money. Money rules the elections that seat the men. And money rises above parochialism, above party and ideology, in allegiance to those mechanisms of its own reproduction that political parties and their officeholders finally function to serve. Like siblings, the judiciary and the executive have their differences, but they usually answer at dinnertime to the same parental call. Thus two branches of our tripartite system are predominantly uninterested in checking each other; while together they outbalance the third.

The judiciary's illicit ties are no secret to those involved. It is a relationship sometimes even regularized. California law, for example, declares that a judge is disqualified in those cases where it appears "probable that, by reason of bias or prejudice . . . a fair and impartial trial cannot be had. . . . Bias or prejudice is a state of mind of a character calculated to impair impartiality and to sway judgment."[145] Explicitly excluded as factors that might shape such biased state of mind are the Bench's links to executive and financial power. For neither "hostility between a party [to the litigation] and the governor who appointed the judge [nor even] *the judge's indebtedness to a bank of which the plaintiff was a director*"[146] (emphasis mine) have been held to be sufficient cause to disqualify a judge under law. His Honor must be free to serve where highest duty calls.

So long as we consider His Honor impartial, those ties are no concern.

Though justice may be variant, judicial mediocrity endemic, and bias rampant, faith in the existence of perfect impartiality—somewhere—persists. Whatever reproaches are leveled at the judiciary: justice too soft, too hard, too inconsistent—the fault is held to lie strictly with the Bench's lapse from the ideal. That ideal remains the passive interpreter, eyes fixed on Law, blind to circumstance, immune to predilection. But the impartial judge does not exist. Nor can he.

Judicial behavior may be more or less self-consistent, and relatively predictable. It can never be entirely self-consistent, nor without variation from one person to another.

Individual reaction is as idiosyncratic as fingerprints. It is a compendium of the biological and the social, the inherited and the learned. It is a product of life-experience and family history, of attention span as well as value system, of doctrines internalized as well as theories intellectualized. It is a mix not only of an infinity of factors, aware and unaware, determinable and indeterminable, definable and indefinable, measurable and immeasurable—but of all those in response to a particular circumstance at a particular moment in constantly changing space-time. The result cannot but be unique. Unique for each person; and for each person, each time.

Biases are the essence both of that particularity and that variation. In statistical aggregate biases may tend to cancel; in single instance they cannot. They may be minimized; that may be taken into account. But the judge can never bring to bear judgment that excludes them. Nor can anyone else.

His Honor may begin without concluded *prejudgment;* he cannot begin free of *leaning,* conscious and unconscious. "The ideal of a government of laws and not of men is a dream," a legal scholar said, that will be realized only when "law becomes calculus."[147]

The central issue, however, is larger. Even if His Honor might conceivably *begin* without bias above a tested, preagreed level in areas at issue—under adversary procedure, he *cannot finish without it.* For adversary approach must create a preponderance of bias against the "other" and for the self in order to produce its "win."

Attend as he will to law, to facts emergent and "truth revealed," the judge hears predominantly not law, facts, or truth; but absolutes, sophistry, blame. He must choose eventually between two mutually exaggerated, selectively represented, misrepresented, hyperbolic sides. Prejudice is adversary method's beginning, chief means, and end. The lay person is its ultimate victim, but the judge (alone or with a jury) is its immediate target. He must buy the shoddy goods. Judicial ruling in adversary proceeding is a decision not so much by cerebration, as by brainwash.

The judge may be the best or worst. No matter: he must finish a partisan. His Honor may be a scholar and a gentleman; Her Honor a model of erudition, reason, comity. No matter: scholarship, erudition, reason, and gentility are of adversary interest only as they join the partisan pack.

Their Honors may be nonpareils of probity or remain in hock for all of their professional lives to the governor who appointed them, the machine that pushed them, the mob that bought them. The judge may tyrannize over his courtroom fief or painstakingly defer to procedural propriety. He may bend to every breeze of constraint or, Gibraltar of courage (there are more than a few), place fair play above carrot, stick, or popular odium. The central point remains: the Bench must choose finally the warp of one perspective or the other. No third is offered.

Judicial tools in adversary procedure are scant. The avenues of judicial discretion, though wide, are mostly dead end: not investigatory but exclusive, not exploratory but categorical, not open but restricted within those boundaries the lawyers draw. The judge has not a maximum of information but a minimum. The judging atmosphere is not discussion, cooperation, nor tempered reflection, but battle. His Honor must clutch his skirts above the strife, while about him the combatants seed pestilence, cry Apocalypse, and vie at pulling him into the vortex. At last he must succumb. He has nowhere else to go.

Judicial decision in adversary procedure is a product not of immunity, but of contamination; not of cool—but of heat.

The elimination of bias is judicial show; but its maximization is adversary reality. Like the shell-man's pitch, the judicial ritual distracts the litigant's eye from the switch. The Bench fronts the claim and shills the game. Other and better ways can be designed.

14

THE FICTION OF
THE IMPARTIAL JURY

Jury trial, some hold, is that other, better way; in fact the "one serious and significant alternative" to trial by judge.[1] But its aura is something weightier. The jury carries a burden of special meaning: the common man raised to mythic dimension—either of acumen or plain tomfoolishness. Juries tend to be invested with the import of democracy itself.

That import has been easily maintained, for there are few fields about which so little reliable knowledge exists.[2] Unlike lawyers and judges, who are long-term stars of the legal repertory show, the jurors are hired for a single run. Unlike the dramatically visible professionals, the jury is relatively anonymous (by requirement a group whose personalities do not individuate within the courtroom), passive and mute. Jurors are untutored in the arcanities of law and their occupational, economic, and educational status is, on the average, not notable.

Juries work in secret. There has been remarkably little investigation of what juries actually do, how and why they do it, nor to what degree they are competent in the process. Jury workings are, as a matter of course, shrouded in mystery.[3] Early studies largely employed simulated juries;[4] an air of impropriety hung over efforts to study real ones.[5] When, in 1947, two of Jerome Frank's students tried to survey juror response to specific trials in which they had served, all those judges whose cooperation in the probe was asked, refused.[6] Judges have been "induced to cover juryroom deliberations with legal shrouds calculated to protect them from close scrutiny."[7] The most impassioned declarations on the jury system's value, pro and con, are based not on data concerning observed jury process, but rather on deduction from jury decisions, on jury myths, and the infrequent posttrial statements of ex-jury members gleaned from interviews and letters to Dear Abby.[8] The book *The American Jury,* written by professor of law Harry Kalven, Jr., and professor of law and sociology Hans Zeisel, was called by its authors "essentially an empirical study of the jury *in operation*"[9] (emphasis mine) and was acclaimed as "up to now, the only significant attempt at a scientific study of the differences in the ways judges and juries decide criminal cases."[10] Yet that book was based "for methodological convenience"[11] upon response to 3,576 questionnaires sent—*not* to jurors, but to *judges*.

Jury operation remains, in other words, a nearly blank page upon which may be written, as one wishes, epic, travesty, tragedy—but always a drama of social significance.

Juries arouse a heat of feeling. For Alexander Hamilton, the jury was ". . . a safeguard to liberty, the . . . very palladium of free government."[12] For Blackstone, it was "the glory of the English law."[13] Others called it "Heaven-taught,"[14] ". . . one of our most cherished democratic institutions . . .,"[15] a "vital artery in the bloodstream of the democratic process,"[16] in fact, ". . . one of the most important, most vital, most sacred of the institutions which maintain our free and popular government. . . ."[17] The jury system is not merely ". . . one of the really great achievements of English and American jurisprudence,"[18] but is "adapted to the investigation of truth beyond any other the world can produce."[19] Perhaps the most intemperate view of all is voiced by lawyer Joseph T. Karcher, who ascribes America's "growth and strength and development"[20] largely to the jury system. "No other nation in history has gone as far, or grown as great or strong or rich in such a short span of less than 200 years. England grew to be the leading world power during the period in which she had a similar system for the administration of justice and the enforcement of law and order."[21] However, Karcher declares, since England's relative abandonment of the jury, "It is noteworthy that there has been a steady decline in [her] power and prestige . . . not only economically and militarily, but politically, socially and morally as well. . . ."[22] A bar journal article puts matters somewhat more bluntly: If the jury should be abolished, "the remaining oasis which is keeping the independent practitioner alive will dry up," for most private-practice lawyers receive "the major part of their income" from personal injury cases[23]—which are generally tried (and cried) before juries.

The opposition sees the jury otherwise: as one of barbarism's relics.[24] "The 'jury tradition' has been the people's sacred democratic cow . . . [but] it is in one sense the antithesis of democratic government. . . . This strange spectacle of an anonymous body of twelve men playing the role of one of democracy's chief symbols may well prompt examination."[25] The jury is "antiquated . . . and inherently absurd—so much so that no lawyer, judge, scholar, prescription-clerk, cook or mechanic in a garage would ever think for a moment of employing that method for determining the facts in any situation that concerned him."[26] "A better instrument could scarcely be imagined for achieving uncertainty, capriciousness, lack of uniformity, disregard of former decisions—utter unpredictability. . . ."[27] According to a lawyer and scholar, our ". . . boasted trial by jury, which affirms that all grades of capacity above driveling idiocy are alike fitted for the exalted office of sifting truth from error, may well excite the derision of future times."[28]

Our concept of the jury might have excited the derision of past times as well. That "anonymous body" has not always been one of democracy's chief symbols; it began, in fact, as a form of "royal inquisition."[29] The jury remains uniquely useful to adversary mythology: a prop that—despite the most extraordinary obstacles—occasionally and miraculously produces a reasonable decision. Such result must surprise all concerned.

THE ROYAL TOOL

Legal historians disagree as to whether the jury's roots were initially Anglo-Saxon, Norman, or possibly even Scandinavian.[30] The predominant view is that the jury originated in 9th-century France in the *inquisitio*, the ancient inquisition of the Carolingian kings.[31] The *inquisitio,* which originally forced witnesses (called *recognitors*) to swear to information used to establish royal land and tax rights, eventually required information or *verdicts* in private controversies also.[32] Those *verdicts* (from the Latin *vere dictum,* "truly said") were based neither on evidence presented nor arguments heard, but solely on personal knowledge and opinion derived from the witnesses' familiarity with events.[33] *Inquisitio* was in effect inquiry, accusation, and judgment at once.

That "royal tool for prying into the affairs of common people"[34] was carried by the Normans into England in 1066. There, the conquerors found several Anglo-Saxon judicial usages with which the Norman import was somewhat congruent. These were *secta* witnesses, neighbors who once more knew the persons and circumstances of controversy; *official* witnesses, specifically appointed to attend all private business transactions in order to be able to testify about them if need arose; and *compurgators* or "oath-helpers," required to swear *with* the parties in support of their word, rather than to give information. (The value of a *compurgator's* oath was rated according to his rank. For instance, that of a thane was, by a kind of class-mathematic, equivalent to those of seven yeomen.)[35]

Recognitors, secta, official witnesses, and *compurgators* were initial variations on the juror concept. Unlike modern jurors, however, they were all actor-participants, all witnesses to the original fracas. Contrary to today, personal knowledge of the facts was the major qualification for all except *compurgators;* for whom personal acquaintance with one of the parties was requisite.[36]

Inquisitio was first employed in England on a grand scale in 1086—still solely for the crown's benefit.[37] It was extended in the latter part of the 12th century, again for the crown's purposes. Henry II, engaged in a power struggle with church and feudal lords and sensing ". . . the potentialities of judgment by neighbors . . . ,"[38] made *inquisitio* or "inquiry" the prevailing means of deciding whether or not people were paying the taxes they owed him.[39] In 1166, Henry expanded inquiry once more, this time into the criminal area, via the historic Assize (edict) of Clarendon. At this point, inquiry's accusatory and judgmental functions were, for the first time, nominally separated. Under the Assize, a body of "the most lawful men"[40] regularly presented to the authorities the names of persons suspected of serious crimes. That "presentment" rested, as before, upon prevailing *belief* as to the accused's guilt.[41]

The accused was then sent to the judgment of ordeal—which settled the matter.[42]

(It did not help much if the victim came through ordeal unscathed. The Assize, leaving as little as possible to chance, declared that "The Lord King also wishes that those who . . . clear themselves shall nevertheless forswear the King's land if they are of bad renown . . . and cross the sea within eight days unless detained by the weather . . . and never come back to England save by the King's permission. . . .")[43]

Thus the Assize, together with a subsequent edict in 1176, effectively brought "the royal presence into the lucrative field of the criminal law,"[44] where the fines and forfeitures that (one way or another) followed presentment provided new additions to the royal treasury. In addition, inquiry was now a means of eliminating, in law-and-order's name, opposition to the increase and centralization of royal power.[45]

In the Assize's distinction between accusation and judgment lay the genesis of our grand and petit juries. That distinction remained fuzzy, however, for the next two centuries, during which time the accusing (or indicting) jury still frequently declared guilt or innocence as well.[46] After all, as a judge pointed out in 1341, "if the indictors be not there, it is not good for the King."[47] Not until the mid-14th century did separation between the two functions formally occur in the shape of two different jury bodies. The grand jury, "instrument of royal power,"[48] now accused, while the petit, or trial jury, judged.

Meanwhile, the role of the juror-witnesses had also begun to change: witnessing and judging functions started to dissociate. Lawyers increasingly brought their own witnesses into court to support the parties' claims of fact, and the juror-witnesses took backseat to those party-witnesses. More and more, over time, the jurors simply audienced the facts as presented by the parties. Nonetheless, the principle that a verdict must be based solely on evidence presented in court, rather than on the jurors' prior knowledge or belief, was not officially established until the end of the 17th century.[49]

From Norman *inquisitio* through the 17th century, juries grand and petit continued predominantly the crown's right arm. During the Tudor-Stuart reigns (1485–1649) the concept of the jury's role began to change. Slowly, the jury system began to be seen as possible protection *against* the crown. But that vision did not yet derive from the jury's actual performance. On the contrary. In the Tudor-Stuart period the administration of justice in England had "sunk to the lowest degradation, and the judicial bench had become the too willing tool of an unconstitutional and unscrupulous executive."[50] In particular, several infamous tribunals had been created for suppression of treason and heresy: among them, the Court of the Star Chamber. In those tribunals no jury was allowed. By inverse reasoning then, popular feeling grew that, if juries were anathema to Tudors and Stuarts, they must be good for everyone else.

In other words: a remedy for despotism was needed. The jury, by default of obvious alternative (or possibly of lesser evil) was nominated.

Magna Carta, with its reference to "the lawful judgement of his peers," was now summoned to validate as "immemorial" the jury's new reputation as the people's shield. In fact, Magna Carta, which addressed itself to the rights of "freemen," had meant thereby only the barons, lesser knights and burgesses, not that majority who (at the time of Runnymede in 1215) were still serfs and land slaves.[51] Nevertheless, the political imperatives of the 16th and 17th centuries required the legend still current: that the jury has been "always" a bulwark of liberty.[52]

For the duration of the Star Chamber, that bulwark remained more hope than fact. Jurors who dared to bring a verdict against the crown's interests were themselves often called before the Star Chamber, imprisoned, or fined.[53] Ordered to reverse verdicts, jurors were often locked up without food, drink, or communication with the outside world until they complied.[54] Although the Star Chamber had disappeared by 1641, not until 1670 did the Bushel Case declare that jurors were no longer to be punished for acquitting a defendant.[55]

In 1681 occurred the particular case that was to symbolize thereafter the jury's refurbished reputation. In that year, the crown accused the Earl of Shaftesbury of treason, and asked a Whig grand jury to hear testimony against him in open court. That jury, unsympathetic to the crown (and perhaps suspecting, with later historians, that the earl was in fact guilty under the laws of the times) deemed it wiser to hear testimony behind closed doors—following which they refused to indict.[56] This notable refusal finally confirmed the grand jury's new image as a people's, rather than a royal, tool.[57]

That updated exterior, however, was superimposed upon a machine built for very different purpose: indeed upon a "relic of another condition of society"[58] that still employed compulsion, secrecy, and inquiry-accusation essentially undifferentiated. The Star Chamber's most salient characteristics had simply taken new cover. The grand jury retained them all.

THE GRAND JURY

America inherited the jury system from England. Inherited too, and dear to the hearts of those freshly escaped from Europe's monarchies, was the "immemorial" tradition of the jury, petit and grand, as freedom's bulwark.

Though Article III of the Constitution initially guaranteed jury trial in criminal cases, broader cover was wanted. It was this cry for more extensive jury protection that impelled the popular push for a more comprehensive Bill of Rights.[59] Consequently, the 7th Amendment extended the petit jury to civil matters; and the 5th Amendment firmly ensconced the grand jury as a protection against unjustified criminal prosecution: "No person shall be held to answer for a capital or otherwise infamous crime, unless on a presentment or indictment of a grand jury. . . ."

Anomaly is clear. The grand jury is embedded in the chief document of our personal liberty as a safeguard against government incursion upon that liberty. But judicial safeguards and personal liberties are almost as foreign to grand-jury style as they were to Henry's Assize or the Tudors' Star Chamber.

Folklore holds otherwise. Folklore still insists that the grand jury unearths wrongdoing; that it is "the conscience of the community," a "guardian of justice," the "cornerstone of our criminal jurisprudence," a "buffer between state and nation," and "watchdog of our rights." Thomas Dewey hailed it as a "protection for the innocent."[60] The courts have called it "both a sword and a shield of justice."[61]

Thus, as shield, the grand jury must prevent unjustified criminal prosecution by hearing the state's case before trial is instigated, and refusing to return a "true bill" if evidence is insufficient.[62] As sword, the panel must ferret out criminal activity or wrongdoing (whether by public official or private citizen) and bring accusation if warranted.[63] The first, or indicting, grand jury begins with a bill of indictment, prepared by the prosecutor, accusing a specific person of a specific crime.[64] The second, or investigating, grand jury begins with neither crime nor accused, but only a *question* as to whether a crime has occurred and if so, who may be involved.[65] Both juries must decide whether there exists probable cause to initiate criminal prosecution.[66]

Theoretically, the grand jury's shield and sword are a double check on Authority's power. On one hand, the indicting jury purports to protect the citizenry from repressive government prosecution. On the other hand, the investigating jury itself initiates prosecution—even against government—where officials may be corrupt.[67]

In practice, however, the indicting and investigating grand juries are structurally indistinguishable. Both hear essentially "the witness the prosecutor decides to call asked questions the prosecutor wants to ask";[68] both go no further than the prosecutor—government's employee—wishes to step. The only difference between the two juries is that the investigating prosecutor "does not know the answers ahead of time."[69] Both juries may use crime—real, unreal, or suspected—as pretext for inquiry into the witness's beliefs and associations, rather than into deeds done.[70] For the citizen, in other words, the grand jury still represents less shield than inquisition.

Grand juries, according to ex-Senator Charles E. Goodell, "have always served the interests of whichever political element could control them."[71] Melvin P. Antell, a former assistant county prosecutor, states: "The fact is that the inherent characteristics of the grand jury suit it best for a role which is actually repugnant to its purported mission . . . it has a far greater potentiality as an instrument of oppression."[72] Beneath its theoretical mission, the grand jury remains structured to abet Authority's interests. In result, the wrongdoing unearthed is less likely to be graft, rackets, gun-pushing, drugs, or crime at the highest official levels, than that which frightens Power more: social and political heresy.

That actuality is not widely publicized. Only a sprinkling of lay persons know much of the grand jury's activities and workings; even a surprisingly large number of attorneys have no more than the foggiest notion of its responsibilities and powers.[73] The fact is that the grand jury is a Constitutional body for which the Constitution's 1st, 4th, 5th, and 6th Amendments do not, generally, exist.

* * *

The grand jury is a law-enforcement panel of (usually) twenty-three persons bound by an oath of secrecy; whose work is conducted in secret; and whose records of proceedings stay secret by law. Only the government prosecutor attends its sessions; only the government's story is heard.

Witnesses may be summoned to appear before a grand jury within hours from receipt of subpoena;[74] and despite hardship, in cities hundreds of miles from their homes.[75] No show of reasonableness or probable cause is required for the issuance of a grand jury subpoena.[76] The witness, though subject to unrestrained cross-examination by the prosecutor, must appear in the jury room alone, unaided by counsel[77]—contrary to his 6th Amendment right to legal assistance. The witness has no 6th Amendment right to know the subject of investigation;[78] no right to know whether he himself or another person entirely is its target;[79] no 6th Amendment rights either to confront the witnesses against him or to call his own witnesses,[80] no right to see entireties rather than parts of documents at issue[81] nor to refresh his memory therefrom; no right to explain or controvert prosecution material.[82] He has no right to object to evidence obtained by any search that violates his 4th Amendment guarantee against unreasonable search and seizure.[83] (The grand jury's freedom to use illegally obtained evidence is in effect a direct incentive *for* that illegal seizure.)[84] The witness has no right even to sit in the grand jury room as an observer.[85] There is no limit to the number of witnesses the prosecution may call and virtually no rules of evidence govern the number, immateriality, vagueness, or personal nature of questions asked.[86] And, except in the most minimal way, no 1st Amendment right against abridgement of speech, press, or assembly is recognized.[87]

The grand jury, in other words, strips the citizen of almost all Constitutional protection; denies him almost all reasonable aid; and then confronts him with the investigatory resource and prestige of an entire state or federal government.[88] Far from protecting the innocent, the grand jury more often offers the innocent "no chance to protect themselves from their accusers no matter how false the evidence may be."[89] The witness who resists goes to jail.

In its almost unlimited prerogative, the grand jury is answerable to no one. It is neither checked, balanced, nor reviewed by any outside person, agency, executive or legislative body. But it is in no way either autonomous or impartial. Rather, the "people's panel" is in fact, according to Antell, "the prosecutor's alter-ego."[90] Prosecutors, Goodell says, ". . . are virtually unchecked in abusing the panel's compulsory process and its rule of secrecy."[91]

Indeed, the rare grand jury that, doing what it is supposed to, resists the prosecutor's armlock, is called with some dismay a "runaway jury." In the federal courts, not even that is possible, for no indictment the jurors bring is valid without the prosecutor's signature. Thus, that Watergate grand jury which—wishing to indict President Nixon as a co-conspirator—moved edgily close to Authority's ultimate lair, was told by prosecutor Jaworski that a sitting President was out of bounds ("The king can do no wrong"). When, unseated and a private citizen, Mr. Nixon became officially vulnerable to public laws, the jurors were again undone: Nixon's heir whisked his benefactor beyond legal accountability for good. Though the jurors' reactions ranged from dissatisfaction to outrage,[92] their bewildered foreman commented, "I think any action should be initiated by Mr. Jaworski. . . . Frankly, I'm not a lawyer and I wouldn't know where to begin."[93] Against Authority, the watchdog has little bite.

In truth, the twenty-three grand jurors are "completely untrained in the work they have to do."[94] The only legal requirement "is that they can see and hear and have resided for a prescribed time in the jurisdiction where they have been called. . . ."[95] The government prosecutor tells them what the charge is, selects the facts for them to hear, and shapes "the tone and feel of the entire case."[96] Investigative techniques of examining and collating documents, interviewing witnesses, and analyzing conflicting data are outside the experience of the average juror.[97] Grand jurors are largely unaware of their rights to ask questions or call witnesses of their own; are rarely apprised of those rights; rarely exercise them.[98] (Or, they may accept the prosecutor's response that such a request is "irrelevant."[99]) The grand jurors may be as ignorant as the witness of the nature, scope, or strategy of the investigation they are supposedly conducting.

Thus, ex-Prosecutor Antell says, ". . . the only person who has a clear idea of what is happening in the grand jury room is the public official whom these twenty-three novices are expected to check . . . [the grand jury] must, paradoxically, look to the very person whose misconduct they are supposed to guard against for evidence as to when he is acting oppressively."[100] To that authority, grand jury "autonomy" defers, for the jurors assume "that the prosecutor wouldn't bring [the case] . . . if he didn't feel that he could get a conviction."[101] That belief is self-confirming. *Grand juries disagree with the government they are supposed to monitor in less than 2 or 3 percent of cases.*[102]

The so-called grand jury investigation, Antell says, "is really nothing more than a review of the prosecutor's pre-digested evidence and a ratification of his conclusions."[103] The jurors themselves initiate investigation less than 5 percent of the time.[104] Any protection that does occur may come oftener from the prosecutor than from the jury. Grand jurors (perhaps taking their cue from grand jury law) are not "overly impressed by constitutional guarantees. . . . Personal standards of conduct supplant those established by the legislature and each grand juror looks for a way to suppress what is unacceptable to him."[105] Nor do grand jury handbooks usually inform the jurors of their guardian role.[106] Rather, Antell claims, most commonly "it is the prosecutor who intervenes between the victim and an irate grand jury."[107] Ultimately, then, the grand jury is as effective or ineffective as the prosecutor in charge.

The grand jury is called a "non-adversary forum"[108] and is both acclaimed and condemned on that basis. Critics deplore the grand jury's lack of "adversary environment"[109] and adversary rights,[110] saying that those features which make the adversary trial viable are "utterly and intolerably lacking from the grand jury process."[111] But it is not adversary environment that creates adversary trial's questionable viability. What viability exists derives from Constitutional and evidentiary *limits* upon adversary environment. It is precisely those limits that grand jury procedure lacks.[112] Against the ordinary citizen, the watchdog wears no muzzle; "against" is essentially out of control.

The grand jury, indicting or investigatory, is predominantly "an engine for unilateral pretrial discovery by the government";[113] discovery unimpeded by the embarrassing presence of the accused or his counsel.[114] The grand jury's vaunted secrecy represents less protection of innocence and preservation of reputation than simply "the government's unwillingness to disclose its case to the defendant in advance of trial."[115]

Innocence and reputation need shield against government muscle.

But the grand jury is not the way. For that "nonadversary forum" is in fact one more adversary weapon; a weapon aimed selectively at the weak far oftener than against the strong.

I believe it is no accident that England—whose courts have strongly curbed the adversary environment[116]—has abolished the grand jury. "Relatively few tears were shed and they have long since been dried."[117] English grand jury proceeding was replaced, in 1933, by a public preliminary examination at which both sides are represented and heard.[118] The largely satisfactory character of these examinations has obviated British regret for the grand jury's demise.[119]

The preliminary examination exists in the United States, too. Where used, it may as in England substitute for grand jury action, or instead simply precede it—determining whether sufficient cause exists to hold a defendant for the grand jury,[120] just as the grand jury decides whether there is sufficient cause for trial. Like the grand jury proceeding, preliminary hearing is meant as a bulwark against possible harassment of an accused.[121] There the resemblance ends. For the preliminary hearing offers those basic safeguards the grand jury denies. It is an open proceeding at which the accused, with his counsel present,[122] may cross-examine the witnesses against him, present any testimony he wishes to give, challenge whether probable cause has been established, and obtain some discovery of the case against him.[123]

In this country, however, preliminary hearing is not guaranteed. It is generally entirely optional. That option is the prosecutor's. The criminal procedures of the federal system and of the majority of states do not require that the prosecutor provide a preliminary hearing for the accused.[124] Solely upon his own discretion, the prosecutor may bypass all those procedural safeguards of preliminary examination[125] and go instead straight to the grand jury. Adversary incentive urges he do just that.

Thus, grand jury accusation may bring a defendant to criminal trial before the petit jury with no weightier consideration than prosecutorial fiat—but a fiat ostensibly mandated by twenty-three "independent" good men and true. Those twelve good men and true, the petit jurors, cannot help but accord significance to the "judicious, impartial opinion" of almost twice their number. There lies the grand jury system's "real evil."[126]

Antell says, ". . . that viciousness, if you will—lies . . . in our pretension that [the grand jury] is actually an informed and quasi-judicial organ, a pretension which misrepresents the prosecutor's unilateral action as the product of stately proceedings conducted by judicial standards."[127] That pretense, whose effects are "greatly magnified by the accompanying judicial rites,"[128] lends almost irresistible impact to any accusation the grand jury returns. That pretense deals, in fact, one more blow to the obligatory presumption of innocence; and to that other mighty jurisprudential theme, the prosecutor's responsibility to prove guilt beyond a reasonable doubt. For accusation is itself an adversary act.

Accusation is not exploration, examination, nor discussion—it is attack. Accusation is not question raised, but declaration of opinion *formed.* When that opinion is held by Authority, grounded in the state's expertise and vast instrument of discovery, and backed by twenty-three "autonomous" citizens, it must, too often, have for the petit jurors the emotional force of "fact."

In practice then, the very *act of accusation* tacitly but surely shifts the burden of proof to the defense. In practice, and contrary to adversary theory, it becomes the *defense's responsibility to disprove* the government's charge. The defense is thereby placed in the impossible position of having to prove a negative.

"Where," demanded the prosecution in a recent California trial, "is the evidence that the defendant . . . didn't beat his wife and children?"[129] Despite what the Court called "inept investigation, inefficient preparation and inadequate prosecution"[130]—the state won. Grand jury accusation is a prosecutorial first-move in the adversary battle plan.

THE PETIT JURY

Petit jury selection is the next big move. It is a move open also to the defense. Though like the grand jury the petit jury is an adversary tool, that tool is available to both sides.

Choice of trial by judge or by jury is generally optional. But, a legal rule-of-thumb counsels, "If you have a weak, long-shot case with the law against you, always demand a jury."[131] Clarence Darrow held, "All property rights are much safer in the hands of courts than of jurors," whereas conversely, "Every lawyer who represents the poor avoids a trial by the court."[132] In the 1950s, defendants in political trials tended to prefer judges; today juries are more frequently trusted.[133] In law school, ". . . it is stressed that . . . cases are won or lost by merely the picking of a sympathetic jury. Nothing is said . . . of seeking a jury that will do justice."[134] In the Patricia Hearst trial, lawyer F. Lee Bailey demanded: "Do I want a fair jury? No, I want an acquitting jury!"[135]

Like the judge, the trial jury is called "impartial." That claim is underwritten by the Constitution's 6th Amendment. Although, as some suggest, impartiality may mean only "random bias," adversary method works at rendering meaningless even that minimum guarantee. The petit jury is no more likely to be an impartial body than the grand jury—nor do prosecutor, plaintiff, or defendant wish it to be, any more than any of them wishes an impartial judge. Bias is the adversary aim.

Lawyers jury-shop at least as diligently as they judge-shop. One writer explains, "The object of jury selection is to choose those individuals who will be most influenced by the emotional displays of the attorney in his presentation of the case and by the participants in testifying. In presenting his case to the jury, the attorney resorts to these emotional displays *in order to divert the attention of the jurors away from the legal concepts and legally admissible evidence. . . .*"[136] (emphasis mine)

A judge says, "The attorney, in most instances, prefers a jury which is prejudiced, or at least leaning, in favor of his cause."[137] A lawyer states, ". . . I submit each attorney is attempting not only to exclude those jurors prejudicial to his side, but is attempting to secure and develop those prejudiced for his side."[138] Officially, that jury-shopping is called *voir dire*.

Voir dire (Old French: "to speak the truth") is a verbal examination whose public goal is the securing of impartial jurors. *Voir dire* is considered an art among trial attorneys, an art to which whole volumes have been devoted.[139] Although *voir dire* examinations are theoretically intended to detect and eliminate bias, "they are almost universally employed for quite different objectives. Most counsel seek to employ any bias in favor of their client and eliminate only such bias as is directed against him."[140]

Nor is selection for favorable bias the entire story. Such bias must be created where it does not yet exist. Thus, *voir dire* is a forensic art by which the lawyer aims not merely at securing a favorable jury initially, but also at ensuring the jury's favor "by verbally—almost subliminally—injecting bias" into it.[141] *Voir dire* is therefore also specifically a tactical device to indoctrinate the jury, the questions themselves "designed to have an influence on the juror. . . ."[142] Now and then an attorney will use *voir dire* constructively: to circumvent the adversary prohibition of contextual information. "Great trial lawyers throughout United States history have used the *voir dire* to educate individual jurors . . . and the public in general, about the social issues behind the arrest and trial of the defendant."[143]

Hints for jury-shopping abound: Clarence Darrow recommended, "Never take a wealthy man on a jury. He will convict unless the defendant is accused of violating the anti-trust law, selling worthless stocks or bonds or something of that kind. . . . An Irishman is emotional, kindly, and sympathetic. . . . . Keep Unitarians, Universalists, Congregationalists, Jews and other agnostics. . . ."[144] A judge counsels, "Fat people are said to be jovial; a fair complexion evidences a warm heart . . . people with light hair are sympathetic; people with thin, sharp faces are self-opinionated and stubborn . . . bankers are hard and apt to convict; elderly people are lenient, but are sometimes severe in criminal matters; the poor believe that the laws were made to benefit the rich and therefore the poor, when in trouble, should stick together."[145]

Physiognomy counts: Osborn, in *The Mind of the Juror,* wrote: "'. . . the man with a little, puckered-up mouth is naturally unsympathetic' . . . a shrewd defense attorney 'endeavors to get only those with good-sized mouths, and especially those the 'corners' of whose mouths turn up. . . .' "[146] An article in the *Criminal Law Bulletin* suggests, "Generally speaking, the heavy, round-faced, jovial-looking person is the most desirable. The undesirable juror is quite often the slight-underweight and delicate type. His features are sharp and fragile, with that lean 'Cassius' look."[147]

Occupation matters: An article in *Forum* states, "The influence of the occupational background upon the juror is often quite pronounced. For example, butchers are three times as favorable to the plaintiff on liability as are executives. . . . However, on the size of awards, butchers are 10 per cent below national average. . . . Retired workers and salesmen are the least desirable jurors for the plaintiff on liability. . . . Retired real estate salesmen are very unplaintiff-minded and vote for the plaintiff only 32 per cent of the time and are 6 per cent under average on awards. . . ."[148] *Selecting a Jury* advises, "In most actions involving personal injuries, the plaintiff should eschew ex-policemen, investigators and bank clerks as jurors. Former policemen and investigators are likely to have acquired the habit of tearing down stories of plaintiffs. . . . Bank clerks . . . are notoriously tight-fisted, probably having acquired the habit of safeguarding other people's money while they themselves receive relatively small salaries."[149]

Gait is significant: *Goldstein's Trial Technique* notes, "It is always good policy for the trial attorney to closely observe each prospective juror as he walks to his seat in the jury box . . . . The aggressive and positive walk of some, the slouched, sliding movement of others . . . should all be looked for and considered in trying to determine those desired."[150]

Physical disability, sex, and dress are handy guides: "Look for physical affliction," a prosecutor urges. "These people usually empathize with the accused. . . . I don't like women jurors because I can't trust them. . . . Young women too are usually unstable. . . . Conservatively dressed people are generally stable and good for the state."[151]

In short: it is susceptability to "extraneous, non-legal influences" that is wanted.[152] Juries, like judges, are selected not for dispassion, but in order to win.

Jury selection does not, however, depend solely upon folklore. More sophisticated techniques are increasingly in use. Personality profiles predicting a prospective juror's attitudes, values, leadership or sycophancy, rigidity or malleability, may be drawn from a mass of data—in the collection of which few citizen privacies remain beyond reach.

Among those criteria of interest, and easily ascertainable, are the juror's age, job, marital status, number and age of children; his place of employment, previous court litigation, religion, political affiliation, status as a property owner, accident record, type of home, neighborhood and length of residence; his union membership or activity, credit rating and background, and standard of living.[153] Indeed, "the only limitations are a lawyer's ingenuity, available time and available funds."[154]

With those limitations, government has no problem. Government lawyers have access to, and use, a vast array of information, including Internal Revenue Service files, FBI reports, and the records and experiences of colleagues and predecessors who keep data on jurors from past cases.[155] Government has available, further, the vast resources of its law enforcement and crime detection network.[156] The FBI, for example, can secure information from banks, stock brokerage firms, insurance companies, and other institutions that would not make their records available to private investigators.[157]

The private citizen, defendant or plaintiff, cannot match government's means. But for those few persons who can afford them, extensive information channels still exist: private detectives, commercial jury-investigation services, and police reports.[158] Sufficient funds may even command the evaluative-predictive skills of graphology (if access to the jury commissioner's questionnaires can be had[159]), and of sociology, psychology, and psychiatry as well. Dr. William Bryant, for instance, helped F. Lee Bailey pick the jury that finally acquitted Dr. Samuel Sheppard of murder after over ten years of trials, appeals, and retrials. Bryant's record since then has been "virtually perfect in some of the most spectacular cases of the past decade."[160] His tab has been known to reach $50,000.[161]

Similarly, trial defense for ex-Nixon-officials John Mitchell and Maurice Stans hired the president of a communications think tank, who applied to juror selection the principles of marketing research. The plan he drew called for blue-collar workers, primarily Roman Catholic, who earned between $8,000 and $10,000 yearly, and who read the New York *Daily News*. He prescribed people who were "home established, to the right, more concerned with inflation than Watergate"[162] people who preferred actor John Wayne to intellectual television host Dick Cavett. His design had no place for Jews or "limousine liberals" and there were neither. Eleven of the twelve jurors had no more than a high school education. The twelfth, a graduate of Harvard Business School, was on the jury by accident—having originally been an alternate who had moved onto the final panel when a regular juror became ill. Since the defense was given twenty peremptory juror-challenges to the prosecution's eight, that defense design dominated and controlled jury selection. Mitchell and Stans were acquitted. Commented one of the prosecutors, "the case was lost in the *voir dire*." ("Scandal!" one courtroom observer cried. "Hurray for American justice!" cried another.)[163]

Jury partisans deny that such strategems defeat impartiality through production of a weighted jury. Partisans claim rather the production of a group whose "biases cancel." The adversaries, ultimately neutralizing each other's impact, will create a stand-off in the jury box and the facts will emerge. But clearly a stand-off can derive only from equal bank accounts, equal wit in their use—and equal luck. Such coincidence is rare. A favorable jury is more generally bought by the side with the larger purse.

That circumstance is perhaps peculiar to the United states. The jury, though inherited from England, has become in many respects a "distinctive American institution."[164] The United States sees over 75,000 civil jury trials per year, to England's less than 200.[165] American lawyers have almost absolute control in picking out the jurors, particularly in state courts,[166] whereas in England jury selection is made almost entirely by the judge.[167] (In England, twelve people are called, indiscriminately, from a list of persons summoned to jury duty, and are asked almost no questions—not even their addresses or occupations.[168]) With his control of jury selection lies the American lawyer's hope of controlling the trial's outcome. "This is too often what [lawyers] mean when they speak of the democracy of a jury."[169]

Of course, nominally, jury "democracy" means something nobler. Trial by jury is held to be a "people's process" in all the ways that trial by judge is not. Pro-jury rationale ". . . supposes that the judgment of twelve men whose differences are resolved through open-minded discussion is better than the judgment of one man whose trial experience is far more extensive."[170] Kalven and Zeisel state flatly that "most praise or blame of the jury can come *only* by way of comparison of trial by jury with trial by judge."[171] (emphasis mine)

That comparison rests on three chief arguments: first, that the jury affords a unique opportunity for popular participation in our legal system; and second and third, that the jury is uniquely suited both to protect the public interest and to find facts.

The first (and probably most frequently offered) argument calls the jury "the only part of [the] judicial process [in] which the public itself participates. . . ."[172] It is "our way of insisting that citizens visit the court from time to time and report to each other on the administration of justice."[173] The jury indeed is the "sole mechanism for the citizen to act and participate as a rational creature" in that administration.[174] (In actuality, less than one percent of the population sees jury service.[175])

Blackstone praised the jury's protective role as a "safeguard against the arbitrary exercise of power by the government. . . ."[176] The jury, according to other proponents, "was designed and has served always as a protection against judges. . . ."[177] This is not only because the judge may be "compliant, biased or eccentric . . .,"[178] but for philosophical and political reasons also: in a democracy, it is held, the jury is closer to the people, their mores, their attitudes and unquestioned postulates than any judge can hope to be.[179]

The third argument, however, is the clincher: that of the jury's fact-finding ability. The jury's size is claimed to render it better able to "judge motives" and "weigh possibilities" than a single man, however wise he may be, or however broad his trial experience. And unlike the lone judge, the jury brings community standards to bear upon cases. As a "community in microcosm,"[180] the jury is a repository of "downright common sense,"[181] that "plain, practical common sense of the Anglo-Saxon race."[182] The jury is in effect that "reasonable man" whose assumed standard is so often cited by our law as a judgment norm.[183] The finding of facts is the jury's central legal function. But adversary procedure does its best—no matter the jurors' most earnest intent—to prevent precisely that.

Jurors are selected not only for bias. They are chosen for ignorance too. Adversary procedure excludes any juror "possessing the slightest knowledge of the facts he is supposedly summoned to determine. Thus, that which specifically qualified one to act as a juror at the inception of the system now specifically disqualifies him. This evolution has been termed progress."[184] Further: lawyers, via peremptory challenge, regularly deny jury service to anyone at all experienced in the field the lawsuit concerns.[185] In personal-injury or malpractice cases, for example, attorneys routinely eliminate doctors, nurses, or any who have otherwise studied medicine. Were such a person to be seated, *Goldstein's Trial Technique* points out, "all of the other jurors on the panel will naturally turn to this one man and will be governed mainly by his opinion. . . . At first blush it would seem preferable to have some man on the jury who would know all about the issues involved, but . . . there is the possibility of this one man disagreeing with the trial lawyer's theory of the case. . . ."[186] Those best equipped to find fact are excluded from the fact-finding panel.

Often excused also are many of those who might best be expected to overcome the handicap of inexperience in legal matters:[187] lawyers, for instance, as well as those who have ever studied law and "educators of every grade and description."[188] A typical state statute exempts from that "community in microcosm" not only state officials and legislators, but all judges, all clerks, sheriffs, coroners, postmasters, mail carriers, practicing attorneys, all officials of the United States, officiating ministers of the Gospel, school teachers, practicing physicians, registered pharmacists, ferrymen, mayors, policemen, members of the Fire Department, embalmers, undertakers and funeral directors, all veterinarians, and all persons actively employed upon the editorial or mechanical staffs of any newspaper.[189] In brief: the nearer the jurors' minds "approach a blank on questions they must try, the better are they qualified."[190]

Who remain? The "chosen" are predominantly older, retired, nonprofessional, middle-class Anglo-Saxons. They bring no particular talent to the fact-finding job and frequently approach their duty in "a haphazard fashion."[191] Jurors are, in fact, generally as biased, emotionally susceptible, uneducated, and ignorant of the principles and material at issue as the lawyers can manage. Nor do the courts extend themselves much to improve those "qualifications." "Jury-schools are unheard of; we first prefer to test citizens on litigants."[192]

To that particular forum, then, the science of law brings its case. To those ears, the lawyers tell their tales: material withheld, information out of order, objections timed to disrupt the adverse flow. At the same time, the very presence of that gallery stimulates the designed and effective adversary histrionic to heights rarely dreamed of before a judge alone.

Before a jury, the lawyer uses a "broader, heavier, grosser weapon."[193] The attorneys are "allowed—in fact expected—to appeal to the crudest emotions and prejudices of the jurors."[194] Indeed, countless treatises on trial technique urge that the lawyer make the best possible use of the jurors' emotions.[195] That attorney who can successfully "appeal to prejudice, arouse the jurors' passions, and cloud the issues, instead of being pilloried by his associates, is canonized."[196] A Tennessee court declared it a serious question "whether it is not . . . [counsel's] professional duty to shed [tears] whenever proper occasion arises."[197] Appellate courts, concurring, will easily overlook what they dub "mildly inflammatory remarks."[198]

The fact finders may make no participant attempt at ordering the chaos. The jurors, of all upon stage, may not speak. The Court generally inhibits those "twelve people of average ignorance"[199] from asking for repetition, clarification, or definition. (Some judges allow the jury to pass questions, in written form, to the Bench for asking. Yet even here, if the jurors claim that privilege more than a few times, the Bench's displeasure will be clear.) The jurors have no right to inquire either about holes in the evidential fabric, or about questionable testimony; not about issues, principles, motivations, nor contextual circumstance. And—perish forbid—they may certainly never interrogate litigants and witnesses. "Those who will finally have the sole responsibility of deciding the case are asked to sit still and say nothing and wait for enlightenment. . . ."[200] Though the judge may interrupt with many questions, "The jurors are embalmed in silence where they sit like oysters when the tide is out, save as they shift to ease their bodies on the hard, wood chairs."[201]

Like the Bench, and more so, the jurors are limited by the adversary frame. The fact finders must accept whatever case the lawmen present, no matter where else common sense, justice—nor fact-finding—urges. Unlike the judge, however, the jury neither directs nor dominates events. The jury is passive indeed.

That passivity enjoined upon the people's forum is not merely verbal. Of all those involved, directly or indirectly, in the drama— judge, lawyers, litigants, witnesses, clerk, court stenographer—it is *only those persons expressly charged with finding the facts who have no clear right to take notes.* Some judges may, if requested, permit jurors' note-taking. Some judges suggest it themselves. A few states' statutes indirectly imply the right of the jury to take notes.[202] Most jurisdictions expressly forbid it.[203]

The juror, in the words of the Supreme Court of Indiana, must too often register the evidence "on the tablets of his memory and not otherwise."[204] In the federal courts, note-taking is discretionary with the Court,[205] but jurors are generally unaware of this—and are not necessarily told. While jurors, once in the jury room, may ask to see transcripts of specific testimony, transcripts of *all* testimony are not automatically provided them. And, since most of us greatly overestimate the accuracy and and retentiveness of our memories (and underestimate the selectiveness of those notes we take), jurors will inevitably request far less than they should have.

In 1961, a research project in information recall was instituted by psychiatrist Richard E. Renneker at Mt. Sinai Hospital in Los Angeles.[206] Twenty consecutive therapy hours, recorded and transcribed, were individually scored by a group of psychiatrists for the quantity of relevant information units contained in each hour. There was 90 percent agreement among the judges as to what constituted relevant units in those periods. The project therapist, chosen because his recall ability was the highest of fifteen therapists tested, was taught predetermined criteria for relevancy, and preproject testing demonstrated his operational mastery of those criteria. Two days after each hour, the therapist's recall of relevant information units in that hour was examined. Results revealed that for two of the hours, during which he had failed to take any notes, his mean average recall was only *1 percent* ; whereas for the eighteen hours during which he *had* taken notes, he produced a mean average recall of 13.9 percent without referring to them, and 18.7 percent when he added the information his notes contained. Further, one fourth of the 13.9 percent was distorted in terms of addition, subtraction, modification, and rearrangement of sequence. At the same time, a control group of ten other therapists, each recalling one hour without reference to their notes, produced a mean average recall of 9 percent, with almost the same percentage of distortions. Seven days after the hour, both therapist and control group were able to produce a mean recall of only 8 percent, without notes. When all referred to their notes, an average 1.5 percent of previously unremembered data was produced. This additional 1.5 percent, however, was almost exclusively distorted and seemed to serve the function of providing an illusion of "evidence" for those distortions unrecognized (by themselves) in prior recalls.

Meanwhile, in Santa Monica, California, for instance, the average jury trial lasts three to four days. In another jurisdiction, an attorney described a trial that lasted five and one half months: "There were about fourteen thousand pages of testimony and hundreds of exhibits. Not a juror requested permission to take a single note. . . . You can imagine how much of this mass of evidence the jurors could remember when they retired."[207] The judge, of course, not only takes notes but may have a transcript available too. Nevertheless, "Trained as he is, his memory often fails. . . . Some trials last for weeks and scores of witnesses give evidence. All this the jury must remember till they reach a verdict."[208] None of the legal professionals is expected to recall the proceedings unaided. The untrained juror is.

Criticized as "hopelessly incompetent fact-finders,"[209] the jurors have no right to the action that might mitigate their failing, nor above all, to the transcript that might cure it. Jury service is largely a memory game. One excuse for that game is that note-taking would permit "the best note taker [to] dominate the jury."[210] Instead, it is the juror with the best memory—or worse, *claim* to the best memory—who is able to just that.

(What jurors *do* seem to recall with some consistency, however, is specifically that which they have been told to forget. An experiment asked thirty juries to try the same injury case. Those who heard that the defendant carried insurance, but were told by the court to "disregard" that fact, granted the plaintiff awards averaging $46,000, or $9,000 *higher* than the $37,000 awarded when the court did *not* instruct them to disregard the fact of insurance.[211] Out of eighteen jurors in another study, only *one*—who had served as a juror twenty times before—responded as if the court's "disregard" had been anything other than explicit command to remember.[212] In other words: that which is ordered stricken from the record tends to be marked upon the jurors' minds in indelible ink.)

Finally, capping and compounding the jury's confusion, is that end-of-trial ritual intended to clarify what has gone before: the ritual of jury instruction. The Court's instruction speech advises the jurors of those "matters of law" they must apply to the facts they find.[213] Unfortunately, that law is pronounced long after the facts have been heard: facts the jurors may well have ignored until belatedly told by the Court that they constitute the crux of the case.[214] More curious still: those same jurors who have, in the words of a judge, been "treated like children while the testimony is going on [are] then . . . doused with a kettleful of law, during the charge, that would make a third-year law student blanch."[215] Another judge declared,"One of the greatest fictions known to the law is that a jury of 12 laymen can hear a judge read a set of instructions once, then understand them, digest them and correctly apply them to the facts in the case. It has taken the judge and the lawyers years of study to understand the law as stated in those instructions."[216]

The judge's learned understanding, however, seems sometimes

less than readily apparent. What, for instance, is a "determinative issue?" Replied the Bench, "Since I have used the phrase determinative issues, I will attempt to explain it to you. A special or determinative issue is a statement of ultimate fact controverted in an answer. Therefore, in coming to a conclusion as to what a determinative issue is, you, the jury, must find facts from the evidence which have [sic] been presented to this courtroom."[217]

What, in an injury suit, is "a safe place to work"? The Bench replied, "By a safe place to work the Court instructs you as a matter of law, that in this case that means the railroad must maintain its tracks and premises in the same manner as a reasonable man ought to maintain them in the circumstances there prevailing, having in mind the standard of care must be commensurate to the dangers of the business, and is measured by what is reasonable and ordinary care and by what is reasonably foreseeable under the circumstances."[218]

What then is "ordinary care"? The Bench replied, "By the term 'Ordinary Care' as here used, is meant such care as ordinarily prudent persons ordinarily exercise, or are accustomed to exercising, under the same or similar circumstances, in conducting and carrying on the same or similar business, and this applies to the defendant so far as the negligence complained of is concerned, as well as to the plaintiff in regard to contributory negligence on his part."[219]

What do the jurors make of His Honor's clarification? Not much. The judge's instructions have "probably been the most fruitful source of error in our jurisprudence."[220] According to Jerome Frank, jurors "are as unlikely to get the meaning of those words as if they were spoken in Chinese, Sanskrit or Choctaw."[221] Significant numbers of jurors interviewed admit to confusion, at the least. In one study of 185 jurors, 73 forthright souls said they did not understand the judge's instructions.[222] In a second study, of 100 jurors, 20 percent responded similarly.[223] In the trial of Symbionese Liberation Army members Emily and William Harris, Judge Brandler spent nearly an hour reading complicated legal instructions relating to eleven counts of assault with a deadly weapon, kidnapping, and armed robbery. But Brandler refused to give the jury a printed copy of those instructions: it was "against his policy."

Clarity is not necessarily the judicial aim: pretense is. For, a writer comments, while judges "always instruct jurors that they are to be guided by law and justice rather than sentiment, sympathy, passion or prejudice . . . neither the judge nor the attorneys really expect such a result. . . ."[224] The judicial charge pretends, however, that—adversary choler cooled—things in a court of law are what they are supposed to be: learned, Latinate, "objective."

Thus the judge's words may depend for their efficacy (magic again!) "on being uttered rather than on being heard [or comprehended]."[225] Behold: "Time and money and lives are consumed in debating the precise words which the judge may address to the jury . . . every day, cases which have taken weeks to try are reversed by upper courts because a phrase or a sentence, meaningless to the jury, has been included or omitted from the judge's charge."[226] At the same time, the courts usually hold that *no evidence may be introduced to show that the jury misunderstood those same instructions.*[227] Meaning is not the ritual's point.

Having however made it crystal clear that Rosaceae are Rosaceae (genus Rosa), the Court adds one last and critical admonition: "You sit here as judges of the *facts*, and as judges of the *facts* you must . . . sit . . . absolutely free from any bias or prejudice or sympathy or any like human emotion, sit here calmly and judicially and determine first what the *facts* are and then determine from those *facts* the things I have instructed you you must determine, what things can properly and reasonably be inferred from the *facts* that have been adduced here. . . ."[228] (emphases mine). Fact, above all, is the jury's purpose.

Indeed, in such grave regard does adversary procedure hold the jury's fact-finding function, that the jurors are, at trial's end, usually not permitted to report any facts at all. The custom that so ordains is called the "general verdict." It is used in the great run of cases.[229]

That verdict which the jurors (after fact-finding) must reach requires them to state, without explanation, not the facts, but instead the rights, obligations, and culpabilities of the parties.[230] The general verdict declares, for instance, that the plaintiff shall or shall not collect for the accident, and how much; that the defendant is guilty or innocent. Unlike the little-used "special verdict," which requires the jury to report its findings on particular facts specified from among those raised at trial,[231] the general verdict is unsupported, unaccounted for—quite fact-free. General-verdict jurors may not detail their confusion, their compromises, their disagreements either with each other or with the court on what issues matter; nor may they suggest that the evidence raises issues other than those the adversaries and the Bench have posed. What testimony, what exhibits, what judicial instructions have been remembered, considered, and employed in decision, what principles were used, what facts lie incorporated in the judgment—all remains, in the general verdict, forever unknown.

Once more like obedient children, the jurors may in effect answer only "yes" or "no" to those questions the judge delimits. Nor may the Court invade the territory of those "exclusive triers of fact"[232] by asking their reasons. Thus, "In a vast majority of cases, the verdict is a complete mystery. . . . No one but the jurors can tell what was put into it and the jurors will not be heard to say."[233] Throwing "a mantle of impenetrable darkness"[234] over jury-operation, the general verdict provides the broadest possible cover not only for the jurors' noncomprehension, but for possible irresponsibility, bias, and disregard of evidence.[235] That verdict is "the great procedural opiate."[236]

The Court prefers not to hear that the trier of fact may have based judgment upon something other than fact. "It is a fixed and universal rule of the courts not to receive proof of the basis upon which verdicts are rendered for the purpose of showing either error or bias."[237] Neither may evidence be introduced to show that the jury "so understood the facts that, in the light of the judge's instructions, they should have brought in a different verdict; or that they reached their verdict without deliberation, or by lot or some other gaming device."[238]

"Gaming devices" are, in fact, sometimes jury tools. The locking up of jurors, "actually imprisoning them"[239] to force the requisite verdict, may be in effect a coerced decision.[240] In order to escape, or simply get home to dinner, jurors have been reported to cast lots,[241] flip coins,[242] barter this-point-for-that,[243] and in damage suits use the "quotient method"—a technique that produces a "unanimous" monetary award by averaging the twelve juror-estimates, no matter how wildly disparate they are.[244] Nevertheless, the upper courts will not reverse that fact-finding.[245] The verdict reached by coin toss is thus as binding as that reached by the most conscientious deliberation, and in its practical result, every bit as legal.

The finders of fact may leave fact unfound. But they make law as surely as do judges. Jury law, though nowhere codified, though ignoring or overriding those codes that exist, is real law nonetheless;[246] the jury's findings are unregulated and generally unreviewable. (While sometimes appeals courts will reduce a sentence or refuse to uphold a conviction if they feel a jury has been too harsh, an acquittal will not be reviewed no matter how irrational it seems.[247]) Jerome Frank wrote, "Proclaiming that we have a government of laws, we have, in jury cases, created a government of often ignorant and prejudiced men."[248]

Concealment of that reality is the jury's chief service to adversary theory. For the inscrutable but apparently "unanimous decision of twelve different minds"[249] supports, once more, the profession's claim of an impersonal and inexorable legal science. The jury's unanimity, no matter its sham, validates whatever judgment the jurors decree—no matter how at odds with fact or law. In this way, legal rules and principles "remain pure and unsullied—because, while clearly enunciated, they are not applied."[250]

For adversary practice, the jury's function is both more complex, and at the same time indispensable. The jury is at once cause-all and cure-all for the most deplored ailments of our legal procedure. The better to perform that curious role, the jury is cast as the legal system's idiot savant.

The jurors are chosen for their ignorance, but at trial's end will be miraculously wise. The jurors are held incapable of taking proper notes,[251] but will make an informed decision. The jury's "immunity from rationalization" is an "essential ingredient of the system";[252] but the judgment of this panel is "the most satisfactory method the wit of man has ever devised for ferreting out the truth. . . ."[253] The exclusionary rules of evidence (which withhold many important facts of each case) are based for the most part on "distrust of the jury";[254] yet the jury's "knowledge and inherent common sense [is] far superior to that of an individual judge. . . ."[255]

How reconcile these contradictions? Natural law turns the trick. As His Honor is divine law's embodiment, so is the jury natural law's. As natural law is conceived accessible to every man (a matter not of mind but of inscription upon the heart), so may truth be clear even to a jury's "non-enlightened and unreasoning conscience."[256] Thus, through "natural instinct"[257] may jurors find that certainty of fact the law seeks;[258] and thus may they express that " 'socially adapted intuitive law'—which evolves in the communities to which we belong—."[259] In the jury's ancient beginnings, its methods of reaching a decision inherited "the inscrutability of the judgments of God."[260] It remains the jury's "oracle-like character,"[261] based upon a "presumption of wisdom"[262] that gives those "hopelessly incompetent fact finders" the last word still.

In that odd coupling of idiot with savant lies the jury's unique adversary value. Lawyers may find in jury trial the "major part of their income"[263] and the judiciary may consider it a "sort of lightning rod"[264] for animosity that might otherwise be directed against the judge. Yet the jury's greatest practical significance is neither to lawyers, judges, nor even democracy, but to the maintenance of adversary procedure itself. The jury is both scapegoat and panacea for our major legal complaints.

For example: Is the law too often unjust? The fault lies not with adversary procedure, but with the "often ignorant and prejudiced" occupants of the jury box. Are our courts clogged, justice too slow? The drawn-out empaneling and deliberation of juries is responsible. Is the outcome of trial too unpredictable? The fault is not with the premise of legal certainty, but with the untutored laymen who apply law to facts. (At the same time, the jury's unpredictability is a "virtue" leading to more out-of-court settlements.[265]) Is the application of law, on the other hand, too mechanical? The jurors' human touch will ameliorate. Contrariwise, are judges too softhearted? The jury's down-to-earth hardheads will compensate. Is the Bench too calloused? The jurors bring a "fresh, alert [approach to] each and every case. . . ."[266] Do the self-interested litigants present too narrow a picture? The jurors' "composite acumen [and] competence"[267] will see beyond the partisans' bias. Is adversary procedure too brutal? The presence of those "emotionally susceptible" jurors (not the adversary ethic) encourages excess. Are the jurors biased? Jury *voir dire* is at fault. Does adversary procedure ignore context? *Voir dire* will inject it. Are the Court's instructions bypassed? The jury has capriciously nullified them. Does adversary procedure offer only bipolar solution? That same "jury nullification" is an escape hatch. Clearly, if juries did not exist, adversary procedure would invent them.

Jury nullification is perhaps the most crucial jury paradox of all. Nullification (called both "jury lawlessness"[268] and the jury's democratic job[269]) is only another name for jury law—but law specifically dictated by the jury's political and philosophical functions.

Jurors may most often ignore the Court's instructions because they fail to understand them. Or jurors may override both fact and law because the community's temper and their own prejudices accord with a litigant's: as for instance in the case of a white defendant who had, in full view of onlookers, shot and killed a black man on a Mississippi courthouse lawn—and was set free.[270] (Rather than canceling individual prejudices, the jury seems more frequently to confirm prevalent ones.[271]) Sometimes, however, a jury may deliberately bend or repudiate harsh law in order to make its verdict consonant with personal conscience and a wider sense of justice. Jurors may, in other words, take into account those circumstances—motivation, social or political condition—that adversary contextual antipathy avoids. Such action is "jury nullification." The right thus to nullify law is inherent in the jury's vaunted safeguard role: in its power and duty to protect the citizen from government oppression.[272] *But jurors rarely know that power, that duty, or that right is theirs. No one tells them. The lawyer who tries will most usually be stopped short by the Bench.*[273] Jurors, alone among legal functionaries, are ignorant of a major discretional mandate.

The policeman has discretion as to whether to make an arrest; knows that discretion and uses it. The prosecutor has discretion as to whether to bring a matter to trial; knows and uses it. The trial judge has discretion as to whether to allow a case to be brought into court, discretion as to how the trial will be conducted, discretion as to sentence; and uses that discretion. The jurors have choice, too. They may choose not merely among degrees of guilt, but also whether to *ignore* the Court's directive and refuse to find guilt or honor harsh law at all.[274] (This is why appellate judges may not review acquittals.[275]) Exercise of such choice may well be a path for prejudice; but it is at the same time a rare alternative to bipolar limits, as well as a potential buffer against Authority's demand for political orthodoxy. Nullification constitutes, in fact, jury trial's most vital superiority to trial by judge alone—for the jurors are independent citizens, while the judge is in government's pay. But the jury's discretion is rarely so used.

Indeed, the Court constantly tells the jurors they have no discretion at all, but only (as in California) the duty "to follow the law as I shall state it to you."[276] Though the jury's obedience to the judge's dictate deprives defendants, and the community as well, of a protection intended, there is nonetheless method in the Bench's command. Authority's team player is not eager to tell the jury it may ignore either government's game plan, or his own. His Honor wants a rubber stamp—which appears self-activated. That is largely what he gets.

The "impartial" petit jury is very much a judicial vehicle. The judge's instructions state the law (as the judge sees and prefers it) and delimit the jury's choices within that law. At the same time, the jury's prejudice or lack of it generally defers to the Court's directive. Even when the jury is not biased initially, the judge "with a know-how born of experience, may render it so."[277] Conversely, some hold that since "the prejudice problem [is] far more pronounced in the case of juries,"[278] it is in fact typically the judge "who restrains the jury, not the other way around."[279] For better or worse, His Honor rules his realm.

An ex-judge says, "We have all seen judges repeatedly indicate their belief or disbelief of the testimony of a witness, without saying a word. . . . The power of the judge is something to be reckoned with. . . . Few cases can be won against the apparent attitude of the court. . . ."[280] A lawyer says, ". . . woe betide the advocate if he gives the jurors the impression that the judge is against him."[281] And in the words of a juror in the Pentagon Papers case, Judge Byrne "was like God up there. He was the Big Man. . . ."[282]

It is not surprising, then, that Judge Richard Hartshorne, keeping records of 523 cases before him over a twelve-month period, declared that from his standpoint, "the jury's verdict would appear to have been unquestionably right more than 85 per cent of the time."[283] It is not surprising that Kalven and Zeisel discovered that judges report agreement with juries, overall, 75.4 percent of the time. Nor that in criminal cases alone, agreement stands at 81 percent.[284] It would be surprising if agreement were less. As the grand jury is the prosecutor's alter ego, the petit jury is very much the judge's.

Perhaps in acknowledgment of that reality, opponents of the jury system call for its abolition and the substitution of trial by judge as "the only alternative"[285] to the jury's defects—precisely as the jury's proponents call for the opposite: the substitution of across-the-board trial by jury as the "one serious and significant alternative" to the defects of the judiciary.[286] Judge-jury, jury or judge; the bipolar box is small.

But the jury, whether earnest, honest, and keen; or lazy, bigoted, and dull, is not the prime courtroom mover; no more than is His Honor. It is the lawyer who "arouses passions, clouds the issues."[287] The attorney directs his "designed and effective"[288] histrionic at judge and jury together.

A judge points out, ". . . no lawyer would want to prejudice a jury against his opponent without also wanting to prejudice the judge . . . prejudice him by emotional means . . . the judge is as much the victim of his human condition as is the jury of its human situation, and the advocate would play equally well on both of them if he is a good advocate. So it would not be surprising that the results would be similar if the judge and jury decided the case as a result of the skill of the man who directs that same *extra-rational weapon* against *both of them*."[289] (emphasis mine)

Judge and jury alike are ultimately prisoners of adversary bounds; victims of battle's selection, deceit, and contagion. But equally so is the law-man. Just as judge and jury are both "possessed of no other means of knowledge than the testimony of interested witnesses and the perverted deductions drawn from it by counsel . . . ,"[290] just so are counsel "precluded from impartiality by the *ethics of their profession*."[291] (emphasis mine)

That adversary ethic is not peculiar to the legal calling. To some degree, it governs and reflects us all. "The basic notion of an adversary system," Judge Marvin E. Frankel comments, "isn't confined to the courthouse. Starting at least as early as Adam Smith we've had the idea that if every man seeks out his own selfish interest, everything will turn out fine for everybody. Sooner or later we're going to have to do some revising. . . ."[292]

"Is there a better way . . . ?" asks a lawyer concerning the jury system. "If there is, no one yet has found it."[293] No one yet can have tried very hard. Other ways, better ways than the polarizing adversary method, can be designed—for our law, our society, and our lives.

PART SIX

The End of the Beginning

Now this is not the end. . . . But it is, perhaps, the end of the beginning.

—*Winston Churchill*[1]

15

OTHER AND BETTER WAYS: LEGAL, EDUCATIONAL, POLITICAL

Although remedies for the symptoms of our legal disorder abound, few identify adversariness as the disease. For example: Jerome Frank (political liberal) called for a variety of reforms. Among them were special education for trial judges, the provision of wider pretrial discovery for defendants in criminal cases, the use of nonpartisan experts to be called by the court, the requirement of fact or special verdicts in all jury trials, and education in school for jury service. But though Frank questioned what he called our "fight theory" of trial, he urged only a reduction of its "excesses."[2]

John Frank (political conservative) in *American Law: the Case for Radical Reform*, makes thirty-eight recommendations. These range from the alteration of legal education so as to "reduce dilatoriness in lawyers,"[3] to the elimination from the court system entirely of "vast areas of present legal work...automobile cases are the most likely candidate."[4] *This* Frank even suggests that "a suitable organization" should sponsor a new national conference on our American legal system.[5] But eradication of adversary procedure is not on John Frank's list.

Former U.S. Attorney and State Senator Whitney North Seymour, Jr., in *Why Justice Fails*, suggests many changes in the areas of criminal, civil, and social justice. These include procedures for the elimination or strict supervision of plea bargaining, equalization of defendants' access to qualified counsel,[6] and expansion of the courts' activist role in social-problem areas, such as equal job opportunities, consumer protection, welfare and poverty programs, health services, housing care for the aged, and public school funding.[7] But through 228 detailed pages, Seymour nowhere considers the failure of adversary method.

Ralph Nader relates the "spectacular increase in the breakdown of the legal system"[8] in large part to the legal establishment's "fettering of imagination," "inhibiting reform," and making "alienation the price of questioning its assumptions...."[9] Legal education must—in Nader's eyes and those of several other critics, too—take its lumps. Nader calls legal education "...a highly sophisticated form of mind control that trades off breadth of vision and factual inquiry for freedom to roam in an intellectual cage."[10] Law professors "delight in crushing egos in order to acculturate the students to what they call...'legal reasoning' or 'thinking like a lawyer.'"[11] The study of actual law cases, almost always at the appellate court level, "combines with the Socratic teaching sequence in class to keep students continually on the defensive,"[12] for that Socratic method "is a game at which only one [the professor] can play..."[13] Karl Llewellyn adds, "The hardest job of the first year [of law school] is to lop off your common sense, to knock your ethics into temporary anesthesia. Your view of social policy, your sense of justice—to knock these out of you.... You are to acquire ability...to see only, and manipulate, the machinery of the law...it is an almost impossible process to achieve the technique without sacrificing some humanity first."[14] Even the skills of analysis, the law schools' ultimate pride, are, according to Nader, seriously deficient[15] in that "great questions [go] unasked, and therefore unanswered."[16] That ideational poverty inheres in the schools' case method of legal study, which uses past case decisions, rather than principles, as the chief means of legal instruction. The case method, an article in *The Texas Review* comments, repudiates "ideas as a basis for the law because ideas might be dangerous. Instead it relies upon precedent, which, because it is based on the experience of the past, tends always to be conservative."[17]

From that intellectual cage, Nader says, lawyers emerge "severely unequipped except for furtherance of their acquisitive drives."[18] Thus are they prepared to labor,

> ...for polluters, not anti-polluters, for sellers, not consumers, for corporations, not citizens, for labor leaders, not rank and file...for highway builders, not displaced residents, for, not against, judicial and administrative delay, for preferential

business access to government and against equal citizen
access to the same government, for agricultural subsidies to
the rich but not food stamps for the poor, for tax and quota
privileges, not for equity and free trade."[19]

The conceptual system and adversary ethic which have built that
cage and inform those legal and social behaviors remain unspecified.
Nader's solution for that "silent violence" rests upon equalizing the
legal battle, rather than upon abolishing it. His aim, another attorney
explains, is "to develop administrative law negotiations into adversary
proceedings, to give public interest advocates an equal voice from the
beginning...."[20] Although Ralph Nader has "done more as a private
citizen for our country and its people than most public figures do in a
lifetime...,"[21] he leaves unchallenged (to date) the intrinsic violence
of polarity itself.

Similarly do most of the public-interest lawyers. The new breed,
taking seriously the old game, means to make the adversary theory of
fair contest work—at last.

Even Professor Rodell, who took on the entire legal establishment,
did not (perhaps for tactical reasons) directly confront the sacred cow.
Rodell advocated "Getting rid of all the lawyers"[22] and making "the
practice of law for money (or for anything else) a crime."[23] Calling for
abolition of "all the legal language and all the legal principles which
confuse instead of clarify the real issues that arise between men,"[24] he
suggested that litigants tell their own stories, themselves,[25] before
arbitration boards or panels of experts in each field of dispute.[26] Yet
while abandonment of adversary procedure is implicit in Rodell's
advice, it is not, as such, explicitly discussed or urged.

Even some of those who appear to speak the crucial words have,
after all, something else in mind. Earl Warren, for example, declared:
"In actuality, the 'exaggerated contentious procedure' is at the heart of
the malfunctioning of our urban courts. The sparring of the litigants;
the tactics employed for delay; the use of the courts as lever in settlement...." But then he added, "[these] all *demean the adversary
process*.... Only when the courts are properly called upon to furnish a
genuine forum for disputed facts and doubtful legal questions will the
adversary process reach its full strength..."[27] (emphases mine)

In other words, the reformers of all shades (Rodell probably except-
ed) wish to restore a mythical "lost dignity" to adversary ordeal. By
reducing battle's excesses and placing the contestants on a similar

footing, they hope for a genuine forum in which truth may emerge. It cannot be done.

The most sophisticated legal mechanisms and benign procedural remedies cannot surmount an ethic that makes them artillery. Nor can the most constructive laws imaginable rise above a destructive legal method that applies those laws to actual problems; a method structured to produce neither new questions nor new answers, but only victors and vanquished. Psychic violence cannot lead beyond violence.

Our adversary procedure, together with its idiosyncratic concepts of lawyer, judge, petit and grand juries, is no longer tolerable. All must go. We must start over.

Nothing less than a new legal system is necessary: a system no longer the haphazard bequest of history and habit, but one deliberately designed. We must establish—for the first time in America's history—a legal system integrated into a cohesive, nonadversary social approach. For that purpose, the summoning of a Special Assembly is requisite.

That Assembly would optimally include the least culture-bound, most free-flying minds from all fields of human behavior and welfare: social psychology, anthropology, sociology, psychology, psychiatry, general semantics and epistemics, philosophy, history, political science, comparative and practical law, education, social welfare and public health; persons chosen, perhaps, by nationwide vote of all matriculating students, teachers, and practitioners in each field. There must also be lay persons: community activists representing geographic areas. There must surely be representatives of the major underrepresented subgroups of our society: among them, Native-American, Chicano and Latino, African-American, Asian, poor, women; the 18-25 group and the over-65; as well as those who have been imprisoned and have since led productive lives. The single fixed condition is that legal professionals, drilled in polarity, must comprise only a small minority of the Assembly's membership.

That Assembly (after experimenting, on a feedback basis, in selected small jurisdictions, with a range of models and over a period of time) must be directed by Congress not merely to design, but specifically to make operative at the federal level, a new legal system; a system we must then, through local legislatures, direct our states to emulate.

Among the Assembly's working premises would be these:

FIRST: *While ours may or may not be the best legal system extant, it is not the best devisable.* A writer in *The Yale Law Journal* says,

"...the cultural arrogance of our society and the inbred elitism of our profession stand squarely in the path of any effort to restructure the legal system to meet even the current demands we place upon it."[28] Habitually, legal invention dead-ends at "ours versus theirs." Thus even "scientific legal scholar"[29] Hans Zeisel asks, "The adversary system has admitted shortcomings. The question is, *Is there a better one*? The European continental one, the so-called inquisitorial system, makes the judge a more powerful director of the proceedings because he decides the order of proof and he does the bulk of questioning. The English judge, though more like the American than the continental judge, is somewhat more active than the American trial judge. The question is: *Which is the better system....*"[30] (emphases mine). A lawyer echoes, "...it helps to view [adversary procedure] with the same jaundiced eye that Churchill had for democracy when he called it the worst system of government except for all the others ever tried."[31] Single perspective is blind to new paths. Therefore,

PREMISE TWO: *In constructing a new legal system, the either-or frame must be shed as a conceptual tool.*

PREMISE THREE: *An effective legal system must be conceived as an instrument for society's health and welfare,* rather than as predominantly punitive. It must be understood as integral with the entire social fabric, rather than as an isolate. The problems of our courts, as well as the disputes they see, inexorably reflect our adversary economic, political, and interpersonal policies. Those policies not only direct each man to be his brother's competitor in pursuit of his own selfish interest, but exalt "private over public enterprise."[32]

Take, for example, the single matter of court congestion—almost universally acknowledged to be quite desperate.[33] That congestion is daily fed by a complex of laws, priorities, and public-policy decisions, all deliberately undertaken, militantly defended.

For instance: In this country, by the year 1977, guns had killed over 800,000 civilian citizens; a toll then already exceeding the total of all war fatalities since the American Revolution.[34] In the last three years, guns killed more Americans than were killed in battle during eight and one half years of the Vietnam war.[35] In 1991 alone, 38,317 American citizens (more than 100 per day) died by firearm—more than the total number of Americans killed in battle during the entire Korean War.[36] According to the Justice Department, there was in 1992 in this country a 50 percent increase over the prior five years in the use of handguns to commit crime.[37] In that year, handguns were used in the murders of 33 people in Britain, 36 in Sweden, 128 in Canada, 13 in Australia, 60 in Japan and 13,220 in the United States.[38] Firearms, increasingly stockpiled as home protection ("The right to possession of weapons is the cornerstone of all human liberties")[39] kill, in those homes, half of all children shot in the United States accidentally, each year; an additional 38 percent are shot in the homes of relatives.[40] (A child in this country is fifteen times likelier to die in gunfire than a child in Northern Ireland. Some thirteen children die daily, in the United States, of gunwounds; thirty more are injured—at a hospitalization cost of $14,434 each.)[41] Yet despite the documented correlation between America's laissez-faire gun laws and ever-rising firearm death,[42] despite the Brady Bill's prevention of some 45,000 felons from handgun purchase, the manufacture and sale of arms and ammunition—whose possession makes every psychopath, every grudge-bearer, and every depressive, as well as every criminal, any man's master (drive-by knifings do not exist)—grows. There are today almost twice as many gun dealers (194,000) in the United States as there are convenience stores.[43] (Nor can it be irrelevant that, by the age of eighteen, most adolescents will have spent more time in front of television than in a classroom; and there have seen—and become terminally desensitized by—over 1,000 murders, rapes, and assaults.[44] The big screen offers little, if any, better.) These are the crimes that jam our courts.

Or, for instance, 42 percent of this country's over 40,000 traffic deaths in 1994 involved alcohol.[45] Yet the connection between that statistic and our lax relicensing of drunk-driving repeaters, between that statistic and our habitual plea-bargaining of drunk drivers to lesser charges—remains unadvertised, largely undecried, remains unstopped. Similarly do we fail to connect, on one hand, the lack of sufficient free treatment centers for our estimated 18 million alcohol addicts and problem drinkers and, on the other hand, the almost 17,000 alcohol-related car deaths recorded in 1994.[46] These are the lawsuits that jam our courts. Or, for instance: In 1992, victimless crimes, such as prostitution, vagrancy, drunkenness, gambling, and drug use, accounted for 1.8 million arrests nationwide[47]—more than all arrests for larceny theft, motor vehicle theft, arson, embezzlement, murder, and nonnegligent manslaughter combined.[48] Despite the fact that these behaviors involve *no nonconsensual infringement* upon the body rights or property of any other person, we categorize them as criminal. That categorization, the National Council on Crime and

Delinquency declares, "so preoccupies the criminal justice system that it prevents it from dealing effectively with real crime"[49]—such as the estimated 310,000 per-year acts of heterosexual rape.[50] Nor, at the same time, is there any serious talk of criminal sanction against those "corporate criminals"[51]—from auto makers through drug companies to polluters—whose acts "can be far more widespread and devastating than [those] of even the most ambitious criminals."[52] These are the cases that jam our courts.

Or, for instance: Eighteen percent of all violent crime and one third of all larceny theft committed in the United States is perpetrated by persons under eighteen.[53] The chief factor in that juvenile lawlessness appears to be a lack of family cohesiveness, including a failure of supervision and home discipline.[54] (Forty-three percent of male state prison inmates grew up in single-parent households.)[55] Those same factors influence susceptibility to drug addiction[56] (the absence of a father figure has been found to be one of the most common and prominent characteristics in the background of male addicts);[57] *while at the same time* the search for money to buy drugs accounts for approximately one third of all robberies and burglaries. *Half of the violent offenders in state prisons and two-fifths of the youth in long-term state-operated facilities said they were under the influence of drugs when they committed their crime.*[58] Nevertheless, our welfare laws largely continue to require a father's absence from the home before his family is eligible for aid. And our grossly inadequate minimum wage—together with economic policies that hold it "good for the economy" for twenty million people to be out of work[59]—combine to convince many a marginally paid or unemployed father that the kindest deed he can do his family is to leave them. At the same time, our tax laws grant mothers who stay home with their children no tax deductions at all—on the ground that what they do there is "worthless";[60] nor on the other hand are child-care centers available to mothers who seek jobs outside—those marginally existent jobs new welfare policies demand they take. (According to a 1993 Cornell study, a woman's housework, including child care, is worth approximately $10,000 per year,[61] or an annual total of 213 million for the 21.3 million currently nonsalaried wives and mothers.[62] "If only," said economist Carol Clark, "work done in the home by women were added, GNP would rise by 25 percent to 40 percent.")[63] The rich, meanwhile, receive subsidies innumerable.

Or, for instance: Seventy-five percent of our state and federal prison population lacks basic reading and math skills, and 85 percent of juveniles appearing in criminal court are functionally illiterate.[64] Yet our almost exclusively punitive "correctional" system schools inmates in crime and little else. Within two to three years of prison release, 40 to 60 percent of offenders will be rearrested;[65] some studies estimate the figure at closer to 94 percent.[66] Recidivism's price, however, is measurable not merely in social violence, but in tax dollars. The average cost of incarcerating a federal prisoner is $20,072 per year, or approximately $55 per day.[67] As of 1994, Federal prison inmates alone numbered over ninety-four thousand[68]—at a budgeted cost for that year of $1,691,623,861.[69] Thus we subsidize criminals in their acquisition of graduate-level criminal skills—while deploring the rise in crime.

That self-evident interrelationship between our courts and the society in which they rest is one the legal profession has consistently failed to acknowledge. Almost to a man, the profession has viewed court congestion not as a function of the larger social context but as essentially an administrative problem, to be solved within the legal framework alone; a problem for which such techniques as shifting victimless crimes from the criminal to the civil courts,[70] or supplying more judges (the "ultimate remedy")[71] will do.

They will do no longer.

The Assembly must not only acknowledge the indivisible interdependence of personal, social, economic, and legal ethics, values, interests, standards, policies, and goals; but must explore and prescribe for them together. Over three decades ago, the President's Crime Commission unanimously said: "...the most significant action that can be taken against crime is action designed to eliminate slums and ghettos, to improve education, to provide jobs...."[72] Programs begun to do just that stand today almost totally abandoned. Twenty-seven members of the Carnegie Council on Adolescent Development—scholars, scientists, congressmen and former cabinet officers—conclude, after a nine-year study, that ten-to-fourteen-year-old children are being abandoned by their governments, communities, schools, and parents: are in danger of becoming "lifelong casualties" of failed educations, of teen pregnancy, of drug and alcohol abuse, of violence, AIDS, and suicide.[73]

Inevitably, since 1970, prison populations have skyrocketed. As of 1995, one out of every thirty-eight adult Americans was under some form of correctional supervision—yet our streets grow meaner every day. (Between 1990 and 1993, the murder rate among young adults between eighteen and twenty-four rose 14 percent, and for teenagers jumped "a whopping and tragic 26 percent," writes the dean of the College of Criminal Justice at Northeastern University. "Complacency and myopia in preparing for the coming crisis of youth crime will almost certainly guarantee a future blood bath—one that will someday make 1995 look like the good old days."[74] According to the National Council on Crime and Delinquency, "Punishment alone will never be a comprehensive solution to America's crime problem. The underlying social issues contributing to the growth of crime—poverty, breakdown of the family unit, excessive school drop-out rates, lack of meaningful job opportunities—must be addressed. [We must] ensure that all of our children enjoy at least a minumum standard of health and security....we should provide every citizen a full opportunity to lead a productive life. And, for those who do commit crimes, we must have a responsive and cost-effective corrections system which will reduce the likelihood of recidivism and increase public safety."[75]

A society that relentlessly presents violence as entertainment will increasingly find violence entertaining—and its courts overflowing. The freedom to do as one will with one's own body or business, to make one's own moral and life decisions, must be limited only—but surely—at that point where threat to the health or welfare of another is shown to begin. The rights to a job, to a sufficient diet, to decent housing and adequate clothing, to education from preschool through trade or graduate schools, to medical care as needed, and to appropriate aid for the variously handicapped (physically, mentally, or emotionally) must be guaranteed as the only soil from which a healthy society can possibly grow; a society in which justice and equity inhere in daily life experience.

PREMISE FOUR: *As means and ends are inseparable, the new legal system must exemplify that ethic it claims to value.* A legal system that eulogizes reason and human dignity must find adversary conduct, in all its aspects, impermissible. The new legal model must be multi-referrant rather than bipolar, relativistic rather than absolute. It must be neither accusatory nor litigious, but preventive, ameliorative, information-seeking; not argumentive, but discussional; not punitive, but constructive.

The dispute-settlement assumptions and methods of other societies need exploration in depth, that we may select, from the widest possible range of choices, those approaches best suited to our particular needs and idiosyncratic heterogeneity. For the Far Easterner, for instance, resolution of conflict ideally centers around the mediator instead of the legal professional.[76] The Chinese, considering litigation disreputable, emphasize persuasion far beyond the point found in the West.[77] In Japan, the person who asserts "rigid legal rights

> is thought to be "inflexible" and selfish.... Introduction of a lawyer into a business conference is thought to be an unfriendly act...equal to an explicit threat of litigation.... When acts such as drafting a contract or the bringing of a suit are unavoidable, the contract is made as short and flexible as possible, or the act of suit is viewed as deplorable, even by the plaintiff.... The law...goes directly contrary to the Japanese feeling that relations (even business relations) should be based upon a warm subjective relationship which can solve every practical problem by mutual compromise and accommodation, regardless of formal rights and obligations. *The most notable practical result of this attitude is a paucity of litigation in Japan.*" [78] (Emphasis mine.)

(There are relatively fewer attorneys, too: 14,901 Japanese out of a population of 125 million are lawyers,[79] while in the United States 896,140 out of 250 million are lawyers[80]—some thirty times as many, proportionately.) In Korea, those "nonlegal considerations" preferred to rules in dispute settlement emphasize feelings and values: loyalty, filial piety, "human-heartedness," good faith and affection; "concrete expressions of interpersonal commitment" that render "life worth living."[81] Significantly, "No specialist in adjudication has been counted among Korea's national heroes, and no professionalization of such specialists has materialized...adjudication has never attained that degree of formal rationality...central to the modern legal thought of the Occident."[82]

PREMISE FIVE: *Archaic laws must be excised from the books.*

PREMISE SIX: *Our new legal system must not be the exclusive province of a legal profession.* It should rather engage the equal, regular, participative experience and responsibility of every adult citizen, and enlist the support, involvement, and ingenuity of local communities.

For instance, Native-American penal codes are generally put into the hands of every member of the tribe, widely read, and discussed.[83] In Des Moines, Iowa, a former Community Corrections program successfully provided community-based alternatives to a spectrum of standard criminal procedures.[84] It provided alternatives to traditional pretrial bail as well as to the usual pretrial incarceration of those unable to afford bail. It provided alternatives to posttrial confinement in county jail or state prison, as well as to customary probation practices. The Des Moines program, offering supervised release into the community of those accused and convicted persons who met specified prognostic and safety criteria, produced significant benefits for all concerned. Supervised release of nonviolent offenders can permit the maintenance of family and community ties crucial to individual rehabilitation, to family health and to eventual reintegration into the community. Such release avoids the jailing that dehumanizes and scars, and that, schooling the inmate further in criminal skills, ultimately escalates the community's endangerment. Allowing the released person to hold a job outside prison walls can promote continuity with positive aspects of his past life and thus help create the self-esteem basic both to rehabilitation and prevention. Supervised release avoids the family indigence generally attendant upon a chief wage-earner's imprisonment. Finally, such release saves society money: the cost of supporting the individual's nonremunerative prison confinement, together with the loss of wage-earned tax dollars consequent upon jailing. Under the Des Moines program, community resources were additionally utilized, at pre-and posttrial levels, in employment counseling and job placement; in vocational training and educational upgrading; in entertainment and recreation; in marital, financial, and psychiatric evaluation and counseling; and in physiological diagnosis and treatment. Wherever possible throughout, extensive use was made of nonprofessionals. The Des Moines program was called exemplary by criminal law experts in its significant reduction of crime and improvement in the quality of justice.[85]

Premise Six also suggests that our new legal system abandon bench and robe, arcane language and ceremonial behavior; replacing those trappings of a pretended objectivity and a given law with an atmosphere that encourages ease, openness, natural response, and understanding; and that acknowledges law as man-made.

PREMISE SEVEN: *The new legal system must employ, at levels of prevention, conciliation, mediation, evaluation, and treatment, the expertise of a wide variety of human-behavior fields*, including trained conciliators and mediators, as well as professionals in mental health, anthropology, sociology, social psychology, epistemics, economics, penology, education, and vocational guidance.

PREMISE EIGHT: *It is essential for the entire justice system to stand at the greatest possible remove from Authority's thumb.*

Consonant with those eight premises, there are innumerable ways to shape a legal system. I offer the following sketch *only as a place to start*. More particularly, I offer it as a *means of inviting dialogue* (and a new beginning) outside old frames.

CITIZENS' JUSTICE DEPARTMENT

Dispute settlement might be the province of a Citizens' Department of Justice: a department administered entirely by nonlegal personnel (an open mix from professional administrators through economists to anthropologists, social psychologists and other social-health and welfare practitioners) independent of any branch of government: with state and local sections loosely joined beneath its wing in order to promote consonancy of justice, nationwide, insofar as practicable. The Department's autonomy might be guaranteed by direct-tax funding. (Alternatively, and I believe preferably, the co-Deans of Antioch Law School some years ago suggested a justice system owned by those it serves, as a kind of corporate democracy. Chapter 16 will detail their unique proposal.) The selection of the Department's administrative personnel by direct vote, at frequent intervals in each local area, would aim at preventing bureaucratic entrenchment as well as at rendering the Department responsive to the electorate as a whole—and its sections responsive to the customs, values, and norms of local areas.

Many present legal concerns would be so no longer: Family matters, such as divorce and child support, would be handled outside court means, elsewhere; injury damages would be the responsibility of a health-care system, as would be drug and alcohol addiction. Those behaviors now characterized as victimless crimes would be no one's business but the consenting parties'. (Native American tribal codes, for instance, contain no catchall provisions such as vagrancy or conspiracy under which almost any unpopular person may be charged with crime.)[86]

In addition to civil and criminal dispute-resolution, the Department would perform three further roles:

1. As *Social Ombudsman* or "people's general representative," the Department would contain a section set up to respond to citizen complaints in those societal areas where people feel now essentially helpless. Matters heard would include complaints of industrial hazard or pollution; complaints of price gouging on those resources or technologies basic to life or welfare (such as fuel, food, medicine, transporta-

tion). Ownership of all such resources and technologies would be considered to inhere in the entire citizenry, and control by private groups would be considered a privilege (perhaps in the form of a lease) dependent on the supplying of those resources to the public at no more than a moderate profit, as well as on responsible safety-management. The Citizens' Justice Department would be empowered, upon adequate showing of dereliction of those responsibilities, to reallocate control (with compensation for loss). The Department's focal purpose, here, would be to afford *remedial recourse in those daily but life-critical areas* we currently perceive as beyond personal reach.

2. As *Social Guardian*, the Department would encompass a section permanently authorized to receive complaints and investigate charges of infringement, by government or business, upon personal privacy and civil rights. The Department would also pursue charges of official misconduct, harassment or corruption. Findings would be presented to the public for action.

3. As *Social Workshop*, the Department would provide a continuing opportunity for the social and human-behavior sciences to address themselves—no longer chiefly to each other—but directly to those reciprocal relationships between social values, public policies, and individual problems; and to prescribe for, oversee, and report upon that ever-changing process. The Workshop's focus would be predominantly upon those overt behaviors that physically threaten others: from drunk driving, mugging, and burglary, to rape, spousal abuse, child molestation, carjackings, and murder; as well as to the mushrooming possession (and use) of firearms. (Increasingly—from ghetto to suburb—juveniles are armed and kill.) Civil and criminal dispute-settlement would proceed through three stages: Preadjudication, Adjudication, and Postadjudication.

PREADJUDICATION

Preadjudication would be neighborhood or community-based, and would precede all litigation. In civil matters, its purpose would be to avoid court action in favor of compromise. In criminal matters, it would replace the grand jury in guaranteeing that no person stand trial without sufficient cause. (Special safeguards must be designed to protect the defendant who might be unpopular in his community.)

For civil cases, a Preadjudication Panel would comprise nonlegal personnel trained in conciliation, mediation, and arbitration. Norway, for instance, provides in each community a conciliation committee of three persons elected by a district council;[87] these settle a majority of civilian disputes.[88] China has People's Conciliation Committees.[89] Japanese judges bring pressure for settlement rather than litigation.[90]

For criminal matters, a Preadjudication Panel would employ nonlegal experts in specific areas, such as financial, criminal, medical, and psychological detection, under the procedural supervision of one or more layman-administrators. This Panel would hear, consider, and investigate criminal complaints; would in that process honor every Constitutional safeguard; would make their skills available equally to suspects and complainants, and render witnesses, evidence, and procedure open to question by all concerned. In France, for example, the job of evaluating and preparing the case is in the hands of a neutral officer, the examining magistrate, rather than of an "avowedly adversary prosecutor."[91] A finding of "reasonable suspicion" would replace indictment or accusation. All preadjudication proceedings would be tape-recorded, and those tapes made requisite to any subsequent action.

ADJUDICATION PANEL

Both judges and juries would give way to an Adjudication Panel. That Panel would be at the same time both widely representative and eminently trained and qualified.

1. The Adjudication Panel would join lay persons with legal professionals. Joint lay-and professional bench-service, usually called the "assessor system," is common in Europe. (Norway provides lay judges at all levels except the Supreme Court.[92] All Hungarian courts of first instance consist of one professional and two lay judges.[93] Germany has two systems: for the most serious crimes, six lay persons form one bench with three professional judges, but for one trial only. For lesser matters, two lay persons sit with one professional judge, but serve for two-year periods on a regular, part-time basis.[94] France draws lay persons by lot from a list of local inhabitants, who must be over thirty and able to read and write. Seven of them, serving for one trial only, sit with three professional judges; the group decides both guilt and punishment by majority vote.[95] Italy also employs a variation of the assessor system, as do many Swiss cantons.)[96]

2. Lay judges on the Adjudication Panel would always significantly outnumber professionals, in some proportion as four to one or five to two. A panel's total membership, however, would increase in direct

relation to the gravity of the matter at issue; beginning perhaps with no fewer than three for the most minor civil concern, and graduating to perhaps as many as fifteen for the gravest criminal offense. (The magic jury-twelve rests on no known mathematical or other rationale. Theories are several, but history offers no sure basis for any of them.)

(a) Lay judges: Ideally, every adult citizen would serve at least one term as a lay judge. Lay-service periods would include a refresher course in skills initially made part of every citizen's schooling: skills of listening, of differentiating description from opinion, assumption from evidence; of thinking, question-asking, and hypothesizing multipossibilities; and of education in the principles of our law. Examination in these matters would precede actual lay-judge service. Lay judges would be sought from every household recordable, and would serve, possibly, for no less than three months at a time, perhaps longer. Ways must be found to dignify the job with great honor, and at the same time to ensure that no financial or professional hardship incurs. Exemption would be rare: students, for example, might be given a choice either of postponement or school credit for service.

And ideally, again, *lay judges would be chosen in each trial on the basis of having some background or expertise that might equip them to deal knowledgeably with areas at contention*: from financial matters to medical ones to such new technologies as DNA—unlike our current demand that jurors be as ignorant of the case, its circumstances, and issues, as possible. In the 1995 trial of sports celebrity Orenthal James Simpson for double murder, for instance, Judge Lance Ito eliminated from the jury pool any of those who admitted to listening to radio, watching television, or visiting bookstores. (One juror stated that she read nothing other than the racing form.) "That tended to leave jurors who...might be less able to ingest arcane scientific evidence."[97]

(b) Professional judges: Professional judges must be untied from politics, power, and money. They would be neither appointed by any person or group, nor elected in any political campaign. Judicial training would include techniques of listening, thinking, and questioning, together with some overview of the complexities of human behavior and feeling. Training would also include emphasis upon the relationship between principles of law and current social, political, and economic issues. In other words, the inevitable realities of judicial discretion and man-made law must be dealt with as an acknowledged—and educated—social force.

Professional judges would qualify for service in three ways: first, via formal examination in judicial skills and studies; second, via an on-job apprenticeship; and finally, through a record (manifest during student days as well as in apprenticeship) of demonstrated humanity, imagination, perceptiveness, and zeal in behalf of information and understanding. That record might be reviewed and perhaps scored by the multidiscipline personnel of the Citizens' Justice Department; themselves responsible to the entire electorate. (Both the French and Japanese require that law graduates who wish to mount the bench combine theoretical with practical training: the French for three years, the Japanese for two. In both cases, training is preceded and followed by examination. The Scandinavian nations variously demand on-job apprenticeships and assistantships. Denmark and Sweden offer seminars for assistant judges in a wide range of subjects, as well as visits to prisons and mental hospitals.)[98]

Professional judges might serve terms of five to seven years, after which they would return to the ranks for renomination. It is possible that after a given number of service periods, their election (by members of the electorate-responsible Citizens' Justice Department) might be for life tenure. On the other hand, it may be found preferable to have in the highest courts, too, some continually rotating mixture of age and experience.

3. Psychological tests would profile all candidates for both lay and professional judgeships, in order to delineate (as well as currently possible) bias in obvious areas such as race, sex, ethnic and occupational backgrounds. That data would be permanently available to any litigant (and should perhaps be updated at regular intervals in recognition that people change). Further, upon request of any trial-principal, a panel might be retested regarding prejudice on matters specific to that case (such as a defendant's conviction record, political history, or community reputation). Bias-profile configuration would serve as a ground for disqualifying any member from a particular case in order to seat, in each dispute, the least-partial panel achievable; as well as to bring into the open the nature and degree of what bias exists.

LAWYERS

The lawyer's current conflicts of interest—his/her allegiance to his client on one hand versus truth on the other, and to his client versus his own gain—must be precluded insofar as can be. Corporate wealth and private riches must be prevented from buttering the attorney's bread. Such behaviors as withholding of evidence, avoidance of discovery, the use of formal accuracy and technical truth to misrepresent a larger issue; those perjurious accusations habitual in written pleadings and those falsifications common to summations; plea bargaining—all must bring the attorney no profit. To that end:

1. Though engaged by the client (private or state) the lawyer would be paid only by the Citizens' Justice Department, whose employee all lawyers would be, and to which they would be responsible. All litigant fees would go directly to that Department. Fees in civil matters would be scaled to ability to pay. In criminal matters there might be no fee at all, or perhaps a fee (again scaled to economic means) would be part of the sanction against those found criminally culpable. In criminal cases, *the victim too would be entitled to representation by a lawyer*, and here there would surely be no fee.

2. The lawyer would function strictly as his client's assistant in presentation. He would be neither a champion nor his client's proxy, neither prosecutor nor defender. He would speak for his client only when, and where, the client was unable or unwilling to speak for himself. The lawyer's job would be to organize discovery, research law, advise concerning rights, customs, precedents, and meanings. He would be a seeker of information and enlightenment (as differentiated from the game playing of adversary law). His duty would be not to any position taken and intransigently maintained, but strictly to exposition *wherever it might lead.* The lawyer's pay scale would correlate positively with a record of diligence in producing data, legal and evidential; with habitual thoroughness in exploring the personal and social implications of issues; and with responsibility in representing fully and accurately, with humanity but without choler, his client's emotional and situational circumstances (where the client wanted such help). His reputation would rest upon all of these positive skills, and for them he would be sought out. His pay scale would correlate negatively with a record of adversary behavior. Complaints of legal adversariness would be investigated by nonlegal personnel and a minimum number of complaints substantiated would (if confirmed by a hearing) mean automatic disbarment.

3. Legal education would be utterly reconceived. Law school would be a forum where historical, sociological, anthropological, psychological, ethical, and legal concepts meet. It would be a forum where such concepts cross-fertilize and join toward practical appli-

cation. Ideas of social welfare and individual equity would be paramount to case precedent; the machinery of the law would be subsidiary to, and the servant of, ethical and social considerations. The lawyer would be trained chiefly as a participant in the realization of social goals as well as in individual conflict-solution. In that participation, habits of manipulation, sophistry, and tactical maneuver would be held profoundly dishonorable.

ADJUDICATION PROCEDURE

Underlying assumptions:

In both civil and criminal adjudication procedure, consensus through cooperative exploration would replace the concept of truth through battle. The assumption of adverse sides would give way to the assumption (as in a family model) that all concerned have a stake in fullest discovery and fair disposition. In criminal matters, the presumption of innocence for the suspect (no longer the *accused)* would be augmented by the presumption, first, that *something* has happened; second, that all parties are telling the truth (since there is only "reasonable suspicion" that the suspect has committed a crime); and third, that all parties are responsible for accurate delineation, insofar as can be, of what (if anything) in fact occurred. The prevailing ethic throughout all adjudication would include fellowship in mutual endeavor for the common good, together with personal accountability. An understanding of emotional, social, and circumstantial context would ultimately be considered almost as important as any assignment of guilt, innocence, or responsibility. *Information must be the goal.*

1. *Conceptual-procedural frame*: That frame would be multipossibilitied, investigatory; all cards on the table in open view. Perjury, for instance, together with either overt or covert misrepresentation, would be gravely penalized. The production of all possible relevant data would be obligatory upon all persons involved—including the defendant in criminal actions. The atmosphere would be not win-punish, but clarify-resolve. (So long as our legal system remains government's arm, the 5th Amendment's protection against self-incrimination will most probably remain necessary. On the other hand, *if* dispute settlement were handled by a system independent of the state, and directly responsible either to a Citizen's Justice Department or to local communities; and *if* the method of procedure were nonadver-

sary; and *if* law avoided such amorphous catchall charges as conspiracy or vagrancy and confined itself to overt acts; and *if* the means of resolution substituted (where reasonable) some form of direct restitution for the classical forms of punishment—then silence would be no longer appropriate. Rather, an obligation to respond to all questions concerning the matter at hand would be requisite.)

2. *Responsibilities*: Conduct of trials would no longer be the sole responsibility of the contesting parties. Trial responsibility would rest jointly on all: litigants, Adjudicating Panel, lawyers and perhaps, in criminal matters, the state. (The victim, or the victim's family or friends, might well replace the state as plaintiff in criminal actions; or the Social Ombudsman or Social Guardian branches of the Citizens' Justice Department might bring action.) Responsibility for maintaining order, courtesy, and balancing conflicting interests would be the Adjudicating Panel's. The Panel would be required to join actively in questioning parties and witnesses, and to request whatever additional material, further witnesses, or expert testimony it might wish. Likewise, persons not called but who believed they might offer relevant testimony would be urged to come forward. Note-taking by the Panel might be obligatory; but in any case, a full transcript of proceedings would be automatically provided them as each matter progressed (as it is never now).

3. *Physical circumstances:* Judicial robes and bench would be dispensed with, together with the deferential term, "Your Honor." Dress would be entirely optional and as casual as the participants wished. Court would be held as a conference, in a warmly furnished, informal room, with a circular table about which all involved would sit.

4. *Procedure:* Where appropriate, proceedings might be held not in a courtroom, but in the physical context of the act or circumstance in question: in ghetto, suburb, hospital, factory, or farm. More important, proceedings would take place, insofar as possible, before lay judges of the litigants' or defendant's cultural-linguistic peer group (or some appropriate mix, if the disputants came from disparate backgrounds).

The bringer of action would begin with a statement of belief as to facts that were to be demonstrated. The respondent would do likewise. The case would then proceed according to that plan and those facts, in time sequence, point by point. Disputants, Panel (and possibly witnesses too) would interrupt where necessary to request clarification, as well as to correct misinformation, misunderstanding, or evidentiary inaccuracy. However, interruption as a disruption device would be impermissible, as would be argument. The parties would close with a summary of the case (or event) as each sees it. That summary would obligatorily deal with all the data elicited in trial, not just selected aspects that suited each side. Argument would be permissible in summary, but that argument would be confined to interpretation of the data on record. *Humiliation of, or attack upon, litigants and witnesses would be forbidden.* Rather than consistency between summaries and opening statements, possible differences would be expected and encouraged, as a result of that information which has emerged.

5. *Findings*: The Adjudicating Panel, confining itself to description, would decide only *who did what*, where, when, and how. It would not sentence or dispose.

(a) Civil findings would not relate to "fault," "right," or "wrong." Instead, findings would state belief as to *what in fact happened*, and individual *degree of responsibility in that event*. Thus one party, both, or neither might be held significantly culpable. (The Koreans emphasize those "special circumstances" unique to each case.)[99]

(b) Criminal findings would state belief as to three points: first, what occurred; second, guilt or innocence of the suspect in that event; and third, the *degree of probability* of significant *event elements* (in murder, for instance, such elements as premeditation, intent, diminished responsibility, psychosis). However, *no attempt would be made to use those elements* as *defenses*; they would be rather illuminating *explanations*, to be considered by the Postadjudication Unit. (The finding of "not guilty by reason of insanity" would, for instance, no longer be possible.)

(c) Although something less than total unanimity in the Adjudication Panel's findings might be permissible, any failure of unanimity would be regarded as potentially signifying a need for further exploration of a matter; and, together with any demonstrable disregard of data or misunderstanding of testimony, would be basis for appeal.

The humanly fallible court reporter would be augmented (if funds permit) by videotape of all proceedings (or at least a tape recording), and all deliberations would be taped. Those tapes would be a requisite accompaniment to any appeal. All Adjudication Panel tapes, together with findings, facts, and conclusions both civil and criminal, would be turned over to the Postadjudication Unit for educated disposition of the particular matter.

POSTADJUDICATION UNIT

Postadjudication would have three functions: settlement or sentence; probation or parole; and Social Workshop (prevention).

1. In settlement or sentencing, a board of persons skilled in the human behavior, social health and welfare fields would attempt, exercising trained discretion, to dispose of matters in ways appropriate both to the offender and the nature of the offense. In civil cases, persons knowledgeable in the field of dispute (for example, property, business, or medicine) would attempt to balance individual interests with an eye to the long-term welfare of the disputants, of those familially or economically dependent upon them (employees, suppliers); and of the community at large. In criminal sentencing, mental health personnel, social psychologists, and penologists would replace classical forms of punishment with a variety of techniques ranging through restitution, hospitalization, education, and job apprenticeship to—for the crimes of murder, repeat rape, child molestation and abuse, as well as *any crime committed with a gun*—incarceration for life, with *absolutely no possibility of parole.*

(a) In civil and criminal case disposition, the rule of "one law for all" would ignore the specific variables of power, status, and privilege (any bow to which would provide a basis for a citizens' suit through the Citizen's Justice Department). On the other hand, the open and educated exercise of that discretionary power now largely hidden would take into account the multiplicity of other personal and social variables that characterize each situation. Discretion would invent (where it seems advisable) individually appropriate sentences and, where indicated, offer therapy, as well as vocational and educational training. (Though fixed, predictable sanctions, known in advance, seem clearly to inhibit certain kinds of infractions, such as parking violations, with other offenses advance knowledge of the penalty seems to make little difference. For instance, in Scandinavia, where the drunk driver is uniformly punished by a jail term, a deterrent effect upon drunk driving has been marked. However, the deterrent effect of fixed, uniform penalties upon violent acts such as murder, sex crimes, and child abuse, is debatable at best.)[100] Native American penal codes

give the court great leeway in adjusting the penalty to the circumstances of the offense and of the offender.[101] The Des Moines facility
attempts a problem-solving approach for each of its residents.[102]

(b) Specifically, Postadjudication would deemphasize monetary
sanctions, alone, in civil offenses, and physical punishment for criminal acts, in favor of a creative attempt to reeducate individual behavior in a normal community setting wherever possible. As in Des
Moines, supervised work and educational release would be used
where practicable as alternatives to prison; and various forms of
restitution—which emphasize the offender's functional responsibility to the victim—would be prescribed. Native American codes, for
example, typically require that the culprit labor for the benefit of the
tribe or of the victim of the offense.[103] Similarly, a Miami judge sentenced a nineteen year-old confessed murderer to life in prison, but
put him on partial probation so that he might work and support his
victim's wife and five children. The judge ordered, "He would have
to support the children until they could earn their own living.... We
would see he got training for a job and even assist him in finding
employment...he would become economically productive rather than
a drain on society...."[104] A Maryland judge sentenced a rape-robbery
defendant to probation and a suspended sentence conditional upon
his working and paying the victim and her children 40 percent of his
earnings.[105] In Minnesota, juvenile offenders who lack the financial
resources to pay monetary restitution, are allowed to work off the
debt with community service hours, for which the offender's modest
wages ($3.50 an hour) are paid into a common fund until the debt is
covered. The victim is thereby compensated, the juvenile has enjoyed
a positive functional relationship to his community (as well as specific work experience), and the community has been to a degree
repaired.[106]

Restitution seems, in fact, a justice concept whose time may have
returned. An unpublished paper[107] sets forth in convincing detail the
advantages to the victim, to society, and to the criminal as well, of
restitution as a new paradigm of criminal justice. Another article[108]
effectively uses a systems analysis approach to urge the same idea.

(c) At the same time, Postadjudication would speak in behalf of life
and guarantee society against the release (*ever*, short of new evidence
of innocence) *of those who have committed any murder except that
committed accidentally or in self-defense, as well as of all repeat
rapists and all child molesters, and any criminal who has used a gun*

in any criminal act. For such crimes, lifetime segregation at self-supporting and preferably socially useful work would replace any possibility of parole.

2. Postadjudication's probation and parole functions would require that the Unit apply informed, in-depth judgment to each case, together with continuously reevaluative supervision. The Unit would (again as in Des Moines) mobilize the wide resources, as well as support and pressures, of local communities, and of the subject's family and local peer group.

3. Postadjudication would, finally, function as our new legal system's in-process Social Workshop. Specialists in such fields as economics, statistics, and political science, as well as in the behavioral professions, would examine through their various lenses, and evaluate, data concerning disturbed or antisocial interpersonal behavior funneled from all branches of the justice system. Those data would be viewed as symptoms and indices not of interpersonal difficulties alone, but of societal malfunction, too. Thus Postadjudication would attempt to correlate, insofar as possible, individual problems, interpersonal conflicts, and antisocial behaviors with social policies (economic, political, legal, ethical, normative, etcetera). The Workshop would formulate changes, observe their results, and again—in a process of continual feedback—redesign new approaches, new policies. Aiming at prevention of those interpersonal conflicts that erupt in violence against persons and property, the Workshop would attempt to midwife ameliorative change, in ways as nonabrasive as possible. (A number of groups, countrywide—detailed in the following chapter—are currently engaged in doing just that.)

But more will finally be necessary. Our courts do not stand alone. Restructure of our legal system will not, by itself, be enough. Those who effectuate that system will eventually need new habits: new values, standards, concepts. They must be trained, as *creative social critics,* for participative citizenship. Our educational system needs restructuring, too.

At some point the Special Assembly must map the ways in which, from preschool on, nonadversary morality may become ingrained. In that new behavioral model, joint goals would balance competitive ones, students would be encouraged to compete primarily against their own records and academic excellence would be valued for its own sake, rather than relished as a "win" at others' expense. The pleasures of effective functioning would, throughout, be emphasized; and sports and games give primary vent to the joys of prevailing. Effort would be as prideful as excellence, accountability for one's own acts would replace blame, and mutual obligation would become the ethical norm. In that schooling of citizens for a democracy, consensus would, wherever practical, replace authoritiarianism: the governed have a voice in their own governance. Principles of desirable behavior would be the product of reasoning between class and teacher, standards be jointly agreed. Contextual particulars would weigh together with rules. Deviations, disagreements, conflicts would be returned to the group for exploration, understanding, compromise, equitable resolution where possible. *The educability of every child would be presumed* and performance expectations not diminished but raised.

Diversities—ethnic, religious, cultural—would be no longer ignored or excluded but *valued as educational tools*: a means not only of educating about "the other," but of widening, enriching, and rendering *inclusive* each student's view of the world.

In every student's middle school years, a semester of intensive training for the civic duty of lay judgeship (as well as for the duty of responsible citizenship) might be requisite. That training would include practice in *listening, in thinking and questioning, in constructive skepticism and resistance to the automatic acceptance of what-is as "best."* It would include practice in perceiving the sounds of bias in oneself and others, and in hearing the assumptions underlying statements. There would be thoughtful examination of the principles of our law in relation to social ideals, and of the gaps between ideals and actualities. In high school, a second semester might elaborate, on a more sophisticated plane, those same techniques and considerations. At this level, emphasis would be on the tenets of our Constitution and Bill of Rights, in terms of current social and legal issues and events, so that citizens learn to consider critically those tenets' daily meaning, interpretation, and application. The *imaginative critique* of political, economic, social, and legal goals, and the probe of connections between them, would no longer be the special preserve of experts but the *responsibility of every citizen*—a continuous process meant to carry through adult life. Valued above all, in that process, would be the ability to step outside one's own perspective: to walk that mile in another's shoes.

And valued as highly, through all those years, must be those who teach. Teachers must no longer be a lip-praised but practically discounted group but be valued among the foremost in our society, potentially formative in all our lives as well as in our nation's future. They must be, for the first time, paid accordingly.

Yet neither will restructure of our educational system sufficiently change the shape of justice. Gradually, power must change hands from few to all. Social change, like it or not, is accelerating: we can choose to guide that change in beneficent ways or be victimized by it. Nonadversary justice ultimately requires that we have *access to channels of control over our own lives.*

So long as the private sector (any private sector, whether of money or ideology) nominates and buys the officeholders who create the adversary policies that serve them both, that concentration of power at one end of the scale will maintain a polarized, adversary society. So long as our political system remains largely nonrepresentative, special interest's single perspective will be, streets and courts, the violent norm. Private interest will continue to rule at public expense. Historian Henry Steele Commager points out,

> Corporation executives, not educators, sit on the boards of colleges and universities; business-men, not artists and musicians, run museums and orchestras; captains of industry and finance dominate the hospitals, not doctors or scientists.... Positions of influence are reserved for corporate executives, and it is they who sit in the President's Cabinets and in the U.S. Embassies abroad, head the powerful administrative commissions and determine what is to be seen on television or in films.[109]

According to economist and Nobel Prize winner Wassily Leontief, it is the disparity between rich and poor that, in the long run, bars world peace.[110] Those disparities of political power and money have the polar ethic's blessing.

Changes in personal orientation and our institutional structures must be reciprocal: "against" replaced, at every possible level, by "with." Toward that end, we must one day have in our hands the mechanical means of directing, insofar as possible, our own destinies. A new political system is necessary.

Finally, we must consider a *direct-nomination, direct-vote* political system in which authority flows not from the top down, but from the grassroots up. We need to shape a system that discards the mediation of professional politicians who owe their souls to the company store, and instead summons the resource of every citizen in a federation of mutual responsibility.

Under that new political system, adversary political mechanisms—from party nominating-conventions, through the electoral college and private campaign funding, to political campaigns themselves (as we now know them)—all would go. Local geographic areas would replace political parties as the nominating units. Nominees would be less often career office-chasers than persons qualified in matters of concern: city planners, agronomists, engineers, tax and financial specialists, conservationists; health, welfare, energy, and transportation experts; as well as widely based generalists. Political parties might function as platforms for programs and social critique, rather than for candidates. Ideas would begin to replace divisive rhetoric. Candidates and electorate alike would be spared the hawking of nominees like meat on bargain sale, and the reduction of questions of global import to Advertisements for Myself.

The polarizing hard sell of political campaigns might be replaced by equal-time detailing of issues, records, beliefs, proposals: a detailing in public forums (chiefly radio and television) on time *freely, frequently, and mandatorily provided as a public-service condition of network licensing*. (What better, more obvious, and simpler way of reducing prohibitive campaign costs?) Emphasis would be on questioning, answering, and discussion—candidate-to-candidate and voter-to-candidates—in order that the office seekers (rather than their speechwriters or journalist-interpreters) might be limned clear. Electronic voting devices set up in neighborhood centers might permit the direct election of officeholders, as well perhaps as the direct expression of popular will (subsequent to the safeguard of sufficient preceding public debate) on such major issues as taxation, fiscal policies, conservation, toxic disposal, health care, and—above all—war. Congress might then function chiefly in a leadership capacity: researching, constructively criticizing, reporting, inventing proposals, recommending and drafting legislation.

Voting would not be limited to the ballot box, however—even an electronic one. Voting would be understood to consist also in those daily acts by which lives are lived, and whose accretion ultimately determines, for better or worse, the nature of our cities and freedoms, and the quality of our world.

In Australia, for example, building-trades laborers have refused to work upon projects they consider detrimental. They have thereby saved half a dozen historic sites from demolition. They have delayed a proposed multimillion dollar freeway extension and tied up $3.5 billion worth of construction projects by imposing forty-seven "green bans" for environmental reasons. An ex-officio union leader explained, "...what good is building highways in cities that are polluted, that have no parks, that are devoid of trees? What's the sense of winning a 30-hour week if we have to live someplace unlivable for 168 hours a week?"[111] The builders' union employs a sociologist, an architect, and a conservationist to advise the workers concerning what projects they might accept or reject. A union-employed social planner has lived with the inhabitants of a proposed redevelopment district, helping determine what form that redevelopment should take. The workers "vote" in other matters, too. When a student was expelled from MacQuarie University after making public his homosexuality, Building Laborers' Federation members were pulled off a building site on campus. The student was reinstated. When the board at Sydney University refused to permit women to teach a course on women's philosophy, construction of a new building stopped. The board reversed itself.

From the brand names we buy or avoid, to the violence-as-thrill films we encourage with our tickets or refuse to subsidize—every day, in many ways, we vote. *The individual is the irreducible political unit.*

Thomas Jefferson wrote in 1820, "I know of no safer depository of the ultimate powers of the society but the people themselves."[112] A direct democracy seems implied. But in 18th and early 19th century America, when communication took weeks and months over a population spread afar, only the indirect representation of a republic was feasible. Historians Charles and Mary Beard comment, "At no time, at no place, in solemn convention assembled, through no chosen agents, had the American people officially proclaimed the United States to be a democracy. The Constitution did not contain the word...when the Constitution was framed no respectable person called himself or herself a democrat."[113]

It is a Republic to which we still pledge allegiance, continuing thereby to cede our franchise to representatives—whose interests (from President down) are rarely ours.

Ex-Senator Ernest Gruening said, "...the nineteenth century American dream of inevitable progress has been negated by evidence of regression, mounting crimes and man-made deterioration of the environment."[114] And the words of John Gardner, former Secretary of Health, Education and Welfare, written in 1972, bear repeating: "We are plunging headlong into an unknown future, dragging with us the outworn slogans, attitudes and institutional apparatus of a world that is vanishing."[115] A majority of people seem to agree—and have felt that way for some time. According to a Harris poll released in December of 1973, 53 percent of Americans interviewed believed there was "something deeply wrong with America."[116]

Indeed there is. Polar conceptualization, in all its personal and institutional manifestations, is more and more inappropriate to ever-complexifying social and technological requirements.

At the same time, in that Harris poll, Americans by and large indicated a desire to participate more widely, and effectively as well, in the democratic process.[117] Though the national mood may be today little better, I believe that the desire to participate more widely remains. The practical means for that participation is at hand: the means finally to rest our society's ultimate powers in the people themselves. Modern communications technology can, for the first time in our dispersed society since the New England town meeting, directly enfranchise every adult citizen. Further franchise lies in an awareness that—since no act is without consequence—*each public act is, yea or nay, a political statement.*

If that activized redistribution of power is accompanied by escape from our bipolar limits and a leap beyond the adversary ethic, this Republic may become a democracy at last; a democracy appropriately equipped to enter the space-age, nuclear-powered 21st century. Two decades after the 200th anniversary of our nation's founding, and on the brink of the century's turn, the time is ripe; the need imperative; the opportunities perhaps boundless. There is no more practical place to begin than with our legal system: analogue of the larger society.

16

WHAT TO DO UNTIL THE FUTURE COMES, AND HOW TO GET THERE FROM HERE

But what to do until that future comes? And how do we get there from here?

Willing or nilling, tangling with our courts in their present adversary state may become unavoidable. A settlement may fail, a situation grow intolerable, an accusation arrive at your door. What then? Unless you are wealthy or have friends in high places, your best bet lies in attempting to disarm the adversary machine. Until choices exist outside of win or lose, your wisest course lies in altering the method by which the victory and loss are achieved.

On only two occasions, after a trial experience as defendant or plaintiff, have I liked myself the next morning. Both times I appeared as my own attorney of record: *pro per*. The first appearance was in Small Claims Court, where obligatorily I spoke for myself. The second was in Superior Court, where by choice I did the same—but with benefit of offstage technical help and advice from a lawyer friend. The victories I won both times were relatively uncorrosive.

That go-it-yourself route is the unorthodox, but I believe likeliest way, for the ordinary citizen to escape the adversary crunch. You will create a special circumstance for which the professionals' adversary reflexes are largely unsuitable.

You need not, however, be David confronting the legal Goliath. If you prefer, find a lawyer willing to backstop you. You will pay that attorney to help with or handle the research, the written pleadings, interrogatories and answers, the filings and technical mysteries; to discuss with you, explain, advise. But keep the right to decide, the rights to act, and to speak directly in court, in your own hands. Represent yourself.

Here is how: Essentially, you must not play the lawyer. You must do the opposite: tell your story straight and simply, chronologically, in layman's language (you may ask permission to read a written statement if you are nervous). If you have a jury, you will request that the judge direct them to take notes. You will produce what supporting evidence you have and detail what holes you see in the opposition's case. You may elicit information from witnesses on the stand and point out discrepancies to the court; but you *must not* cross-examine in the adversary sense. You will eschew leading questions, bombast, sarcasm, name-calling. You will treat answers, even when disadvantageous to your position, with respect. You will refuse to battle. That rejection of adversary behavior increases the probability of your truth's being apparent. And it declares that your case can speak for itself.

Your effect will be threefold: First, the adverse attorney will usually deem it wise to cool his/her spleen—in order to avoid appearing a bully whose case, unlike yours, cannot stand on its own feet. Second, the judge will usually deem it politic to assume a more helpful role toward your inexperience and a more engaged stance in behalf of the material—in order to protect his own image on the record. Otherwise, should you lose and appeal, the judge may find himself held derelict by his superiors. (Too many reversals handicap a judge's reelection chances. Remarked one member of the Bench,[1] "Seventy-five percent of judges' lunchroom talk is complaint about their *pro per* cases that morning. *Pro per* makes us think!") Third, the jury (if you have one) will be inclined to grant you the moral advantage of having dispensed with weapons in favor of facts; the practical advantage of having summoned their intelligence rather than their prejudice.

Most lawyers will discourage the layman from going *pro per*. Most will view with horror, warn disaster. Don't listen. *Pro per* will pay: less pain, humiliation, anger; personal fences less rudely torn, more easily mended; less time in trial; far less money spent—and the balance tipped toward equity.

But the fear of facing the courtroom-unknown alone may yet outweigh for you its advantages. If so, there is another path. Hire as your representative a lawyer who will accept you as a partner in your own case. It is you who know it best. Choose a lawyer who will accept without rankle or disdain your joining in research, in preparation of arguments and questions; and most particularly in the making of decisions. It is you who will live with them. A small but increasing number of younger lawyers will buy this approach.

Such lawyer-client partnership does not dispense with adversariness; but it may limit it—and be the best that we can do until the future comes.

How do we reach that future from here? How can we effectuate those other and better ways—in our law, in education, in the distribution of power and access to channels of control over our own lives? We may already have begun. People are starting to step outside old assumptions.

In Los Angeles, for instance, former Judge Armond M. Jewell a number of years ago suggested that developing an "informal trial system" in nonjury civil and criminal cases might begin to free us from "the absolutism of the formal adversary procedure."[2] Former federal Judge Shirley Hufstedler has proposed "economy courts" with simplified procedures, where (though lawyers would be permitted) emphasis would be on oral presentation and paper filings would be kept to a minimum.[3] Dorothy W. Nelson, former Dean of the University of Southern California Law Center and now on the United States Court of Appeals, called for creation of "institutional alternatives to the present court system."[4] Specifically, she suggested "neighborhood mechanisms to settle disputes, dispense remedies and enunciate norms of conduct," the model for which would be the family and not confrontation between adversaries. Emphasis would be on resolving problems by consensus, and "situational justice" would be the aim. The Los Angeles Superior Court has instituted a voluntary arbitration program in civil cases. Under that Court program, a litigant can expect a verdict within ninety to one hundred and fifty days, instead of the usual two-to three-year wait for judge or jury. That program (which in 1994 alone processed some 25,350 cases) has become a model for other communities.

Edgar S. and Jean Camper Cahn, former co-Deans of Antioch Law School, called for a highly innovative redesign of the entire "Justice Industry." Using an economic model, they wrote that we currently have "an inefficient system for dispensing an unsatisfactory product which is kept in unnecessarily short supply by a monopoly-created scarcity of manpower." [5] In a detailed proposal, they offered an alternative which begins with a Neighborhood Court System. "The neighborhood concept...[implies] a preference for local accountability, local resolution of disputes—and a commitment to provide the aggrieved with a source of remedy that does not subject him *unnecessarily* to the perils of a foreign jurisdiction...."[6] Their neighborhood tribunal would incorporate at least four arms: a neighborhood arbitration commission, a panel of hearing referees with independent investigative resources, a youth division run and administered *by* youth, and a referral bureau. Each of these arms would be manned primarily by neighborhood inhabitants—lay advocates, trained and "appropriately selected."[7] Such a court system, the Cahns suggested, might come into being as decentralized branches of existing small claims courts, magistrates courts, domestic relations courts, and juvenile and landlord tenant courts. That system would deemphasize rules and precedents in favor (once more) of a situational justice which would contribute directly to the parties' well-being.[8] Among further ideas, the Cahns proposed the formation, within the Justice Industry, of a Research and Development division whose purposes would include treating disputes as possible symptoms of a social pathology; they suggested the development of mechanisms of control, disclosure, and accountability of the industry to the consumer. Finally, the Cahns proposed vesting the Justice Industry's ownership in the consumer, in the form of a nonprofit membership corporation. "There is reason to believe that corporate democracy can be made to function...where ownership rests in the consumer...and where all owners have an abiding interest in the caliber of the product," in its availability, and in the innovativeness of the total enterprise.[9] Those owners would have a direct, personal, and daily stake in the corporation's reduction of internal community conflict, in its serving as a bulwark against external threats to privacy, dignity, and self-determination, and in its functioning as a champion, Ombudsman, and lobbyist in areas where so many (middle class as well as poor) are now without representation.

Across the country, new approaches to conflict resolution—and violence prevention—have been spreading. Victim-offender mediation programs, for instance, are beginning to receive wide attention; there are now some 150 such programs in the United States—dealing typically with property crime and nonviolent offenses—although a small but growing number of victims of serious crime have begun to choose to participate. (Mediation has, however, been shown to be inappropriate for use in such crimes as sexual assaults, incest, and battery.) Those who participate say that mediation offers a degree of satisfaction to victims, while allowing criminals to witness firsthand the hurt they have caused; some of these programs seek to effect not just restitution agreements, but actually some "reconciliation" between viction and offender. In 1994, the American Bar Association House of Delegates urged, in a resolution, that victim-offender mediation be used and studied.[10]

Teen Courts offer another new approach, this time to sentencing. These courts, which began in Odessa, Texas, in 1983 and provide peer jurisprudence, have now spread to over 160 jurisdictions, countrywide. The typical teen court consists of an adult judge and a jury of six to twelve teenagers, usually students who have volunteered from local high schools as well as some prior defendants who have completed their probation. The defendants present their own cases, while probation officers present the charges and the jurors do all the questioning. The defendant must have agreed, beforehand, to abide by whatever sentence is prescribed. Punishment can include community service and essay assignments and must be completed within a six-month probation. The charges are then removed from the defendant's record. Supporters of this approach believe that it prevents teenagers who have committed petty crimes from becoming repeat offenders whose crimes may escalate. The thirty programs operating currently in Texas reported in 1994 their yearly recidivism rates were less than 5 percent, as against 30 to 50 percent in the state's juvenile courts. In Los Angeles County, only 3 percent of the juveniles who appeared have been rearrested, as opposed to the recidivism rate in the Los Angeles City courts where recidivism ranges from 10 percent (when community service is required) to 30 percent under probation only. According to a spokesperson for the American Bar Association, "Courts like [these]...are not just handling kids who would straighten out on their own...teen court is turning them around before it's too late."[11]

In some dozen Chicago-area schools, a pioneering program involving over 5000 students aims at preventing juvenile violence by teaching children, and in some cases their parents, amicable ways of resolving disputes. Financed by the National Institute of Mental Health, the Chicago project is only one of thousands of antiviolence and dispute-resolution programs that have sprung up in schools, clinics, churches, and neighborhoods around the country in the past few years. A growing number of experts agree that the threat of longer and longer sentences has little impact on adolescents, especially those from poor, already stressed families. The best hope, they believe, lies with early intervention—working with children as young as six to head off antisocial behavior. Treatment is seen as most effective between the ages of four and nine. According to Gerald Patterson, psychologist and cofounder of the Oregon Social Learning Center in Eugene—an agency widely respected for its work with antisocial youth—"After fourteen, it is extremely hard to make any changes." Such conflict-resolution programs now exist in cities from New York and Boston to Washington, Tucson, and Los Angeles.[12]

John Cuie, professor of psychology at Duke University and founder of FAST Track (Families and Schools Together), points out that violence has complex roots: It can arise out of living in poor areas where violent crime, unemployment, and drugs are rampant. It can spring from families where the parents are abusive or negligent. Or it can develop out of the difficulties an impulsive child has on entering school and being suddenly required to sit still and learn to read.[13] "A successful intervention needs to attack all these factors at once." FAST Track combines training for parents, home visits by trained staff members, and special enrichment classes for those students seen as most troubled. A report on participants in a similar program initially conducted in the 1960's among poor black students, found that at age twenty-seven, graduates of the program were five times less likely to have serious arrest records than those in a control group.

"The evidence is overwhelming," says Joan McCord, professor of criminal justice at Temple University in Philadelphia, "that incarceration does not work as a deterrent, especially for kids, for whom life is an adventure." There must be, she believes, a change in current family court policy—under which judges often dismiss a juvenile's first and second offenses—in favor of "penalties for first offenses, and serious consideration to restitution, like service kinds of work."[14]

The National Association for Mediation in Education (NAME) establishes and sustains school and university-based conflict resolution programs and curricula that, among other goals, aim at decreasing violence and improving the school climate.[15] The Partnerships for Youth Project of the American Friends Service Committee offers a Conflict Resolution Program that works together with community-based youth groups such as a job-training program in East Harlem, a youth leadership program in south Brooklyn, and a Youth Action

Council in Queens—to teach critical thinking, communication and problem-solving skills as well as emotion management.[16]

The Center for Nonviolent Communication works with adults as well as young people to promote greater tolerance between ethnic and racial groups. During the sixties, the Center trained civil-rights activists to facilitate, with mediation and communication skills, the peaceful desegregation of schools and other institutions. The Center has more recently mediated between landowners and migrant workers in California, and tutored teams of citizens in San Francisco, California, Norfolk, Virginia, and St. Louis, Missouri (as well as in war-torn areas abroad).[17]

In 1992 the National Institute for Dispute Resolution (NIDR) launched a three-year project sponsoring mock mediation competitions for secondary-school students, and is shaping a blueprint with which principals can develop their own school dispute-resolution programs. But NIDR considers community justice centers the "grass roots of dispute resolution." Operating at more than 400 locations nationwide, volunteer mediators settle disputes within families, among neighbors, between merchants and consumers, landlords and tenants, and even government agencies and citizens. Tens of thousands of Americans use them yearly to devise solutions to specific problems.

Among these NIDR-affiliated justice centers: The Community Board Program in San Francisco has mediated disputes ranging from a conflict between police and neighborhood youth to the siting of a mental health facility. The Justice Center of Atlanta coordinated mediation of a dispute over a highway proposed to cut through a residential district. In Connecticut, Community Mediation, Inc., has helped establish community justice centers throughout the state. The New Mexico Institute for Dispute Resolution in Albuquerque has established networks, at levels both local and national, between youth service, community justice, and juvenile justice organizations. Overall, NIDR focuses special attention on lessening conflict-related problems of the poor and other disadvantaged minorities—guided by the principle that tensions inherent in conflict situations can, if dealt with creatively, produce positive results.[18]

A number of organizations focus specifically on at-risk youth. JACS (Joint Action In Community Service) is a national group of community volunteers directed at helping such youth enter the work force and become self-reliant adults. The organization believes that "the personal tragedy and social ills spawned by youth unemployment are major problems in our society. The economic costs to the taxpayer and to the nation are staggering." JACS works together with such federal programs as Job Corps, and in collaboration with business, labor, and educational institutions, to bring cost-effective educational and vocational training to thousands of economically disadvantaged young men and women throughout the country.[19]

The YAR (Youth at Risk) programs of the Breakthrough Foundation serve inner cities, suburbs, and rural areas through a network of affiliated organizations jointly directed at reclaiming endangered youth, healing families, and restoring communities. "We live in a time," they state, "when every day 135,000 teenagers bring guns to school, 5000 drop out of school, 1800 are arrested for serious crimes, and 7000 children are neglected or abused." Issues dealt with include failing in school or dropping out; joining gangs, committing crimes, dealing drugs or becoming addicted; becoming teen parents; being neglected, abused physically, sexually, or emotionally; or being abandoned."We work with the whole child—youths examine their attitudes, behaviours, beliefs, values and thinking processes, and empower themselves...with an increased sense that their future is determined by their own behavior, rather than by fate or other people." Since 1982, YAR has worked with more than 3000 young people in over 25 communities, and has trained some 3000 mentors. Evaluations by Breakthrough of YAR programs indicate a statistically significant reduction of serious-offense recidivism of up to 54 percent, as well as reduction of overall arrest rates; a reduction of 25 percent in marijuana use and of 62 percent in the sale of heavier drugs; and increases of 250 percent to 550 percent in employment hours.[20]

"Aftercare" programs—directed at helping teenagers make the transition from an institution to life outside—are, though the concept remains fairly new, seen as a key to preventing juvenile recidivism. "If Aftercare prevents even a few young people from being reincarcerated, at a cost of up to $100,000 a year, it's worth it," says an expert in the field.[21] Aftercare—going far beyond traditional probation or parole—ranges from programs in which counselors meet with youths several times a day, to ones in which they telephone the young people and their families once or twice a week in order to facilitate their getting back into school, finding jobs, or generally managing their lives. Gatherings are arranged where successful adults share their experiences. "Now we realize," says Dr. Barry Krisberg, president of the

National Council on Crime and Delinquency, a private research center in San Francisco, "that the process of helping youths return to their community is of even greater importance than the institutional experience."[22]

Federally sponsored Aftercare programs have been established in New Jersey, Virginia, Colorado, and Nevada. And the Robert F. Kennedy Memorial Juvenile Justice Project, in Boston, has started or expanded the Aftercare concept in Nebraska, Connecticut, and Washington, D.C., as well as in Los Angeles, California, and Wayne County, Michigan.[23]

On many levels, action is under way. People are joining together *and being effective* concerning issues and through means that transcend ideological labels and partisan stands. That self-empowerment phenomenon is growing. In John Gardner's words some twenty years ago, it was foreshadowed

> ...in the 1950's in the civil rights movement. In the 1960's the students raised the cry of "participatory democracy." Among the poor the phrase was "community action."...As a result, in the 1970's what we are seeing are the beginnings of a powerful movement to call the great institutions of our society to account. The ombudsman concept is being tried in various places....Consumerism...is essentially the same kind of effort. All of the groping efforts at neighborhood organization are part of the same phenomenon.[24]

Those efforts are "groping" no longer.

There are, for example, nonpartisan, state-level organizations like California's Center for Law in the Public Interest. The Center's targets, in its own words, are "pollution of our air, water, pollution by noise. [The Center] is concerned with transportation, land use, and the preservation of open spaces, with urban planning. It focuses on matters of fair employment practices, education, corporate responsibility, fair access to communications media, elections reforms."[25] In all those areas, the Center has achieved landmark successes. There is Ralph Nader's Public Citizen, which among other goals "wants to show millions of Americans how they can get many...public problems solved at the local, state or national level..."[26] And there is Common Cause, another "grassroots people's lobby" with a membership of over 250,000 nationwide. Common Cause aims, "by linking the long tradition of citizen action with the skills of professional lobbying,"[27] to introduce a "new ingredient into the political system...a means of voting between elections." Common Cause aims to organize the citizenry to grasp the instruments of self-government. For unless the citizen "turns again to those instruments... repairs them, and resharpens them, perhaps even redesigns them, he will not regain control of his society."[28]

It's really very simple. Lengthy, perhaps. Complex and arduous, surely. But simple—in the sense of a goal clearly within reach.

From the Declaration in 1776 of our revolutionary purposes, people's movements have changed the face of our nation again and again. Gardner reminds us

> The Populist Movement in the nineteenth century altered both of the major parties before it ran out of steam. Citizens' movements led to the abolition of child labor and to the vote for women. A popular movement foisted Prohibition on the nation and a second popular movement repealed it. Relatively small groups of crusading citizens launched the labor movement, the civil rights movement, the peace movement, the conservation movement, the family planning movement. All of these welled up from the ranks of the people. None was launched by government action.... But they made government respond.[29]

Organizations exist, or can be formed, through which to do just that again.

In 1973, the National Advisory Commission on Criminal Justice Standards and Goals called specifically for creation of neighborhood governments to give political and economic strength to the otherwise powerless: "The real need is to allow neighborhood groups to control their own destinies, to participate in the systems affecting their daily life and to create and manage their own policies."[30] The Commission suggested that neighborhood officials be elected by residents of their areas, and be responsible for matters directly affecting community life such as health, education, and welfare services, zoning, land use and development, and crime and juvenile delinquency programs. Across the United States, communities have been exploring a variety of grassroots strategies directed ultimately toward just such ends.

For example:

The Association of Community Organizations for Reform Now (ACORN), started in 1970 in Little Rock, Arkansas, has spread from a federation of some 100 neighborhood groups with a membership of

6000, in five states, to well over 500 neighborhood groups, now boasting a membership of 85,000, covering twenty-five states. Those members, primarily low-to-moderate-income urban families, have in each area organized from the ground up. Making decisions by consensus and addressing themselves first to whatever local issues were uppermost, from drainage problems and loose dogs to stop signs, traffic lights, traffic patterns, or the resurfacing of an elementary school yard, these community groups have gone on to create neighborhood parks and recreational facilities, to improve health care and school district safety measures. They have variously halted blockbusting by real estate interests, reduced or limited utility rates, equalized property taxes, required industry responsibility in the handling of dangerous waste, improved environmental safety and conservation measures and have put ACORN endorsed candidates on city and school councils. A sign on an ACORN office wall reads: "Mouth—good; Action—better." An organizer says, "We like to encourage our members to dream. What would they like to see happen to their lives, their communities?"[31]

ACORN has established a number of affiliated organizations to complement its work: The ACORN Housing Corporation and ACORN Community Land Association both work to foster decent and affordable housing for low and moderate income people. The Institute for Social Justice conducts special research and educational projects, and carries out local, regional, and national training programs for ACORN leaders. The Affiliated Media Foundation Movement is developing a network of community-band radio stations with the goal of giving low-and-moderate-income people access to the airwaves.

Other communities are adopting similar means for bringing about social change: In Nevada, where the United States Department of Energy wants to site the nation's first high-level nuclear waste dump at Yucca Mountain, Citizen Alert has joined both the state and groups from other states in calling for a scientific—rather than political—approach to nuclear waste disposal. Additionally, Citizen Alert organized farmers, ranchers, Native Americans, recreationalists, hunters, and small business owners against water grabs by the cities of Las Vegas and Reno, grabs that could deplete springs and groundwater, and destroy adjacent ecosystems. The organization has also established a Native American program to listen to, educate and work with native communities on military, nuclear, and environmental issues that affect their areas.[32] Believing (with the former chairman of the

Atomic Energy Commission) that "...the rash proliferation of atomic energy plants has become one of the ugliest clouds overhanging America,"[33] Citizen Alert declares that "the obvious solution is to quit generating radioactive waste."[34]

In Tennessee, SOCM (Save Our Cumberland Mountains), organized initially to eradicate strip mining and to bring more revenue into mineral-rich, revenue-poor counties by taxing land companies' mineral reserves, today includes over 2000 members. It has expanded its efforts to oppose illegal toxic dumping and irresponsibly placed solid and hazardous waste facilities, and to develop jobs that will benefit communities.[35]

In the Black Belt of the American South, the National Association for the Southern Poor (NASP) has enabled more than 200,000 persons in forty-one cities and counties across Georgia, North and South Carolina, and Virginia to transform their communities and ultimately their lives. In the words of one of their spokespersons, "Hope, opportunity, and renewal are coming to regions of the South where despair, poverty, and resignation have defined the human condition since the Civil War. This revolution is rooted in volunteerism, self-help, and grassroots decision making. Its expression is the newfound unity of tens of thousands of Black Southerners who are taking responsibility for their destinies and tackling their communities' most urgent needs." In Surry County, Virgina, for example, NASP has created partnerships with business and government leaders. Their appeals for improved education resulted in a $3 million dollar elementary school and a $4.6 million dollar high school with an award-winning vocational program. Local banks stopped discriminating on loans. Older homes were winterized and new ones built with FHA loans. A modern health clinic now operates where health care had been negligible, and the community boasts a new recreational facility. The high-school dropout rate fell from 15 percent to 2 percent, and test scores soared; a growing number of Surry students attend college—and graduate. The crime rate has dropped so dramatically that the county jail has closed.[36]

In Louisiana, the Southern Mutual Help Association's special focus is on agricultural and pervasively poor communities—particularly those of sugarcane workers—women and people of color. The aim is to help these citizens develop sustainable, healthy, prosperous environments. "People," says SMHA, "become the agents of their own empowerment to overcome the effects of racism and poverty; to assure the well-being of children, youth, and families; and to bridge the fault lines of race and class." SMHA helped organize the Louisiana Farmworker Project, a corporation defending the legal and civil rights of farm workers, dealt with health concerns associated with intensive chemical farming methods that affected both sugarcane workers and the broader rural community, and initiated such projects as St. Jules Apartments for Retired Citizens, Better Homes, Inc., and Plantation Adult Education Program.[37]

In Washington, D.C., there is the multiracial, interdenomination group called Interfaith Action Communities whose principle is simple: let each community group identify its priorities, focus on "winnable" targets, build trust and relationships between people of different races and classes, and train lay leaders in an effort to avoid dependence on one charismatic personality. In five years in St. George's County, the group raised $3 million dollars to build eighty-five affordable townhouses; passed legislation requiring developers who build fifty or more homes to set aside 10 percent as moderately priced units; successfully lobbied for effective community policing; and confronted the school board over inequitable distribution of funds.[38]

In Illinois, over 150,000 citizens support Citizens for a Better Environment, which calls itself "the first organization in the country to go door-to-door and talk to people about pollution in local communities." Among their victories: the discontinued use of radium-contaminated drinking water; the country's first ban on shallow burial of radioactive waste; proof that "Nu Earth" fertilizer was toxic; the winning of a court decision classifying incinerator ash as hazardous waste.[39]

In New York, the National Committee for Independent Political Action has called for a vision of a "new society that places sustainable quality of life for all people in our communities the true measure of the health, wealth and success of our nation" and aims to build "a genuinely multi-racial, grass-roots, mass-based, independent progressive movement and party in this country."[40]

In Little Rock, Arkansas, the Women's Project aims at helping create "a world where opportunity is not determined by gender and race, and where there is true democratic equality in which women and people of color have self-determination at every level of society." Working on a project-by-project basis, the community-based organization has since 1981 provided community education and helped women mobilize around a range of matters: The Prison Project, for example, provides support groups for battered women in prison and a transportation program for the children of these mothers. Women and Aids develops strategies for working with women and caregivers around AIDS issues. The African-American Women's Institute for Social Justice creates strategies for overcoming the barriers that hinder African American women's efforts toward power and self-determination. The Women's Watchcare Network organizes community response to acts of racist, religious, sexist, and antilesbian and gay violence. "We believe that we cannot work for all women and against sexism unless we also work against racism, classism, ageism, anti-Semitism, heterosexism, and homophobia. We see the connection among these oppressions as the context for violence against women in this society."[41]

In Chicago, the National People's Action (NPA), founded in 1972, is "about neighborhood people doing what it takes to save their neighborhoods." A coalition of over 100 neighborhood groups, church organizations, labor unions, and farm, senior's and disabled-rights groups, NPA works on a range of issues that immediately affect their communities. Among these are affordable housing; community policing and alternative sentencing; creation of jobs by negotiating with agencies that spend federal money on job creation, such as the Private Industry Councils; making affordable energy available; stopping the use of neighborhoods as dumping grounds for toxic waste and requiring the polluters to clean up the communities they have fouled.[42]

In Los Angeles, Women Against Gun Violence (WAGV) focuses on "an issue that crosses racial, ethnic and economic lines and has become one of the leading social problems of our time...a health, safety, social and economic issue that costs thousands of lives and billions of dollars every year." According to WAGV, six handgun manufacturers in Southern California produce 80 percent of the "Saturday Night Specials" made in the United States and used in thousands of crimes each year across the country. By 1994, Californians were buying an average of 1800 guns *every day*—often from "kitchen table" dealers operating from their cars. Gun ownership as a form of self-protection is, WAGV believes, a myth: for every one woman in the United States who uses a handgun to kill a stranger, over 200 women are murdered with a handgun—often their own. WAGV organizes educational forums and mobilizes a broad spectrum of women and men in action against the mushrooming gun plague in their communities.[43]

There are innovative technological approaches to social problems, such as that of CAN: In 1985, CAN (Community Action Network) created a unique community-oriented data bank that collects and disseminates solutions—solutions to practical problems—that have proved successful in communities nationwide. Conceived initially by the publisher of *Marketing and Media Decisions*, who believed that the vast majority of solutions to community social problems were known only in their communities of origin, CAN represents an advertising and media partnership in formation of a data bank available to all. Among those critical community issues initially identified by Dr. Daniel Yankelovich, one of America's foremost social researchers, and to which CAN offers practical answers, are street crime and criminal justice, rape, drug and alcohol abuse, housing and homelessness, unemployment, missing children and teenage suicide, medical care and care of the elderly, drunk driving, child abuse, and AIDS.[44]

There are, too, successful partnerships across unlikely lines, between people who once viewed one another with suspicion, at best. Partnerships such as that between longtime liberal, black social activist C. Delores Tucker and William J. Bennett, advisor to Republican presidents—joined together against the corporate sponsors of hate and sexist rap lyrics. Increasingly, writes journalist Marlene Cimons, "People from very different places and perspectives—indeed, people who agree on little else—are separately concluding that something is destroying the nation's moral core. More amazing still, they agree on remedies." According to Rabbi Eri. H. Yoffie, vice-president of the Union of American Hebrew Congregations, "People of all persuasions are very troubled. They are troubled by the fact that a million teenage girls get pregnant every year, that somewhere between 130,000 to 200,000 kids bring guns to school every day....There are certain basic consensus values we can all agree on, recognizing that they are essential to building a decent society."[45]

And then there are heroines: remarkable individuals—brave and determined, though without wealth, or significant education, or backing by those in power, or any apparent background in activism at all—who have yet managed to impact signficantly the world in which they live:

There is Juana Beatriz Gutierrez, sixty-three years old, mother of nine, an immigrant from rural Zacatecas, Mexico—and cofounder of the now politically potent Mothers of East Los Angeles Santa Isabel. Formed in 1986 in protest against a state plan to build a prison in their neighborhood, Mothers of East Los Angeles almost single-handedly stopped the plan—and the state—cold and went on to successfully fight construction of a hazardous waste incinerator nearby. Constructively, the organization now runs a water conservation program that offers free low-flush toilets and recycles old ones; a program that currently employs twenty people and has earned enough money to award $20,000 in college scholarships to local students in one year. The group's lead-poisoning education program employs ten youths, and a graffiti-removal program employs another fifteen. Juana Gutierrez' activism began in the 1970's with the PTA and Neighborhood Watch: "I was worried for my kids." In 1995 she received the year's Mujer Award—a national honor bestowed by the National Hispana Leadership Institute.[46]

And there is sixty-four-year-old Myrtle Faye Rumph—mother of Al Wooten, Jr., killed in 1990 in a drive-by shooting. A woman forced to drop out of high school to help her family pay its bills, a woman who initially came to LosAngeles as a single mother with $5 in her pocket and three small children in tow, a woman who worked all day, took in ironing at night, and studied for her high school diploma after her children were asleep—Myrtle Rumph has single-handedly done an apparently impossible thing. Eschewing the revenge urged upon her, she instead, with extraordinary dedication and imagination, and almost no money at all, created a magnificent gift to her South-Central community in her son's name.

After young Wooten's death, angry relatives talked of tracking the killers down. But at a family meeting, Myrtle Faye Rumph declared that she did not want to avenge her son's memory—she wanted to honor it. In 1990, she emptied her savings account and opened a tutoring and educational center in a small storefront office on a busy street. She named the center the Al Wooten Jr. Heritage Center. She had no government funding, no grants, no donations; no students, no teachers, no classrooms. She had only a vision of the way in which she wanted to memorialize her son. The following year, she sold her house to raise additional funds.

Five years later, the Center—in a still-grim neighborhood—is a remarkable success story. It receives $200,000 in annual funding via donations from individuals, businesses (including the Kellogg Company and Rhino Records) and grants from such groups as the Ralph M. Parsons Foundation and the California Wellness Foundation. It has well-appointed offices, a computer-learning center, and a recreation room; it boasts eight paid employees, fifteen volunteer tutors (white, black, and Latino professionals) and some 125 children enrolled—children who stream in, after school, every afternoon. Some of those children were born in jail, some were crack babies. Most are from single-parent homes or live with grandparents or in foster homes. Some are good students, some are far behind, and a few can barely read.

The Wooten Heritage Center offers an alternative to the streets, a place where children can play in safety and find refuge from the gangs. But it is also a place where those children can learn, can get help with their homework, and obtain the tutoring and individual attention unavailable in crowded public schools or often enough not at home. The Center's volunteers teach such courses as African-American history, introduction to computers, mathematics, and study skills, and reading. Drum corps and choir are offered; and after classes, sports are played.

"I wanted to set this center up, and I didn't want to wait around for the city, the county, or the state to give me the money to do it. It's up to black people to change our own destiny. That's what I'm trying to do."[47]

All of these groups, all of these individuals, have abandoned passivity and reliance upon the conflicting opinions of experts. They are taking responsibility for their lives into their own hands in behalf of their own well-being and that of generations to come.

Karl Hess (a major architect of the Republican Party's 1960 platform) wrote: government "can operate on a human scale, with local interests represented in regional and national federations or forums called for particular purposes...do we really run a great risk by experimenting with a new scale of economic and political organization? The real risk, it seems to me, is in placing so much trust in leaders who must attempt to manage institutions which are unmanageable and counterproductive."[48]

Everywhere, potentially effectuating assemblages can be created or found: unions, church groups, educational and student groups, recreation and professional groups, issue-oriented groups. And we all have neighbors.

Through such means can we enfranchise ourselves. It only takes understanding that we can. No one need give us power over our own lives. We possess it already. We need only join in its use.

Acceptance of helplessness can kill: organisms or societies. Rats, physically restrained until they stopped struggling and then placed in a tub of water, dived to the bottom and drowned.[49] Societies whose citizens find their votes, protests, pleas, in effect change nothing, and who fail to find alternate ways of ending their powerlessness, disintegrate and die—or fall prey to some false Rescuer.

Gardner wrote, "There's no point in talking of the dignity of the individual if we tolerate institutions that diminish and demean him."[50]

More recently, Archibald Cox, chairman emeritus of Common Cause, asked, "What can you or I do? Alone, almost nothing. Yet one person—you alone—can make the difference....The failure of just one person to join, to participate, to do whatever he or she can—your failure or my failure—may mean that there is just one too few to win the fight for sanity, and so leave the world on the road to destruction. Each of us, all of us, must do what we can."[51]

The United States is not the only adversary society on our globe. But it *is* the one Americans can change. It only takes wanting to enough. That end will be our new beginning.

NOTES

Shortened forms of titles are sometimes used after the first reference. First names are dropped after the first reference.

Abbreviations: *ABA=American Bar Association; ABLJ=American Business Law Journal; ACLQ=American Criminal Law Quarterly; ABLR=American Business Law Review; ACLR=American Criminal Law Review; BJ=Bar Journal; GLJ=Georgetown Law Journal; HCR=Harvard Civil Rights and Civil Liberties Law Review; JAJS=Journal of the American Judicature Society; LJ=Law Journal; LQ=Law Quarterly; LR=Law Review.*

PREFACE

1. Franklin Strier, *Reconstructing Justice* (Quorum Books), p.172
2. Alan Dershowitz, *The Best Defense* (Vintage Books, 1983), p.xvi.
3. Ibid., p. xiv.
4. Los Angeles *Times*, May 27, 1990.
5. Washington *Post*, Dec. 17, 1993.
6. Ibid., Jan. 25, 1994.
7. Los Angeles *Times*, April 3, 1994.
8. New York *Times*, Dec. 26, 1991, B–6.
9. *Time* magazine, Aug. 28, 1995.
10. George Regas, Los Angeles *Times*, Oct. 10, 1995, S–8.
11. Gardner, *In Common Cause* (New York, W.W. Norton, 1972), p.250.

CHAPTER 1

1. Pound, *The Causes of Popular Dissatisfaction with the Administration of Justice* (Chicago, American Judicature Society, 1963), pp. 13–14.
2. John Frank, *American Law: The Case for Radical Reform* (London, Macmillan, 1969), p. 182.
3. Freedman, *Time*, July 1, 1974.
4. Freedman, *Lawyers' Ethics in an Adversary System* (Indianapolis, Bobbs-Merrill, 1975), p. 3.
5. Ibid., pp. 3–4.
6. Pound, *Causes of Popular Dissatisfaction*, p. 13.
7. Maurice Rosenberg, "The Adversary Proceeding in the Year 2000," *Case & Comment*, vol. 74, no. 1, p. 3.

CHAPTER 2

1. Bernard Botein, *The Trial of the Future* (New York, Simon and Schuster, 1963), p. 27.
2. Harry A. Gair, quoted in Marshall, *Law and Psychology in Conflict* (Garden City, N.Y., Doubleday, 1969), p. 7.
3. Pete Axthelm, "This Gun for Hire," *Newsweek*, March 1, 1976, p. 25.

CHAPTER 3

1. Henry C. Lea, *Superstition and Force* (New York, Haskell House, 1971), pp. 100–1.

2. Gustave Glotz, in Albert Kocourek and John Wigmore, *The Evolution of Law* (Boston, Little Brown, 1915), vol. 2, p. 610.

3. Ibid., p. 613.

4. E. Adamson Hoebel, *The Law of Primitive Man* (Cambridge, Harvard University Press, 1967), p. 260.

5. Glotz, in Kocourek and Wigmore, p. 621.

6. Ibid., pp. 633–34.

7. Ibid.

8. Ibid., p. 636.

9. Lea, *Superstition*, pp. 24–25.

10. Arthur S. Diamond, *Primitive Law* (London, Longmans, Green, 1935), p. 385.

11. Hobhouse, in Kocourek and Wigmore, *The Evolution of Law*, vol. 2, p. 150.

12. William Holdsworth, *A History of English Law*, 5th ed. (London, Methuen and Co., 1931), vol. 1, p. 308.

13. Lea, *Superstition*, p. 218.

14. Lea, in *Law and Warfare*, edited by Paul Bohannon (Garden City, N.Y., Natural History Press, 1967), p. 236.

15. Lea, *Superstition*, p. 100.

16. Lea, in Bohannon, *Law and Warfare*, p. 240.

17. Ibid., p. 243.

18. Ibid., p. 247.

19. Ibid., p. 244.

20. Lea, *Superstition*, p. 132.

21. Ibid., p. 138.

22. Ibid.

23. Ibid., p. 140.

24. Ibid., p. 141.

25. Lea, in Bohannon, *Law and Warfare*, p. 251.

26. Ibid., p. 240.

CHAPTER 4

1. Glotz, in Kocourek and Wigmore, *The Evolution of Law*, vol. 2, p. 621.

2. Lea, in Bohannon, *Law and Warfare*, p. 245.

3. Ibid., p. 242.

CHAPTER 5

1. Gabriel Tarde, in Kocourek and Wigmore, *The Evolution of Law*, vol. 2, p. 691.

2. J. W. Ehrlich, *The Lost Art of Cross-Examination* (New York, Putnam's, 1970), p. 49.

3. Norbert Savay, *The Art of the Trial* (New York, Conway, Bogardus, 1929), pp. 4–5.

4. Francis Wellman, *The Art of Cross-Examination* (New York, Macmillan, 1931), p. 19.

5. Percy Foreman, preface to Ehrlich, *The Lost Art*, p. 8.

6. Ibid., p. 9.

7. Ehrlich, *The Lost Art*, p. 17.

8. Ibid., p. 18.

9. Ibid., p. 27.

10. Ibid.

11. Rosengren, *ABA Journal*, vol. 55, Dec. 1969, p. 1158.

12. Savay, *The Art of the Trial*, p. 21.

13. Ibid., pp. 23–24.

14. Ibid., p. 41.

15. Learned Hand, in *Cases on Pleading and Procedure*, 2nd ed. (Mineola, N.Y., Louisell and Hazard, Foundation Press, 1968), pp. 1262–63.

16. Ehrlich, *The Lost Art*, p. 97.

17. John Wigmore, *Evidence in Trials at Common Law*, 2nd ed. (Boston, Little, Brown, 1923), vol. III, #1368.

18. Simon Greenleaf, *Law of Evidence*, 16th ed. (Boston, Little, Brown, 1899), vol. 1, #446.

19. Harry Bodin, *Principles of Cross-Examination* (New York, Practicing Law Institute, 1955), pp. 1–2.

20. 58 *American Jurisprudence*, #610.

21. Ehrlich, *The Lost Art*, p. 96.

22. Wigmore, *Evidence*, vol. III, # 1367.

23. Lea, *Superstition*, pp. 294–95.

24. Ibid., p. 323.

25. John Appleman, *Cross-Examination* (Fairfax, Virginia, Coiner Publications, 1963), p. 1.

26. Lewis Herman and Mayer Goldberg, *You May Cross-Examine* (New York, Macmillan, 1937), p. 151.

27. Ehrlich, *The Lost Art*, p. 50.

28. John Munkman, *The Technique of Advocacy* (London, Stevens and Sons, 1951), p. 112.

29. Savay, *The Art of the Trial*, p. 42.

30. Quoted in John Frank, *Courts on Trial* (Princeton, Princeton University Press, 1950), pp. 84–85.

31. Savay, *The Art of the Trial*, p. 43.

32. Irving Goldstein, *Goldstein's Trial Technique* (Chicago, Callaghan and Co., 1975), #26.66.

33. Asher Cornelius, *Cross-Examination of Witnesses* (Indianapolis, Bobbs-Merrill, 1929), p. 58.

34. Ibid., p. 56.

35. Goldstein, *Goldstein's Trial Technique*, #19.34.

36. Ehrlich, *The Lost Art*, p. 100.

37. Cornelius, *Cross-Examination*, p. 121.

38. Ibid., p. 127.

39. Wellman, *The Art of Cross-Examination*, p. 123.

40. Rufus Choate, quoted in Lewis Lake, *How to Cross-Examine*, (Englewood Cliffs, N.J., Prentice-Hall, 1957), p. 207.

41. Rolla Longenecker, *Some Hints on the Trial of a Lawsuit* (Rochester, N.Y., Lawyers Co-operative Publishing Co., 1927), p. 109.

42. Ibid.

43. Alexander Rose, *So You Are Going to Be a Witness* (New York, N.Y., Institute Press, 1942), p. 115.

44. Herman and Goldberg, *You May Cross-Examine*, pp. 100–1.

45. Harward, quoted in Lake, *How to Cross-Examine*, p. 207.

46. Longenecker, *Some Hints*, p. 111.

47. Keeton, quoted in Lake, *How to Cross-Examine*, p. 206.

48. Cornelius, *Cross-Examination*, p. 139.

49. Savay, *The Art of the Trial*, p. 184.

50. Ehrlich, *The Lost Art*, pp. 31–32.

51. Cornelius, *Cross-Examination*, p. 31.

52. Lake, *How to Cross-Examine*, p. 3.

53. Charles Curtis, *It's Your Law* (Cambridge, Harvard University Press, 1954), p. 21.

54. Goldstein, *Goldstein's Trial Technique* (Chicago, Callaghan and Co., 1935), #559.

55. Ehrlich, *The Lost Art*, p. 18.

56. William Reynolds, *Trial Evidence* (Chicago, Callaghan and Co., 1911), p. 337.

57. Ibid., p. 336.

58. Wellman, *The Art of Cross-Examination*, p. 23.

59. Reynolds, *Trial Evidence*, p. 336.

60. Charles Cusumano, *Laugh at the Lawyer Who Cross-Examines You* (New York, N.Y., Old Faithful Publishing Co., 1942), pp. 214–1⁵.

61. Ibid., p. 215.

62. Freedman, 55 *GLJ* 1033

63. Ehrlich, *The Lost Art*, p. 50.

64. White, quoted by Freedman, 55 *GLJ*, p. 1047

65. Pound, *Causes of Popular Dissatisfaction*, p. 13, and Wigmore, *Evidence #983*.

66. Freedman, 64 *Michigan LR*, p. 1475.

67. Freedman, 55 *GLJ*, p. 1045.

68. Ibid., pp. 1045–46.

69. 5 *ACLQ*, p. 30.

70. 5 *ACLQ*, p. 24.

71. Ibid., pp. 21, 22.

72. Ibid., pp. 14–15.

73. Freedman, 55 *GLJ*, p. 1046.

74. Bella Stumbo, "Rape: Does Justice Turn Its Head?" Los Angeles *Times*, March 12, 1972, Section E, p. 1.

75. Ibid.

76. Freedman, 55 *GLJ*, 1033.

77. Ibid.

78. White, quoted by Freedman, 55 *GLJ*, p. 1047.

79. Freedman, 55 *GLJ*, p. 1033.

80. Ibid., p. 1044.

81. Ibid., p. 1039.

82. Ibid., pp. 1038–39.

83. James E. Starrs, *Professional Responsibility: Three Basic Propositions*, 5 *ACLQ*, p. 21.

84. Vol. 386, U.S. Supreme Court Reports, *Miller v. Pate*, p. 1.

85. Ibid.

86. Freedman, 55 *GLJ*, p. 1038.

87. Ibid., p. 1036.

88. *Look*, March 23, 1971.

89. Murphy, *The Center Magazine*, vol. III, no. 3, May/June 1971.

90. Robert Daley, "How Killers Get Away With Murder, *New York* Magazine, July 22, 1974.

91. Los Angeles *Times*, July 26, 1974, part 1.

92. Richard Harris, "Reflections: The Watergate Prosecutions," *The New Yorker*, June 10, 1974, p. 57.

93. 55 *GLJ*, p. 1037.

94. Ibid.

95. Ibid.

96. Bress, 5 *ACLQ*, p. 23.

97. Ibid

CHAPTER 6

1. Los Angeles *Times*, March 14, 1972, part 1.

2. D. Swett, reported by R. Canter, instructor, Legal Anthropology, UCLA.

3. Ibid.

4. John Phillimore, *Principles and Maxims of Jurisprudence* (London, J.W. Parker, 1856), p. 30.

5. Rodell, *Woe Unto You, Lawyers!* (New York, N.Y., Pageant Press, 1957), p. 127.

6. Ibid., p. 133.

7. Rene Wormser, *The Story of the Law* (New York, N.Y., Simon and Schuster, 1962), p. 234.

8. Vol. 355, U.S. Reports 466, dissenting opinion of Mr. Justice Whittaker, *U.S. vs. City of Detroit*, p. 481.

9. Rodell, *Woe Unto You*, pp. 123–24.

10. Wormser, *The Story of the Law*, p. 260.

11. Rodell, *Woe Unto You*, p. 15.

12. Ibid., pp. 28–29.

13. *Harvard LR*, vol. 85, no. 1, Nov. 1971.

14. Herman and Goldberg, *You May Cross-Examine*, p. 117.

15. Special report, "Justice on Trial," *Newsweek*, March 8, 1971.

16. White, note in Freedman, *55 GLJ*, p. 1047.

17. Carroll, in Bartlett's *Familiar Quotations*.

18. Noonan, *64 Michigan LR*, p. 1492.

19. Braun, *Trial* 3–4, 1967–68, pp. 35–38.

20. Ibid.

21. Ibid.

22. Ibid.

23. Burger, *5 ACLQ*, pp. 14–15.

24. Noonan, *64 Michigan LR*, p. 1491.

25. William Hughes, *Procedure, Its Theory and Practice* (Chicago, Callaghan and Co., 1905), preface, vol. 1.

26. Rodell, *Woe Unto You*, p. 144.

27. Ibid.

28. Ibid.

29. Jerome Frank, *Courts on Trial* (Princeton, N.J., Princeton University Press, 1950), p. 104.

30. Rodell, *Woe Unto You*, p. 142.

31. Ibid., p. 143.

CHAPTER 7

1. Josef Kohler, in Kocourek and Wigmore, *The Evolution of Law*, vol. 2, p. 577.

2. Harry Gair, *Negligence Cases, Winning Strategy* (Englewood Cliffs, N.J., Prentice-Hall, 1957), p. 213.

3. Ibid.

4. Hugh Goitein, *Primitive Ordeal and Modern Law* (London, G. Allen and Unwin, 1923), pp. 193–94.

5. Everett Abbot, quoted in Frank, *Law and the Modern Mind* (Garden City, N.Y., Doubleday, 1963), p. 60.

6. Hooker, ibid.

7. Hughes, *Procedure*, vol. 1, p. 34.

8. Pound, quoted in Frank, *Law and the Modern Mind*, p. 60.

9. Bertrand Russell, *A History of Western Philosophy* (New York, Simon and Schuster, 1945).

10. Lea, *Superstition*, p. 16.

11. Wormser, *The Story of the Law*, p. 161.

12. Kohler, in Kocourek and Wigmore, *The Evolution of Law*, vol. 2, p. 577.

13. Ibid., p. 575.

14. Andreas Heusler, in ibid., p. 638.

15. John Zane, *The Story of the Law* (Ives Washburn, N.Y.), 1927, p. 48.

16. Steward Easton, *The Heritage of the Past* (New York, Holt, Rinehart & Winston, 1966), p. 43.

17. Wormser, *The Story of the Law*, p. 6.

18. Ibid.

19. *Encyclopaedia Britannica* (Chicago, 1960) vol. 11, p. 135.

20. Ibid., vol. 1, p. 571.

21. Wormser, *The Story of the Law*, p. 177.

22. Ibid., p. 183.

23. Ibid., p. 7.

24. Ibid., pp. 6, 7.

25. Ibid., p. 8.

26. *Encyclopaedia Britannica*, vol. 15, p. 839.

27. Easton, *The Heritage of the Past*, p. 100.

28. Bertrand Russell, *A History of Western Philosophy*, p. 309.

29. *The Jewish Encyclopedia* (New York, Funk and Wagnalls, 1901), vol. 10, p. 385.

30. Ibid.

31. Exodus 20:5.

32. Léon Yankwich, *The Code of Hammurabi*, 4 *Southern California LR*, p. 29.

33. Exodus 21:23, 24, 25.

34. *The Jewish Encyclopedia*, vol. 10, p. 385.

35. Menninger, *The Crime of Punishment* (New York, Viking, 1969), p. 192.

36. *The Jewish Encyclopedia*, vol. 2, p. 225, and vol. 10, p. 385.

37. Wormser, *The Story of the Law*, p. 23.

38. Ibid., p. 7.

39. *Encyclopaedia Britannica*, vol. 18, p. 780.

40. Wormser, *The Story of the Law*, p. 308.

41. Ibid.

42. Ibid., p. 203.

43. Ezekial 8:18.

44. Matthew 25:46.

45. 11 Thessalonians 1:8, 9.

46. Jude 7.

47. Wormser, *The Story of the Law*, p. 312.

48. Ibid.

49. Ibid., pp. 309–313.

50. Potter, quoted in Yankwich, *An American Judge Looks at the Talmud* (Los Angeles, Western Jewish Institute, 1936), no. 3, n. 34, p. 7.

51. Kohler, in Kocourek and Wigmore, *The Evolution of Law*, vol. 2, p. 577.

52. Menninger, *The Crime of Punishment*, p. 59.

53. "Justice: Prosecutor's Privilege," *Newsweek*, March 15, 1976.

54. Linda Matthews, "Justices Won't Curb Police Misuse of 'Criminal' Label," Los Angeles *Times*, March 24, 1976, part 1, p. 6.

CHAPTER 8

1. S.I. Hayakawa, *Language in Action* (New York, Harcourt Brace, 1941), p. 166.

2. Bertrand Russell, *Wisdom of the West* (London, Crescent Books), p. 191.

3. Hendrik Zwarensteyn, 10 *ABLJ*, p. 26.

4. Ibid., pp. 30–31.

5. Ibid., pp. 26, 28.

6. Hahm, in Schuberg and Danelski, *Comparative Judicial Behavior* (London, Oxford University Press, 1969), p. 20.

7. Zwarensteyn, 10 *ABLJ*, p. 27.

8. Pyong-Choon Hahm, in Schubert and Danelski, *Comparative Judicial Behavior*, p. 20.

9. Laura Nader, in Laura Nader, ed., *Law in Culture and Society* (Chicago, Aldine Publishing, 1972), p. 84.

10. Frank, *Courts on Trial*, p. 267.

11. Laura Nader, in *Law in Culture*, p. 84.

12. Ibid., p. 86.

13. P.H. Gulliver, in Nader, *Law in Culture*, pp. 26–27.

14. Vilhelm Aubert, in Nader, *Law in Culture*, p. 289.

15. Ibid., p. 290.

16. Frank, *Law and the Modern Mind*, p. 5ʏ.

17. *Encyclopaedia Britannica*, vol. 8, p. 687.

18. Moore, in Nader, *Law in Culture*, p. 377.

19. Ibid.

20. Wormser, *The Story of the Law*, p. 280.

21. Lea, in Bohannon, *Law and Warfare*, p. 240.

CHAPTER 9

1. Eugene Gerhart, *Quote It!* (New York, Boardman, 1969).

2. Hughes, *Procedure*, preface, pp. iv-v.

3. Ibid.

4. Ibid.

5. Kathy Burke, "Imprisoned on False Evidence," Los Angeles *Times*, Sept. 11, 1974, part 1, pp. 1, 3, 32, 33.

6. Hughes, *Procedure*, preface, pp. iv-v.

7. Ibid., p. 288.

8. Ibid., index.

9. Ibid., index.

10. Ibid., p. 19.

11. Wormser, *The Story of the Law*, p. 254.

12. Arnold, The Symbols of Government (New York, N.Y., Harcourt, Brace, 1962), pp. 185, 186.

13. "Where the Defense Went Wrong," *Time*, March 29, 1976.

14. Pound, *Causes of Popular Dissatisfaction*, p. 13.

15. Thomas Szasz, "Mercenary Psychiatry," *The New Republic*, March 13, 1976, p. 12.

16. Louis Joughin and Edmund Morgan, *The Legacy of Sacco and Vanzetti* (Chicago, Quadrangle Books, 1964), p. 190.

17. Goldstein, *Goldstein's Trial Technique*, 1975, #19.21.

18. White, *5 Houston LR*, no. 4, 1968, pp. 575–77.

19. R.J. Walker and M.G. Walker, *The English Legal System* (London, Butterworth's, 1972), p. 320.

20. Charles Dickens, *Bleak House* (New York, Macmillan, 1895), pp. 2–3.

21. Savay, *The Art of the Trial*, p. 36.

22. Commissioner John Alexander, Los Angeles Superior Court, 1970.

23. Canon 17, ABA *Code of Professional Responsibility and Canons of Judicial Ethics*, 1969.

24. Rosengren, 55 *ABA Journal*, Dec. 1969, p. 1158.

25. "Corona: A Mistake," San Francisco *Chronicle*, Oct. 15, 1973.

26. Donald W. Ricketts, "The Rapist Deserves Due Process, Too," Los Angeles *Times*, August 22, 1974, part 2, p. 7.

27. Ibid.

28. Wigmore, *Evidence*, #983.

29. Ibid.

30. Frank, *Courts on Trial*, p. 266.

CHAPTER 10

1. Flavell, *The Developmental Psychology of Jean Piaget* (Princeton, Van Nostrand, 1963), p. 278.

2. Ibid., p. 274.

3. Ibid.

4. Ibid., p. 281.

5. Piaget, quoted in Flavell, *Developmental Psychology*, p. 278.

6. Flavell, *Developmental Psychology*, p. 296.

7. Ibid., p. 292.

8. Ibid., p. 295.

9. Ibid., pp. 295–96.

10. Ibid., p. 296.

11. Piaget, *The Moral Judgment of the Child* (Glencoe, Ill., Free Press, 1932), 1960, p. 324.

12. Flavell, *Developmental Psychology*, p. 294.

13. Ibid., p. 292.

14. Ibid., p. 293.

15. Piaget, *Six Psychological Studies* (New York, Random House, 1967), p. 37.

16. Flavell, *Developmental Psychology*, p. 293.

17. Piaget, *Six Psychological Studies*, p. 38.

18. St. Clair, "The President's Lawyer: A Punishing Adversary," *Time*, March 25, 1974.

19. Flavell, *Developmental Psychology*, p. 294.

20. Frank Browning, "Organizing Behind Bars," *Ramparts*, Feb. 1972, p. 45.

21. Michael Tigar, interview with, *A Lawyer for Social Change*, p. 35.

22. *Newsweek*, Oct. 30, 1972.

23. Ralph Nader, speech to International Symposium on Electromagnetic Compatability, July 15, 1970.

24. Lee Inglis, *IEEE International Symposium* (New York, Institute of Electrical and Electronic Engineers, 1970), p. 170; *Radiation Exposure Overview* (Rockville, Md., U.S. Dept. of Health, Education and Welfare, 1969), p. 7; *Microwave Radiation Hazards* (Berkeley, Calif., California State Dept. of Public Health, 1964), pp. 6, 7.

25. Inglis, ibid.

26. Ibid., p. 171

27. Ibid., p. 168

28. Ibid.

29. Ibid.

30. Thurman Arnold, *The Symbols of Government* (New York, Harcourt Brace and World, 1962), p. 187.

31. Rodell, *Woe Unto You*, p. 152.

32. *The World Book Encyclopedia* (Chicago, Field Enterprises, 1960), vol. 14, p. 747.

33. Piaget, *Six Psychological Studies*, p. 57.

34. Ibid.

CHAPTER 11

1. Rosenberg, *Case & Comment*, vol. 74, no. 1, 1969, p. 9.

2. Noonan, 64 *Michigan LR*, pp. 1486–87.

3. Marc Franklin, *Biography of a Legal Dispute* (Mineola, N.Y., Foundation Press, 1968), p. 94.

4. Edmund Morgan, in Louisell and Hazard, *Cases on Pleading and Procedure*, p. 40.

5. Cound, Friedenthal, and Miller, *Civil Procedure, Cases and Materials* (St. Paul, Minn., West Publishing Co., 1968), p. 2.

6. *ABA Journal*, vol. 44, 1958, p. 1161.

7. Lee Loevinger, in preface to Marshall, *Law and Psychology in Conflict*.

8. Morgan, *Some Problems of Proof Under the Anglo-American System of Litigation* (New York, Columbia University Press, 1956), p. 34.

9. Pound, *Causes of Popular Dissatisfaction*, pp. 12–14.

10. Joughin and Morgan, *Legacy*, p. 184.

11. Arnold, *The Symbols of Government*, pp. 183–85.

12. James, *Civil Procedure* (Boston, Little, Brown, 1965), p. 7.

13. Curtis, *It's Your Law*, p. 18.

14. Goitein, *Primitive Ordeal and Modern Law*, p. 71.

15. Tarde, in Kocourek and Wigmore, *Evolution of Law*, p. 691.

16. *You and the Law* (Pleasantville, N.Y., Readers Digest Association, 1971), p. 37.

17. Alfred N. Whitehead, *Science and the Modern World* (New York, New American Library, 1964), p. 15.

18. Daryl Bem, *Beliefs, Attitudes and Human Affairs* (Belmont, N.Y., Brooks/Cole, 1970), p. 31.

19. Ibid.

20. Wormser, *The Story of the Law*, pp. 185–56.

21. Russell, *A History of Western Philosophy*, p. 449.

22. Marshall, *Law and Psychology in Conflict*, p. 121.

23. Ibid.

24. Chaim F. Shatan, M.D., "How Do We Turn Off the Guilt?" *Human Behavior*, vol. 2, no. 2, Feb. 1973, p. 60.

25. Letters to the Editor, Los Angeles, *Times*, May 27, 1972, part 2.

26. Mrs. G. Gordon Liddy, "Watergate Wife," *Ladies' Home Journal*, Sept. 1973.

27. "Experiment Proves Point," Los Angeles *Times*, May 8, 1974, part 1.

28. Stanley Milgram, *Obedience to Authority* (New York, Harper and Row, 1974), p. 5.

29. Ibid.

30. Ibid., p. 188.

31. Ibid.

32. Ibid., p. 8.

33. Ibid., pp. 8, 9, 187.

34. Ibid., p. 10.

35. Connie Bruck, "Zimbardo: Solving the Maze," *Human Behavior*, vol. 5, no. 4, pp. 25–31.

36. Ibid., p. 26.

37. Milgram, *Obedience to Authority*, p. 137.

38. Jules Henry, in Goldschmidt, ed., *Exploring the Ways of Mankind*, 2nd ed. (New York, Holt Rinehart and Winston, 1971), pp. 180–81.

39. Steinbeck, *Cannery Row* (New York, Bantam Books, 1971), p. 89.

40. Linden L. Nelson and Spencer Kagan, "The Star Spangled Scramble," *Psychology Today*, Sept. 1972, p. 53.

41. "The American Predicament: Truth No Longer Counts," Los Angeles *Times*, Jan. 1, 1972, section G, p. 6.

42. Hand, in Louisell and Hazard, *Cases on Pleading and Procedure*, p. 1263.

CHAPTER 12

1. Cardozo, *Paradoxes of Legal Science* (New York, Columbia University Press, 1947), pp. 33–34.

2. Lea, in Bohannon, *Law and Warfare*, p. 251.

3. Ibid.

4. "Today's Top Lawyers: They Never Had It So Good," *Medical Economics*, Sept. 25, 1972, p. 191.

5. Riley, 38 *George Washington LR* 547, 1970.

6. *Encyclopaedia Britannica; Encyclopedia Americana*, passim.

7. Alexis de Tocqueville in Frank, *Courts on Trial*, p. 256.

8. *Marquette LR*, 50:594.

9. "Today's Top Lawyers: They Never Had It So Good," *Medical Economics*, Sept. 25, 1972, p. 185.

10. Goulden, *The Superlawyers* (New York, Weybright and Talley, 1971), p. 6.

11. Ibid., p. 7.

12. Rodell, *Woe Unto You*, p. 8.

13. Goulden, *The Superlawyers*, p. 13.

14. Curtis, *It's Your Law*, p. 17.

15. Williston, *Life and Law* (Boston, Little, Brown, 1941), p. 271.

16. Ibid., p. 272.

17. Curtis, *It's Your Law*, p. 18.

18. Freedman, 64 *Michigan LR*, pp. 1470–71

19. Ibid.

20. In Freedman, 55 *GLJ*, p. 1032, dissenting opinion, Miranda v. Arizona.

21. Freedman, 64 *Michigan LR*, p. 1482.

22. Braun, 55 *GLJ*, p. 1049.

23. Albert Guerard, "The Testament of a Liberal," in Louisell and Hazard, *Cases on Pleading and Procedure*, pp. 1255–56.

24. Freedman, 55 *GLJ*, p. 1030, and Freedman, *Journal of Legal Education*, vol. 21, no. 5, p. 570.

25. Braun, 55 *GLJ*, p. 1050.

26. Curtis, *It's Your Law*, p. 17.

27. ABA *Code of Professional Responsibility and Canons of Judicial Ethics*, 1969.

28. Noonan, 64 *Michigan LR*, p. 1487.

29. Braun, *Trial*, 3–4, p. 37, Dec. 1967 to Jan. 1968.

30. Freedman, 64 *Michigan LR*, pp. 1471–72.

31. Quoted by Curtis, *Stanford LR* 4, Dec. 1951, p. 14.

32. Freedman, 64 *Michigan LR*, p. 1475, n. 11, quoting opinion 150, ABA, 1936.

33. Ibid., n. 12, quoting *Greenough v. Gaskell*.

34. Ibid., 55 *GLJ*, . 1031, n. 6, quoting Opinion 9, ABA.

35. Ibid., *Michigan LR*, pp. 1474–475.

36. Ibid.

37. Ehrlich, *The Lost Art*, p. 57.

38. Ibid., p. 50.

39. Wellman, *The Art of Cross-Examination*, p. 22.

40. Ibid., p. 123.

41. Bress, 5 *ACLQ*, p. 24.

42. Noonan, 64 *Michigan LR*, p. 1488.

43. Ibid., 1491.

44. Logan Pearsall Smith, in Bartlett's *Familiar Quotations*, p. 822.

45. *Stanford LR* 4, p. 349.

46. Curtis, in *Stanford LR* 4, p. 9.

47. Ibid.
48. Curtis, *It's Your Law*, p. 20.
49. Ibid., p. 16.
50. Curtis, in *Stanford LR* 4, p. 18.
51. Drinker, in *Stanford LR* 4, p. 18.
52. Freedman, 64 *Michigan LR*, p. 1471.
53. Ibid., p. 1469.
54. Ibid., n. 1.
55. Ibid.
56. Monroe Freedman, 55 *GLJ*, p. 1031.
57. Ibid., p. 1030.
58. Braun, 55 *GLJ*, p. 1049.
59. Ibid., p. 1053.
60. Chief Justice Warren Burger, quoted by David P. Riley, 38 *George Washington LR*, p. 559.
61. Burger, 5 *ACLQ*, p. 12.
62. Ibid., p. 16.
63. Riley, 38 *George Washington LR*, pp. 559–70.
64. James Mills, "I Have Nothing to Do With Justice," *Life*, March 12, 1971, p. 57.
65. Ibid., p. 66.
66. Ibid., p. 57.
67. Ibid., p. 66.
68. Ibid., July 28, 1972.
69. "The Law," *Time*, Nov. 22, 1971.
70. "A Court Takes Revenge on an Outspoken Lawyer," *Life*, July 28, 1972.
71. Gene Blake, "Errant Lawyers: More Critical View Emerging," Los Angeles *Times*, Aug. 31, 1974, part 1, p. 20.
72. Gregory Bateson, *Steps to an Ecology of Mind* (New York, Ballantine Books, 1972), p. 420.
73. Frank, *Courts on Trial*, p. 85.
74. Ibid., p. 429.
75. Rodell, *Woe Unto You*, p. 184.
76. Ibid., foreword.
77. Murray Bloom, *The Trouble with Lawyers* (New York, Pocket Books, 1970), introduction.
78. *Law and Society Review*, 1:15, June 1967, p. 19.
79. Ibid., p. 21.
80. Ibid.
81. Ibid., pp. 21, 22.
82. Ibid., p. 22.
83. Ibid., p. 23.
84. Ibid., p. 25.

85. Ibid., p. 26.
86. Ibid.
87. Ibid., p. 27.
88. Ibid., p. 26.
89. Ibid.
90. Ibid., p. 28.
91. Ibid., p. 30.
92. Ibid., p. 30–31.
93. Ibid., pp. 22–23.
94. Ibid., p. 32.
95. Ibid., p. 28.
96. Ibid.
97. Freedman, 55 *GLJ*, n. 45, p. 1041, "The Subin Report."
98. Ibid.
99. *Law and Society Review*, 1:15, June 1967, n. 22, pp. 32–33.
100. Ibid., p. 32.
101. Judge Tim Murphy, *The Center Magazine*, vol. 3, no. 3, May/June 1971, p. 50.
102. Rodell, *Woe Unto You*, p. 164.
103. *Trial Lawyers' Guide*, 10:5, Nov. 1966, pp. 236–38.
104. Ibid., pp. 239–41.
105. Ibid., p. 241.

CHAPTER 13

1. Blackstone, quoted in John Gray, *The Nature and Sources of Law* (New York, Macmillan, 1948), p. 219.
2. James Mills, "I Have Nothing to Do With Justice," *Life*, March 12, 1971, p. 66.
3. Haines, 17 *Illinois LR*, p. 97.
4. Carter, in ibid.
5. Coke, in Dickensen, 29 *Columbia LR*, n. 8, p. 115.
6. Montesquieu, in ibid., pp. 115–16.
7. *Encyclopaedia Brittanica*, vol. 13, p. 168.
8. Radin, 15 *Cornell Law Quarterly*, p. 10.
9. *Canons of Judicial Ethics*, nos. 5 and 34.
10. Max Radin, *Law as Logic and Experience* (New Haven, Yale University Press, 1940), p. 56.
11. Joughin and Morgan, *Legacy*, p. 184.
12. Radin, *Law as Logic and Experience* p. 56.
13. Rosenberg, *Case & Comment*, vol. 74, no. 1, p. 8.
14. Bernard Botein, *Trial Judge* (New York, N.Y. Simon and Schuster, 1952), p. 96.
15. Haines, 17 *Illinois LR*, n.3, p. 98.

16. Los Angeles County Law Library.

17. ABA *Canons of Judicial Ethics*, #20.

18. Gitelson, Los Angeles *Times*, June 15, 1972, part 7, p. 4.

19. Montesquieu, in Dickensen, 29 *Columbia LR*, pp. 115–16.

20. Dicey, in Frank, *Courts on Trial*, n. 6, p. 131.

21. Haines, 17 *Illinois LR*, p. 97.

22. *Webster's Third New International Dictionary.*

23. Walter Moberly, quoted in *Webster's Third New International Dictionary*, p. 211.

24. *Webster's Third New International Dictionary*, p. 1788.

25. Haines, 17 *Illinois LR*, p. 97, and Frank, *Law and the Modern Mind*, p. 223.

26. Haines, ibid., n. 6.

27. Frank, *Law and the Modern Mind*, n. 1, p. 35.

28. *You and the Law*, pp. 36, 37.

29. Leslie L. Conner, Oklahoma Bar Association: *The Journal*, vol. 40, 1969, p. 962.

30. George Everson, American Institute of Criminal Law and Criminology: 10 *Journal of Criminal Law*, 1919–20, p. 90.

31. Ibid., p. 96.

32. Ibid., p. 97.

33. Ibid., pp. 97–98.

34. Ibid., p. 98.

35. Ibid., p. 97.

36. Haines, 17 *Illinois LR*, p. 105.

37. "How Equal Is Justice," *Newsweek*, Oct. 30, 1972, The Cities section.

38. Ibid.

39. Ibid.

40. Ibid.

41. Ibid.

42. William Farr, "Felon's Chance of Leniency Greater in L.A. Courts, Rand Survey Shows," Los Angeles *Times*, April 25, 1973, part 2, p. 3.

43. "Parsing Sentences," *Time*, April 9, 1973.

44. Lewis Isaacs, *The Record* 20, pp. 365–66.

45. Sykes, in Nader, *Law in Culture and Society*, p. 331.

46. Isaacs, *The Record* 20, pp. 365–66.

47. Green, 28 *Columbia LR*, pp. 137–38.

48. John Gray, in Frank, *Law and the Modern Mind*, p. 131.

49. Ibid.

50. Gray, *The Nature and Sources of Law* (New York, Macmillan, 1921), p. 101.

51. Frank, *Law and the Modern Mind*, p. 132.

52. Ibid., pp. 134, 137, 138.

53. Gray, *Nature and Sources*, p. 125.

54. Dickensen, 29 *Columbia LR*, p. 306.

55. Hutcheson, 14 *Cornell LQ*, pp. 285–86.

56. Yntema, 37 *Yale LJ*, p. 480.

57. Pitney, in Frank, *Law and the Modern Mind*, n. 6, p. 115.

58. Gray, *Nature and Sources*, p. 225.

59. Yntema, 37 *Yale LJ*, p. 480.

60. Frank, *Courts on Trial*, p. 177.

61. Frank, 26 *Illinois LR* p. 653.

62. Hutcheson, 14 *Cornell LQ*, p. 287.

63. Frank, *Courts on Trial*, p. 168.

64. Tourtoulon, in Frank, *Courts on Trial*, p. 169.

65. Tim Tyler, "The Ethnomethodologist," *Human Behavior*, April 1974, p. 60.

66. Rodell, *Woe Unto You*, p. 114.

67. Superior Court, County of Los Angeles, 1970.

68. Bacon, in ABA *Canons of Judicial Ethics*.

69. Blackstone, in Gray, *Nature and Sources*, p. 220.

70. Ibid.

71. Ibid., p. 232.

72. Frank, *Law and the Modern Mind*, p. 40.

73. Rhodes, in 17 *Illinois LR*, Haines, n. 60, p. 115.

74. Wykes, in Nader, *Law in Culture and Society*, p. 331.

75. Rodell, *Woe Unto You*, p. 28.

76. Frank, *Courts on Trial*, p. 255.

77. Haines, 17 *Illinois LR*, p. 115.

78. Rodell, 50 *GLJ*, p. 707.

79. Ibid.

80. Ibid.

81. Ibid.

82. Judge Tim Murphy, "His Honor Has Problems, Too," *The Center Magazine*, vol. 3, no. 3, May/June 1971, p. 51.

83. Ibid., p. 49.

84. Gregory, in Frank, *Law and the Modern Mind*, n. 2, p. 111.

85. Kent, in ibid., p. 112.

86. *Law and Society Review*, 1:23, June 1967.

87. Richard Harris, "Annals of Law (Boston Criminal Courts)," *The New Yorker*, April 14, 1973, p. 86.

88. Ibid., p. 88.

89. Ibid., April 21, pp. 76, 77.

90. Ibid., p. 85.

91. Frank, *Courts on Trial*, p. 168.

92. Frankfurter, *The Case of Sacco and Vanzetti* (New York, Grosset and Dunlap, 1962), p. 59.

93. Ibid., p. 87.

94. Ibid., p. 78.

95. Ibid., p. 87.

96. Ibid., p. 78.

97. Ibid., p. 79.

98. Ibid., p. 82.

99. Ibid., p. 84.

100. Ibid., p. 87.

101. Ibid., p. 92.

102. Herbert, Ehrmann, *The Case That Will Not Die* (Boston, Little, Brown, 1969), p. 458.

103. Frankfurter, *The Case of Sacco and Vanzetti*, pp. 92–93.

104. Ibid., pp. 101–2.

105. Ibid., p. 103.

106. Ibid., p. 116.

107. Ibid., p. 89.

108. Ibid., p. 104.

109. Ibid., p. 90.

110. Ibid.

111. Ibid., p. 91.

112. Ibid., p. 116.

113. Ibid., p. 91.

114. Ehrmann, *The Case That Will Not Die*, p. 477.

115. Curtis, *It's Your Law*, p. 31.

116. Arthur Vanderbilt, *Judges and Jurors* (Boston, Boston University Press, 1956), p. 28.

117. Winters and Allard, 48 *JAJS*, p. 144.

118. *The Record* 20:366.

119. James V. Bennett, "Crime: Old Answers Aren't Enough," Los Angeles *Times*, July 8, 1974, part 2, p. 6.

120. Richard Harris, "Annals of Law (Boston Criminal Courts)," *The New Yorker*, April 14, 1973, p. 88.

121. 48 *JAJS*, p. 87.

122. Murphy, op. cit., p. 53.

123. Rodell, *Woe Unto You*, pp. 161–62.

124. Murphy, op. cit., p. 48.

125. *Suffolk University LR*, vol. VI, p. 957.

126. Joel Grossman, *Lawyers and Judges* (New York, John Wiley, 1965), p. 28.

127. James Mills, "I Have Nothing to Do With Justice," *Life*, March 12, 1971, p. 66.

128. Murphy, op. cit., p. 48.
129. Rosenman, 48 *JAJS*, p. 86.
130. Winters and Allard, 48 *JAJS*, p. 138.
131. Ibid., p. 140.
132. Ibid., p. 144.
133. Rosenman, 48 *JAJS*, pp. 88–89.
134. Winters and Allard, 48 *JAJS*, p. 140.
135. *Suffolk University LR*, vol. VI, p. 958.
136. Winters and Allard, 48 *JAJS*, p. 141.
137. Rosenman, 48 *JAJS*, p. 88.
138. 28 *Alabama Lawyer*, p. 169.
139. Ibid., p. 170.
140. *Suffolk University LR*, vol. VI, p. 962.
141. Ibid., p. 967.
142. Ibid., p. 968.
143. Ibid., p. 963.
144. 48 *JAJS*, p. 88.
145. 28 *California Jurisprudence* 2nd, #41, p. 587.
146. Ibid., p. 591.
147. Yntema, 37 *Yale LJ*, p. 479.

CHAPTER 14

1. Harry Kalven and Hans Zeisel, *The American Jury* (Boston, Little, Brown, 1966), p. 9.
2. xvii *Missouri LR*, p. 236.
3. Ibid.
4. 4 *Law and Society Review*, p. 235.
5. Frank, xvii *Missouri LR*, p. 235.
6. Ibid.
7. 21 *University of Chicago LR*, p. 386.
8. Los Angeles *Times*, Oct. 11, 1972; Abigail Van Buren, Chicago *Tribune*.
9. Kalven and Zeisel, The *American Jury*, p. 11.
10. *Criminal Law Bulletin*, vol. 2 no. 9, p. 4.
11. Ibid., p. 10.
12. 74 *Yale LJ*, p. 171.
13. Frank, *Courts on Trial*, p. 108.
14. Dickensen, 74 *Yale LJ*, pp. 171–72.
15. 4 *Columbia Journal of Law and Social Problems*, p. 179.
16. 36 *New York State BJ*, p. 309.
17. Ibid., p. 307.
18. Knox. Frank, in *Courts on Trial*, p. 108.
19. 74 *Yale LJ*, pp. 171–72.

20. Karcher, 45 *Chicago-Kent LR*, pp. 160–61.

21. Ibid.

22. Ibid.

23. *New York State BJ* no. 4, p. 308.

24. 4 *Columbia Journal of Law and Social Problems*, p. 179.

25. 21 *University of Chicago LR*, p. 387.

26. Frank, *Courts on Trial*, p. 124.

27. Frank, *Law and the Modern Mind*, p. 186.

28. Frank, *Courts on Trial*, pp. 138–39.

29. Marcus Gleisser, *Juries and Justice* (South Brunswick, N.J., A.S. Barnes, 1968), pp. 138–39.

30. *Encyclopaedia Britannica*, vol. 13, p. 205.

31. Ibid.

32. 15 *De Paul LR*, pp. 400–1.

33. Ibid.

34. Gleisser, *Juries and Justice*, p. 35.

35. Lea, *Superstition*, p. 42.

36. Gleisser, *Juries and Justice*, p. 36.

37. *Encyclopaedia Britannica*, vol. 13, p. 205.

38. Ibid.

39. Ibid., and Easton, *The Heritage of the Past*, p. 726.

40. 50 *Michigan State BJ*, p. 695.

41. Antell, 51 *ABA Journal*, p. 155.

42. Encyclopaedia Britannica, vol. 13, p. 205; 3 *Portia LJ*, p. 71; 50 *Michigan State BJ*, p. 695.

43. 50 *Michigan State BJ*, n. 2, p. 695.

44. Ibid.

45. 51 *ABAJ*, p. 155.

46. Tigar, 50 *Michigan State BJ*, p. 695; 3 *Portia LJ*, p. 76.

47. Tigar, 50 *Michigan State BJ*, p. 695.

48. Ibid.

49. *Encyclopaedia Britannica*, vol. 13, p. 205.

50. Ibid., vol. 12, p. 994.

51. Wormser, *The Story of the Law*, p. 251.

52. Tigar, 50 *Michigan State BJ*, p. 695.

53. Gleisser, *Juries and Justice*, pp. 40–41.

54. Ibid., p. 41, and *Encyclopaedia Britannica*, vol. 13, p. 205.

55. 3 *Portia LJ*, p. 76.

56. 22 *Cleveland State LR*, p. 140.

57. 3 *Portia LJ*, p. 76; 50 *Michigan State BJ*, p. 695.

58. 3 *Portia LJ*, p. 77.

59. 7 *HCR*, p. 462, and *Encyclopaedia Britannica*, vol. 13, p. 206.

60. *The Record* 22:472.

61. 7 *HCR*, n. 2, p. 432.

62. Ibid., and 10 *ACLR*, p. 817.

63. 7 *HCR*, n. 2, p. 432, and Gleisser, *Juries and Justice*, p. 129.

64. 10 *ACLR*, pp. 809–10.

65. Ibid.

66. 7 *HCR*, p. 480.

67. Ibid., p. 441.

68. Ibid.

69. Ibid.

70. Ibid., p. 435.

71. Charles G. Goodell, "Where Did the Grand Jury Go?" *Harper's* Iay 1973, p. 23.

72. 51 *ABAJ*, p. 154.

73. Antell, 51 *ABAJ*, p. 153.

74. 7 *HCR*, pp. 446–47.

75. Ibid., p. 452.

76. Ibid., pp. 445, 482.

77. Ibid., p. 455, and 10 *ACLR*, p. 808.

78. 7 *HCR*, p. 448.

79. Ibid., p. 465; Donner and Cerruti, *The Nation*, Jan. 3, 1972.

80. 7 *HCR*, p. 455.

81. Foster, *Ohio State LJ*, vol. 32, p. 701.

82. Ibid.

83. 7 *HCR*, p. 456.

84. Ibid., p. 457.

85. Ibid., p. 455.

86. Ibid., p. 454, *The Nation*, Jan. 3, 1972, and *Rolling Stone*, Dec. 7, 1972.

87. 7 *HCR*, p. 454.

88. Ibid., p. 485.

89. Gleisser, *Juries and Justice*, p. 124.

90. Antell, 51 *ABAJ*, p. 156.

91. Goodell, op. cit.

92. *Newsweek*, Sept. 16, 1974, p. 20.

93. Los Angeles *Times*, Sept. 11, 1974, part 1.

94. 51 *ABAJ*, p. 154.

95. Ibid.

96. Ibid.

97. Antell, 51 *ABAJ*, p. 155.

98. Goodell, op. cit.

99. Ibid.

100. 51 *ABAJ*, p. 155.

101. Ibid.
102. Goodell, op. cit.
103. 51 *ABAJ*, p. 155.
104. 7 *HCR*, n. 34, p. 441.
105. Antell, 51 *ABAJ*, p. 155.
106. 7 *HCR*, p. 442.
107. 51 *ABAJ*, p. 156.
108. David Broder, Los Angeles *Times*, Aug. 28, 1973, part 2.
109. 32 *Ohio State LJ*, p. 716.
110. 7 *HCR*, p. 455.
111. 32 *Ohio State LJ*, p. 717.
112. 10 *ACLR*, p. 816, and 7 *HCR*, p. 456.
113. 7 *HCR*, p. 455.
114. 10 *ACLR*, n. 26, p. 813.
115. Ibid., p. 824.
116. Pound, *Causes of Popular Dissatisfaction*, p. 13.
117. 3 *Portia LJ*, p. 90.
118. Ibid., p. 77.
119. Ibid.
120. 10 *ACLR* n. 59, p. 820.
121. Ibid., p. 817.
122. Ibid., p. 810.
123. Ibid., p. 814.
124. Ibid., p. 813.
125. Ibid., p. 815.
126. Antell, 51 *ABAJ*, p. 156.
127. Ibid.
128. Ibid.
129. Walter Steameier, "He Didn't Prove He Didn't Do It," *The Nation*, March 5, 1973, p. 303.
130. Ibid.
131. 5 *ABLJ*, p. 197.
132. "Clarence Darrow: Attorney for the Defense," *Esquire*, Oct. 1973, p. 225.
133. Ginger, 45 *Judicial Reform: The Forensic Quarterly*, p. 375.
134. Gleisser, *Juries and Justice*, p. 299.
135. David Larsen, Los Angeles *Times*, March 21, 1976, p. 1.
136. 15 *De Paul LR*, p. 420.
137. *Trial 5*, vol. 5, no. 1. p. 37
138. *Federal Insurance Counsel Quarterly*, 18:57, 1967
139. 15 *De Paul LR*, p. 419.
140. 56 *GLJ*, pp. 841–42.
141. *Criminal LR*, 1967, p. 563.

142. *Military LR*, vol. 40, 1968, p. 2.

143. *The Forensic Quarterly*, vol. 45, p. 377.

144. *Criminal Law Bulletin*, vol. 1, no. 4, May 1965, p. 4.

145. *Trial 5*, vol. 5, no. 1, p. 37.

146. Ibid.

147. *Criminal Law Bulletin*, vol. 2, no. 4, May 1965, p. 18.

148. *Forum* 5:151, 1969–70.

149. Harry Bodin, *Selecting a Jury* (New York, Practicing Law Institute, 1948), p. 43.

150. Goldstein, *Goldstein's Trial Technique*, #245.

151. *Time*, June 4, 1973, p. 67.

152. 15 *De Paul LR*, p. 435.

153. 56 *GLJ*, pp. 851, 855.

154. Ibid., 851.

155. *Trial* 5:40.

156. 56 *GLJ*, p. 852.

157. Ibid., p. 853.

158. 55 *GLJ*, p. 845, and 38 *Nebraska LR*, p. 753.

159. *Trial* 5:40.

160. Wayne Sage, "Psychology and the Angela Davis Jury," *Human Behavior*, Jan. 1973, p. 56.

161. Ibid.

162. Martin Arnold, New York *Times*, May 5, 1974, and Los Angeles *Times*, April 29, 1974.

163. Ibid.

164. 38 *Nebraska LR*, p. 746.

165. Ibid., p. 745, and conversation with Zeisel, May 1976.

166. Gleisser, *Juries and Justice*, p. 298.

167. Ibid., 299.

168. Kaplan, *Criminal Justice* (Mineola, New York, Foundation Press, 1973), p. 363.

169. Gleisser, *Juries and Justice*, p. 299.

170. 21 *University of Chicago LR*, p. 388.

171. Kalven and Zeisel, *The American Jury*, p. 9.

172. 15 *Chicago-Kent LR*, p. 160.

173. 5 *Vanderbilt LR*, p. 157.

174. 36 *New York State BJ*, no. 4, p. 309.

175. 15 De Paul LR, no. 54, p. 434.

176. VI *Suffolk University LR*, p. 898.

177. 36 *New York State BJ*, p. 307.

178. 16 *Catholic Lawyer*, p. 233.

179. 36 *New York State BJ*, no. 4, p. 306.

180. Ibid.

181. 74 *Yale LJ*, p. 190.

182. 36 *New York State BJ*, no. 4, p. 307.

183. 1 *Valparaiso University LR*, p. 4.

184. 15 *De Paul LR*, p. 418.

185. Goldstein, *Goldstein's Trial Technique*, 1975, #9.39.

186. Ibid.

187. 21 *University of Chicago LR*, p. 390.

188. Ibid., p. 391.

189. Ibid., no. 16, p. 390.

190. Henry Wilcox, *The Frailties of the Jury* (Chicago, Legal Literature Co., 1907), p. 110.

191. 16 *Catholic University*, p. 232.

192. 21 *University of Chicago LR*, p. 419.

193. 44 *Federal Rules Decisions*, p. 193.

194. 5 *ABLJ*, p. 198.

195. 21 *University of Chicago LR*, p. 394.

196. Ibid.

197. Ibid.

198. Ibid.

199. *Criminal LR* 1967, p. 566.

200. Albert Osborn, *The Mind of the Juror* (Albany, Boyd Printing Co., 1937), p. 800.

201. Wilcox, *The Frailties of the Jury*, p. 11.

202. *Journal of Urban Law*, 47:199.

203. 21 *University of Chicago LR*, p. 392.

204. 5 *Vanderbilt LR*, p. 160.

205. 44 *Federal Rules Decisions*, p. 191; 19 *Oklahoma LR*, p. 131.

206. Richard Renneker, MD, *Supervision Project: The Nature of Data in the Therapeutic Process*, read at Annual Meeting of The American Psychiatric Association, 1961.

207. 44 *Federal Rules Decisions*, p. 191.

208. Wilcox, *Frailties of the Jury*, p. 43.

209. Frank, *Law and the Modern Mind*, p. 194.

210. 18 *Oklahoma LR*, p. 130.

211. 38 *Nebraska LR*, pp. 753, 754 and 15 *De Paul LR*, p. 42.

212. XVII *Missouri LR*, p. 245.

213. 21 *University of Chicago LR*, p. 398.

214. Ibid., p. 392.

215. Bok, in Frank, *Courts on Trial*, p. 117.

216. Swain, quoted in 13 *Hastings LJ*, p. 456.

217. Gleisser, *Juries and Justice*, p. 263.

218. Ibid., p. 228.

219. Ibid., p. 229.

220. 21 *University of Chicago LR*, p. 398.
221. Frank, *Courts on Trial*, p. 116.
222. XVII *Missouri LR*, p. 238.
223. 4 *University of Kansas LR*, p. 435.
224. 5 *ABLJ*, p. 197.
225. Frank, *Law and the Modern Mind*, p. 196.
226. Ibid., p. 195
227. Ibid., n. 3, p. 185.
228. Ibid., p. 196.
229. Ibid., p. 184.
230. Ibid., p. 185.
231. Frank *Courts on Trial*, p. 141.
232. Gleisser, *Juries and Justice*, p. 266.
233. Frank, *Law and the Modern Mind*, n. 3, p. 18.
234. Ibid.
235. Frank, *Courts on Trial*, p. 132.
236. Ibid., p. 114.
237. Gleisser, *Juries and Justice*, p. 266.
238. Frank, *Law and the Modern Mind*, p. 185.
239. XX *Oregon LR* 197, n. 40.
240. Ibid., p. 197.
241. Ibid., p. 200.
242. Frank, *Courts on Trial*, p. 115.
243. XX *Oregon LR*, p. 195.
244. Ibid., p. 201.
245. 15 *De Paul LR*, p. 435.
246. Frank, *Law and the Modern Mind*, n. 7, p. 187.
247. 16 *Catholic Lawyer*, p. 227.
248. Frank, *Law and the Modern Mind*, p. 187.
249. XX *Oregon LR*, p. 189.
250. Frank, *Law and the Modern Mind*, p. 187.
251. 18 *Oklahoma LR*, p. 130.
252. 1 *Valparaiso University LR*, p. 4.
253. *Trial* 5:39.
254. Ibid.
255. VI *Suffolk University LR*, p. 897.
256. Frank, *Courts on Trial*, p. 139.
257. Ibid.
258. XX *Oregon LR*, p. 189.
259. 21 *University of Chicago LR*, no. 128, p. 411.
260. Holdsworth, *The History of English Law* (London, Methuen & Co., 1956), vol. 1, p. 317.
261. 4 *Law and Society Review*, n. 9, p. 360.

262. Ibid.
263. *New York State BJ*, vol. 36, no. 4, p. 308.
264. Kalven and Zeisel, *The American Jury*, p. 7.
265. 4 *Columbia Journal of Law and Social Problems*, no. 21, p. 180.
266. 45 *Chicago-Kent LR*, p. 166.
267. Ibid.
268. Frank, *Courts on Trial*, p. 132.
269. 16 *Catholic Lawyer*, 1970, pp. 224–41.
270. 4 *ABLJ*, pp. 102–3.
271. 15 *De Paul LR*, p. 436.
272. 16 *Catholic Lawyer*, p. 227.
273. Ibid.
274. VI *Suffolk University LR*, p. 902.
275. Ibid., p. 903.
276. 16 *Catholic Lawyer*, p. 225.
277. 21 *University of Chicago LR*, p. 420.
278. Ibid., p. 420.
279. Ibid.
280. 8 *Illinois LR*, p. 594.
281. 44 *Federal Rules Decisions*, p. 189.
282. Statement to this writer.
283. 35 *ABLJ*, p. 114.
284. 38 *Nebraska LR*, p. 749.
285. 15 *De Paul LR*, p. 432.
286. Kalven and Zeisel, *The American Jury*, p. 9.
287. 21 *University of Chicago LR*, p. 394.
288. 15 *De Paul LR*, p. 419.
289. 44 *Federal Rules Decisions*, pp. 193–94.
290. 10 *ABAJ*, p. 54.
291. Ibid.
292. "Lying in the Courtroom," Interview with U.S. District Judge Marvin Frankel. *Harper's*, Sept. 1973, p. 10.
293. *Chicago-Kent LR* 15:168.

CHAPTER 15

1. Churchill, in *Bartlett's Familiar Quotations*.
2. Frank, *Courts on Trial*, p. 422.
3. Frank, *American Law: The Case for Radical Reform*, p. 193.
4. Ibid., p. 186.
5. Ibid., p. 191.
6. Seymour, *Why Justice Fails* (New York, William Morrow, 1973), pp. 219, 220.

7. Ibid., p. 221.

8. 54 *Minnesota LR*, p. 493.

9. Ibid.

10. Ibid., p. 494.

11. Ibid.

12. Ibid., p. 459.

13. Ibid.

14. Llewellyn, *The Bramble Bush* (Dobbs Ferry, N.Y., Oceana Publishing, 1960), p. 101.

15. Nader, 54 *Minnesota LR*, p. 495.

16. Ibid., p. 496.

17. 47 *Texas LR*, p. 795.

18. 54 *Minnesota LR*, p. 495.

19. Ibid.

20. 38 *GWLR*, p. 586.

21. Bess Meyerson, quoted in Ralph Nader Public Citizen public relations material.

22. Rodell, *Woe Unto You*, p. 179.

23. Ibid., p. 182.

24. Ibid., p. 167.

25. Ibid., p. 180.

26. Ibid., p. 175.

27. 47 *Texas LR*, p. 619.

28. 79 *Yale LJ*, p. 619.

29. Menninger, *The Crime of Punishment*, p. 58.

30. Zeisel, in ibid.

31. 38 *GWLR*, p.566.

32. Henry Steele Commager, "Where Have All America's Leaders Gone?", Los Angeles *Times*, Nov. 18, 1973, part 4, p. 4.

33. Wright, in Frank, *American Law: The Case for Radical Reform*, p. 3.

34. Editorial, Los Angeles *Times*, Feb. 6, 1973.

35. Subcommittee on Crime and Criminal Justice of the Committee on the Judiciary, House of Representatives, March 1, 1994, p.214.

36. New York *Times*, March 2, 1994, A–15.

37. Los Angeles *Times*, May 16, 1994, A–1.

38. New York *Times*, March 3, 1994, A–15.

39. Los Angeles *Times*, July 7, 1994, Part 1, p.3.

40. New York *Times*, March 2, 1994, A–15.

41. Washington *Post*, Jan. 1, 1994, A–3.

42. New York *Times*, March 15, 1995, A–23.

43. New York *Times*, March 13, 1995, B–1.

44. Los Angeles *Times*, Oct. 20, 1995.

45. Los Angeles *Times*, Oct. 24, 1995, E–1.

46. New York *Times*, Feb. 25, 1995.

47. United States Federal Bureau of Investigation,*Crime In The United States* annual (1992).

48. Ibid.

49. Seymour, *Why Justice Fails*, p. 82.

50. New York *Times*, Aug. 17, 1995, A–10.

51. 38 George Washington LR, p. 574.

52. Ibid.

53. U.S. Federal Bureau of Investigation, Uniform Crime Report, *Crime In The United States*, 1993.

54. Seymour, *Why Justice Fails*, p. 152.

55. Bureau of Justice Statistics, Survey of State Prison Inmates, 1991, p. 9.

56. Sourcebook of Criminal Justice Statistics, 1993, p. 616.

57. Seymour, *Why Justice Fails,* p. 153.

58. *Drug and Crime Facts*, Bureau of Justice Statistics, 1994.

59. *Employment and Earnings*, U.S. Department of Labor, Bureau of Labor Statistics, Sept. 1995, vol. 42 n. 9.

60. Los Angeles *Times*, Nov. 6, 1973, part 4, p. 1.

61. *Christian Science Monitor*, Jan. 13, 1993, p. 7.

62. U.S. Department of Labor, Bureau of Labor Statistics, March 1994 (unpublished tabulation for Current Population Survey).

63. Los Angeles *Times*, Dec. 12, 1991, A–5.

64. Literacy Fact Sheet published by National Institute for Literacy, Washington, D.C., April 21, 1995.

65. Washington *Post,* Feb. 10, 1992, A–9.

66. *Christian Science Monitor*, May 20, 1993, p. 2.

67. Prepared statement of Gerald Goldstein, hearing before subcommittee on Crime and Criminal Justice of the Committee on The Judiciary, House of Representatives, March 1, 1994, p. 8.

68. U.S. Department of Justice, Bureau of Prisons, September 1995.

69. Provided by Federal Bureau of Prisons staff, November 1995.

70. Seymour, *Why Justice Fails*, p. 118.

71. Zeisel, Kalven, and Bucholz in Frank, *American Law: The Case for Radical Reform*, p. 4.

72. Los Angeles *Times*, Sept. 4, 1974, part 2, p. 5.

73. *Time*, Oct. 23, 1995.

74. Los Angeles *Times*, Oct. 30, 1994, B–5.

75. National Council on Crime and Delinquency, San Francisco, position statement, 1995.

76. Zwarensteyn, 10 ABLR, p. 27.

77. Ibid., p. 28.

78. 27 *Business Lawyer*, p. 1272.

79. Japan Statistical Yearbook, 1995, Tokyo Statistics Bureau Management and Coordination Agency; and Chiezo, *The Asahi Encyclopedia of Current Terms* (Tokyo, Asahi Shinbansa, 1994).

80. ABA, March 1995 (verbal report).

81. Pyong–Choon Hahm, in *Comparative Judicial Behaviour*, edited by Glendon Schubert and David J. Danielski (New York, Oxford University Press, 1960), pp. 19–21.

82. Ibid.

83. 2 Minnesota LR, p. 156.

84. National Council on Crime and Delinquency:*Community–Based Alternatives to Traditional Corrections*, February 1974.

85. Foreward, *Community Based Corrections in Des Moines*, U.S. Department of Justice, Law Enforcement Assistance Administration, 1973.

86. 2 Minnesota LR, p. 156.

87. Seymour, *Why Justice Fails*, p. 222.

88. Aubert, in Nader, *Law In Culture and Society*, p. 295.

89. Seymour, *Why Justice Fails*, p. 222.

90. 10 ABLJ, p. 30.

91. 2 ACLQ, p. 173.

92. Seymour, *Why Justice Fails*, p. 222.

93. Ibid.

94. Gleiser, *Juries and Justice*, p. 53.

95. Ibid., pp. 51, 52.

96. Ibid.

97. *Newsweek*, Oct. 16, 1995, p. 47.

98. 52 Judicature, p. 199.

9 9. Pyong–Choon Hahm, in Schubert and Danielski, *Comparative Judicial Behaviour,* pp. 19–21.

100. Kaplan, *Criminal Justice*, pp. 19, 20, 24.

101. 24 Minnesota LR, p. 156.

102. *Community Based Corrections in Des Moines*, p. 9.

103. 24 Minnesota LR, p. 156.

104. Ronald Goldfarb, *An Innovation In The Sentencing of Criminals,* Los Angeles *Times*, Jan. 4, 1974, part 2, p. 7.

105. Ibid.

106. Itasca County, Minnesota, Board of Government Innovation and Cooperation, Probation Department, Grant Program, 1994.

107. Randy Barnett, Restitution: A New Paradigm of Criminal Justice (Harvard Law School, fall, 1975). For private circulation only. Author's common law copyright reserved. Sent to me by the Institute For Humane Studies, Menlo Park, California.

108. Poole, *Criminal Justice: A Systems Analysis Approach,* in *Law and Liberty* (Menlo Park, California, the Institute for Humane Studies) vol. 1, no. 4, 1975.

109. Commager, op. cit.

110. *Rich–Poor Disparity Bar to World Peace*, Los Angeles *Times*, Dec. 8, 1973, part 1, p. 20.

111. David Lamb, Los Angeles *Times*, July 11, 1974, part 3, p. 12.

112. *Bartlett's Familiar Quotations.*

113. Ibid.

114. Robert Kirsch, "The Book Report," Los Angeles *Times*, Dec. 4, 1973, part 4, p. 7.

115. Gardner, *In Common Cause* (New York, W.W. Norton, 1972), p. 250.

116. *Newsweek*, Dec. 10, 1973, p. 4.

117. Ibid.

CHAPTER 16

1. Judge Robert Kenny, Los Angeles Superior Court, comment to this writer.

2. California State BJ, vol. 49, no. 5, p. 463.

3. Los Angeles *Times*, Feb. 15, 1976.

4. Los Angeles *Times*, July 22, 1974.

5. 4 *Notre Dame Lawyer*, p. 936.

6. Ibid., p. 949.

7. Ibid., p. 950.

8. Ibid., p. 962.

9. Ibid., p. 959.

10. *ABA Journal* February 1995.

11. New York *Times*, Dec. 18, 1994.

12. New York *Times*, Dec. 30, 1994, A–25.

13. Ibid.

14. Ibid.

15. NAME literature.

16. American Friends Service Committee literature.

17. Center for Nonviolent Communication literature.

18. NIDR literature.

19. JACS literature.

20. YAR literature.

21. New York *Times*, Dec. 29, 1994, B–7.

22. Ibid.

23. Ibid.

24. Gardner, *In Common Cause*, pp. 73–75.

25. The Center for Law In the Public Interest literature.

26. Public Citizen literature.

27. Gardner, *In Common Cause*, p. 20.

28. Ibid., p. 76.

29. Ibid.

30. Ronald Ostrow, "State, Local Attacks on Corrupt Public Officials Urged by U.S. Panel," Los Angeles *Times*, Nov. 26, 1973, p. 20.

31. *Working Papers*, vol. III, no. 2, 1975.

32. Citizen Alert literature.

33. *Just Economics*, vol. 4, no. 1, Movement For Economic Justice, 1976.

34. Citizen Alert literature.

35. SOCM literature.

36. NASP literature.

37. SMHA literature.

38. Washington *Post*, Feb. 6, 1994, B–1.

39. Citizens for a Better Environment literature.

40. National Committee for Independent Action literature.

41. Women's Project literature.

42. NPA literature.

43. WAGV literature.

44. CAN literature.

45. Los Angeles *Times*, July 5, 1995, A–1.

46. Los Angeles *Times*, Sept. 7, 1995, B–3.

47. Los Angeles *Times*, Oct. 29, 1995, A–1.

48. Karl Hess, "America Has a Crisis of Scale—Not Leadership," Los Angeles *Times*, May 30, 1975, part 2, p. 7.

49. Martin P. Seligman, "Giving Up On Life," *Psychology Today*, May 1974, p. 82.

50. Gardner, *In Common Cause*, p. 103.

51. Common Cause, literature.

INDEX

ACKNOWLEDGMENTS

Acknowledgment is gratefully made for permission to reprint from the following:

54 Minnesota Law Review: excerpts from article by Ralph Nader.

The New Yorker: excerpts from series by Richard Harris: "In Criminal Court," Parts I and II.

Law and the Modern Mind, by Jerome Frank: Anchor Edition. Excerpt permission granted by the estate of Barbara Frank Kristein.

Selections from Jerome Frank, *Courts on Trial: Myth and Reality in American Justice* (copyright 1949 by Jerome Frank; Princeton Paperback, 1973) pp. 84–429. Reprinted by permission of Princeton University Press.

Excerpts from: *The Art of Cross-Examination,* by Francis L. Wellman (copyright 1903, 1904, 1923, 1936 by Macmillan Publishing Co., Inc., renewed 1931, 1932 by Francis L. Wellman, and 1951, 1964 by Ethel Wellman).

Excerpts from: *Trial Evidence,* by Reynolds: Callaghan & Company.

Excerpts from: Starrs, *Professional Responsibility: 5 American Criminal Law Review,* published by the American Bar Association, Section of Criminal Justice.

Excerpt from: White, *5 Houston Law Review,* no. 4, 1968.

Excerpts from articles by Judge Samuel Rosenman, and Winters and Allard: 48 *Journal of the American Judicature Society.* Reprinted by permission from *Judicature, Journal of the American Judicature Society.*

Excerpts from: *It's Your Law,* by Charles Curtis: Harvard University Press, 1954.

Excerpts from article by Fred Rodell: 50 *Georgetown Law Journal.* Reprinted with permission of the Georgetown Law Journal Association.

Excerpts from articles by Freedman and Braun: *Professional Ethics,* 55 *Georgetown Law Journal.* Reprinted with permission of the Georgetown Law Journal Association.

Excerpts from: *The Lost Art of Cross-Examination,* by J.W. Ehrlich. Reprinted by permission of G.P. Putnam's Sons. Copyright © 1970 by J.W. Ehrlich.

Excerpts from: article by Melvin P. Antell, *ABA Journal,* vol. 51.

Excerpts from: *In Common Cause,* by John Gardner. W.W. Norton & Company, Inc.

Excerpts from: *Juries and Justice,* by Gleisser. Barnes and Co.

Excerpts from: 21 *University of Chicago Law Review.*

Excerpts from: *His Honor Has Problems, Too,* by Judge Tim Murphy. Reprinted with permission from *The Center Magazine,* a publication of

ACKNOWLEDGMENTS   294

the Center for the Study of Democratic Institutions, Santa Barbara,
California.

Excerpts from: *Symposium on Professional Ethics:* 64 *Michigan Law Review.* Copyright 1966 by The Michigan Law Review Association.
Used with permission.

Excerpts from: *Law and Warfare,* edited by Paul Bohannon. Doubleday.

Excerpts from: *The Case of Sacco and Vanzetti: A Critical Analysis for Lawyers and Laymen,* by Felix Frankfurter. By permission of Little, Brown and Co. in association with the Atlantic Monthly Press; copyright © 1927, 1955 by Felix Frankfurter.

Excerpts from: *Cross-Examination of Witnesses,* by Cornelius. Copyrighted by The Bobbs-Merrill Company Inc. Reprinted by permission. All rights reserved.

Excerpts from: *Woe Unto You, Lawyers!* by Fred Rodell. Published by Pageant-Poseidon Press, Ltd.